EDEN BY DESIGN

EDEN BY DESIGN

*The 1930 Olmsted-Bartholomew Plan
for the Los Angeles Region*

Greg Hise and William Deverell

Afterword by Laurie Olin, ASLA, AIA

UNIVERSITY OF CALIFORNIA PRESS
Berkeley · Los Angeles · London

*For those citizen planners who,
in their regard for the environment,
are willing to draft big plans and
work toward their implementation.*

University of California Press
Berkeley and Los Angeles, California

University of California Press, Ltd.
London, England

Introduction and Afterword © 2000 by
Greg Hise and William Deverell

Library of Congress Cataloging-in-Publication Data

Eden by design : the 1930 Olmsted-Bartholomew plan for the Los Angeles Region /
Greg Hise and William Deverell
     p.   cm.
     Includes bibliographical references and index.
     ISBN 0-520-22414-0 (alk. paper)—ISBN 0-520-22415-9 (pbk. : alk. paper)
     1. Regional planning—California—Los Angeles Metropolitan Area—History.
     2. Olmsted Brothers.   3. Harland Bartholomew & Associates.
     I. Deverell, William F., 1962–   II. Hise, Greg.
     HT394.L67 E34 2000
     711′.4′0979494 21—dc 21   99-045101

Printed in the United States of America

08   07   06   05   04   03   02   01   00   99
10   9   8   7   6   5   4   3   2   1

The paper used in this publication meets the minimum requirements of
ANSI/NISO Z39.48-1992 (R 1997) (*Permanence of Paper*). ∞

CONTENTS

PREFACE TO A MASTER PLAN

T HE 1930 REPORT SUBMITTED to a committee of the Los Angeles Chamber of Commerce, *Parks, Playgrounds and Beaches for the Los Angeles Region*, is a remarkable document. It is the product of three years of surveys and fieldwork, analysis and synthesis, and the collective expertise of two of America's most prominent landscape and planning firms, Olmsted Brothers and Harland Bartholomew and Associates. In creating this report, these design professionals had to grapple not only with the physical expanse of Los Angeles County and the complexity and range of infrastructure and amenities both existing and proposed that fell within their purview. More trying, they conducted this study in the charged and dynamic context of Los Angeles politics and development at the close of a decade-long boom. The economy then began to falter during the early phases of the Depression, ushering in a time of limited growth and reduced expectations in Southern California as elsewhere. How they conducted their work, their findings and recommendations, and the lessons we can draw from that experience are the principle themes of this volume.

Reprinting *Parks, Playgrounds and Beaches* has been akin to urban archeology. At the most obvious level the analogy is appropriate since the report was printed in a limited edition and the few copies that are available have been lying relatively undisturbed on the shelves of research libraries for the past seventy years. Our endeavor required fieldwork in order to locate the original artifact, bring it to the University of Southern California's digital imaging center, and create a facsimile of the original so that the document can reach a wider audience.

But the archeological features of this project go well beyond the "can you find it?" challenges posed by a rare book. As is the case for any archeological excavation, this project requires an imaginative reconstruction of a site. This is where the real intellectual excitement resides both for us as editors and for you as readers. This imagining has at least four dimensions. Because we are historians, we first tried to figure out how greater Los Angeles developed during the first decades of the twentieth century. What caused the rapid population expansion and changing demographics? More specifically, why did patterns of peripheral and central city growth and the concerns of social reformers generate an appeal in the late 1920s to the premier planning firms in the nation?

Part of our purpose in reprinting *Parks, Playgrounds and Beaches* is to remind people that both the Olmsted and Bartholomew firms, as well as their associates and affiliates, played a significant role in shaping the urban West. With these design professionals as our guides, we needed then to imagine what the Los Angeles region would have looked like had the report been adopted and the recommendations implemented as planned. And because the report met with such focused and effective opposition, we needed to consider what it was about the plan that so worried the very same Los Angeles elites who had requested it in the first place. What implications did they imagine when they considered the wholesale adoption of *Parks, Playgrounds and Beaches*?

For many readers, the most interesting imaginary reconstruction or reconsideration will be from the vantage point of the present day. In and of itself, finding, reprinting, and studying this report is a valuable scholarly exercise; we should know about this plan, understand the reasons it was called for, and analyze the reasons it failed. But is it possible that discovery might lead to a recovery? Can we imagine a Southern California, a San Francisco Bay Area, a greater Chicago or New York where people not only find value in the grand ambitions of this and similar reports but actually use these documents as the basis and means for a renewed public discourse about cities and their futures? Is there a chance the planning, environmental, and political communities might not only learn *about* the Olmsted/Bartholomew report but also learn *from* it? The future of Southern California's landscape was the central focus for the Olmsteds and Bartholomew, and they presented their vision with clarity and confidence. There is much to learn from their study. Our hope is that the discussions this reprint provokes will extend beyond greater Los Angeles and engage students, design professionals, policy makers, elected officials, and all those who have a stake in the future of our cities.

ACKNOWLEDGMENTS

The authors thank Robert Fishman, Paul Groth, Roger Montgomery, Ted Muller, and David Schuyler for their early support for this project and Dell Upton for a critical review of our essay. Peggy Shaffer and Terry Young offered insight regarding the planners and their report; Todd Gish and Mark Wild provided research assistance. Lisa Padilla suggested we interview Laurie Olin, arranged the initial session, and then advised us regarding images and design. Our editor, Charlene Woodcock, guided the project through the press and has been a great collaborator. Thanks to Dace Taube (Regional History Center, USC) for assistance with the Chamber collection and photographs, to Jay Jones (Los Angeles City Archives), and to the curators at the Olmsted Archive in Brookline, Massachusetts, especially Joyce Connelly. The interlibrary loan staff at Caltech secured microfilm from the Olmsted collection at the Library of Congress. Matt Gainer (Information Systems Division, USC) scanned the original report and answered numerous technical queries. Kathleen Much of the Center for Advanced Study in the Behavioral Sciences (Stanford University) provided editorial assistance. We appreciate support from the Andrew W. Mellon Foundation.

PRIVATE POWER, PUBLIC SPACE

Greg Hise and William Deverell

"When I heard this report first explained by these two distinguished planners, Messrs. Olmsted and Bartholomew, I was immediately sold on it."

Oscar Mueller, Los Angeles attorney, 1929

O
N MARCH 16, 1930, the *Los Angeles Examiner* and *Los Angeles Times* alerted readers to a "gigantic county park and beach plan" that the Chamber of Commerce had unveiled the previous evening.[1] The Chamber's public presentation, the prominent newspaper coverage, and the corresponding sense of import were consistent with previous initiatives designed to shape civic opinion and generate support for municipal investment in infrastructure and improvements. This particular event was timed with the publication of a 178-page, clothbound document, *Parks, Playgrounds and Beaches for the Los Angeles Region.* The authors of record were principals in the landscape architecture and city planning firms Olmsted Brothers in Brookline, Massachusetts, and Harland Bartholomew and Associates, of St. Louis.

In their authoritative study, these prominent consultants marshall diagrams, plans, and spare prose to set out a system of neighborhood playgrounds and local parks linked to regional "reservations" along the Pacific coastline and interspersed across the surrounding foothills, mountains, and desert. It was a bold vision, encompassing an area of more than 1,500 square miles stretching from the arid Antelope Valley in the north to the harbor in Long Beach, from the famed beaches of Malibu out to Riverside County. The authors and their cartographers played up the heroic scale. Large-format, color maps fold out of the report to convey how this expansive region with its diverse physiography and broad array of land uses should, or must, be understood as a self-evident unit for analysis, governance, and the exercise of the planners' imagination. Strategically clustered charts and tables tell a complementary story of administration, finance, and policy. This pragmatic account is sketched out with economy and poise in the executive summary. Interested readers could turn to the appendices for sample legislation, a legal opinion on land rights along California beaches, and a table outlining comparable administrative powers, funding mechanisms, and the structure of programs in other metropolitan areas. The report's breadth and attention to detail combined with the authors' insight into the vicissitudes of the planning process sets this document apart from the majority of such studies produced at that time as well as much of the comparable work produced during the intervening seven decades.

Three years in the making, *Parks, Playgrounds and Beaches* was the product of a self-proclaimed "citizens' committee" composed primarily of Chamber of Commerce members and their associates, a diverse group of movers and shakers with representatives from a cross-section of local manufacturing and industry, the financial sector, real estate, and commerce. Membership was by subscription and the funds raised were used to finance a study of publicly-owned playgrounds, parks, and beaches. Committee members rightly viewed this survey as the first step toward identifying future needs, designing a county-wide system, and establishing guidelines for implementation.

To achieve these objectives, Chamber members approved hiring what they considered to be the "best brains in the United States."[2] Beginning in 1927, staff and local affiliates associated with the Olmsted and Bartholomew offices and their technical advisors undertook an exhaustive survey of existing conditions, assayed the relevant local studies, conducted comparative assessments of similar proposals for other metropolitan areas, produced four drafts, and billed nearly $80,000 for their services. The dominant tone of the document they produced and the Chamber's public announcement was one of urgency. The executive committee's letter of transmittal declared that the "situation revealed by the report is so disquieting as to make it highly expedient to impress upon the public . . . the present crisis in the welfare of Los Angeles and the surrounding region."[3]

The crisis they defined was one brought on, in part, by the Chamber and other boosters' success at attracting visitors and increasing

Figure 1. Chutes Park, a thirty-five acre site at the southwest corner of Main
and Washington was first developed in the late 1870s as Washington Gardens.
Over time, it was transformed into an urban pleasure ground, of a type found
in most American cities, featuring dancing and variety shows, amusement rides,
and the consumption of alcohol and tobacco. Reformers imagined city parks and
playgrounds as a substitute for commercial leisure, a place for contemplation
and supervised recreation. In this photograph from 1905, children are playing
on equipment without supervision in the shadow of the "chutes" (a thrill ride
that required a fare) in close proximity to vendors of draft beer. In their report,
Olmsted and Bartholomew classify amusement zones as sites for commercial
exploitation that "corral the crowd" and are "on the whole distinctly deleterious
in character."

numbers of new residents to the Southland. More people meant the
county would become "less and less attractive, less and less wholesome . . . the growth of the region will tend to strangle itself." As the
committee and its consultants emphasized repeatedly, Los Angeles
County had far fewer acres devoted to playgrounds and parks relative
to other metropolitan areas and the ratio of recreation space to residents fell well below national standards. Bridging this shortfall would
become increasingly difficult as more people came to the region and
additional land was developed for residences, business, and industry.
At the very least, a shortage of beaches and scenic mountain retreats
foretold a crisis for the tourist economy. Just as critically, committee
members viewed parks and playgrounds as a means to improve health,
reduce delinquency, and promote citizenship in the city's "congested
districts" (figures 1, 2, and 3). Insuring existing recreational amenities

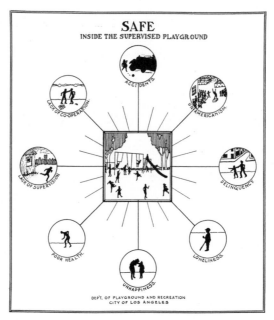

Figure 2. For members of the city's Playground Department, supervised play areas were opportune sites for stimulating right ideals and acculturating youth into the norms of American society. In playgrounds outfitted with the proper apparatus and under the watchful eyes of trained staff, the children of immigrants might be transformed into citizens. According to the commissioners' 1908–10 *Annual Report,* "This is the very essence of democracy. For to know how to associate, how to co-operate with one's fellows is the foundation of our national form of government."

against encroachment and setting aside adequate land where it was needed most for active play and leisure were the solution. Now was the time to act. Suitable sites were becoming ever more scarce and rising property values meant that acquiring this land would become more difficult in the future.[4]

Despite the immoderate pleas for urgency, the report garnered almost no public attention. The response, in truth, was a resounding silence. There were no follow-up stories in the local papers, nor was there discussion of the plan and its publication in the official minutes of city or county agencies and committees such as the Regional Planning Commission, the Los Angeles Parks Department, and the city's Playground and Recreation Department. Each would have been affected directly by the proposal. If the recommendations had

Figure 3. In their report, Olmsted and Bartholomew call for neighborhood-based recreation facilities. Ideally these centers would contain parklike areas for "mental refreshment," a field house and swimming pool, and club rooms or similar structures for community use. The Board of Playground Commissioners (founded in 1904) had established a series of neighborhood playgrounds, initially in the city's Second, Seventh, and Eighth wards (the "congested districts" running along the west side of the Los Angeles River) and then additional sites in outlying areas such as El Sereno (see figure 18). The Apablasa Playground, completed in 1927, the year this photograph was taken, was located on land donated to the city by the Southern Pacific Railroad Company. The site, in the center of Chinatown, had previously been used for stables.

been implemented, the latter two faced consolidation and perhaps elimination in lieu of a new, countywide parks commission. No mention of the report or its findings appear in the bulletins of the Los Angeles City Club or the Municipal League, groups of businessmen and professionals whose members prided themselves on their activism and close attention to policy, planning, and local politics. A search of national publications whose purview encompassed the domains of landscape architecture, urban planning, city design, and public administration finds no mention of the Olmsted-Bartholomew study despite the prominence of both firms in these fields. The report is not even noted in a special May 1931 issue of *Western City* devoted exclusively to urban parks and recreation despite a lead essay on county facilities for Los Angeles penned by Pasadena's superintendent of parks.[5]

Given the report's anemic reception, it is reasonable to ask: Why bother to look at it now? What can be gained through close study of a failed planning document? The black hole into which *Parks, Playgrounds and Beaches* disappeared was so vast it did not even receive the dismissive sobriquet "utopian," a customary response to ambitious, large-scale plans. (Keep in mind that later generations often pluck these plans from the dustbin and reify them as relic reminders of what could have been.)

The question can be posed another way. Suppose you were to visit Los Angeles and head out, reprint in hand, intent on discovering the Olmsted-Bartholomew legacy. Where would you begin? What route might you travel? Toward which destinations? If you travel the surface streets across the basin you are traversing infrastructure put in place along lines first sketched out by the Olmsted and Bartholomew offices (with consultant Charles Cheney) in 1924 as the *Major Traffic Street Plan*. This system of regular north-south, east-west boulevards provides access to a series of sites whose basic design can be traced to the Olmsted office. These range in scale, scope of involvement, and degree of integrity relative to first intention from a schematic diagram for the eventual pleasure boat harbor at Marina del Rey, to consultation on the layout and planting scheme for Torrance and Leimert Park, to the design and implementation of a large-scale community plan at Palos Verdes Estates. You will note how the physical build along major boulevards such as Western, Vermont, and Crenshaw and the experience of traveling through these sections of the region differs from the vision of landscaped parkways depicted in the 1930 report. While it is true these generously-scaled transit corridors continue to serve their primary purpose—moving people quickly and directly throughout the region—regrettably, they do not connect a series of integrated parks and recreation places designed for and used by the majority of residents in and visitors to Los Angeles County.

Another way to address these questions is to note that even though *Parks, Playgrounds and Beaches* achieved limited currency at the time of publication, it has served as a touchstone for subsequent investigations of the region (a lineage we chart in this introduction). That said, we should assure readers that our interest is not in elevating this particular report to iconic stature. On the contrary, our intention is to analyze the planning process, to make transparent the somewhat shadowy and therefore suspect practice by which individuals and agencies with authority identify those "problems" the "experts" will address, how "solutions" are generated, and the way in which the public resources necessary for implementation are accumulated and assigned. This kind of investigation requires a thorough examination of the objectives that motivated Chamber members to take action and the politics that guided their decisions, especially their decision to enlist consultants from outside Southern California. In addition, it is instructive to interpret the 1930 report for Los Angeles County in light of other studies, and we situate this document in a comparative, national context. Ultimately, it is of great utility to understand why this report did not generate an outpouring of institutional and citizen support regardless of the power and prestige embodied in the Chamber of Commerce, despite the undeniable cachet associated with the Olmsted and Bartholomew offices, and in spite of a demonstrable groundswell of opinion that there was a need for public investment in recreation facilities and parkland. This fate was not due to some intrinsic flaw in the plan, nor was it due to a lack of public will, and it certainly was not happenstance. No, what happened in this case was more deliberate, more planned. The Chamber of Commerce and its allies effectively limited circulation of the report and discouraged public discourse.

LINEAGE

In one sense, the Olmsted-Bartholomew report is of a type: it is a metropolitan or regional plan for a coordinated park and parkway system with associated urban pleasure grounds. The Olmsted firm, in particular, made its name with similar, well-known plans for New York and Brooklyn, the Boston park system, and analogous projects for Buffalo, New York; Louisville, Kentucky; Chicago's South Parks, and Rock Creek Park in Washington, D.C. These grand exercises sought to impose order, or at least a diagrammatic comprehensibility, on cities that contemporaries viewed as out of control. The survey was a means to this end. If the perceived shortcomings, often defined as the "problem" (or problems), could be quantified and coded, then surely a corrective could be defined and applied. This technique is scientific; a problem described is a problem solved. Of course urban "problems" have proven far more intractable and cities far more complex than these reformers imagined, and it is valuable to compare the 1930 report and subsequent planning efforts drawn from that study in light of present-day issues in Southern California.

Figures 4 and 5. Two views of Castle Rock looking north from Castellammare record the pace and character of development in coastal areas of Los Angeles County during the 1920s. In 1924 we see the "remains of the old County road," a two-lane thoroughfare graded from a narrow strip of land along the highwater zone between the breakers and the palisades.

The Olmsted-Bartholomew report for Los Angeles County spells out the dangers posed by a more than two-fold increase in population during the 1920s (from 900,000 to over 2,200,000, an average of 350 newcomers per day for ten years) and the seemingly insatiable demand for subdivided property that could be developed as house lots, business parcels, and industrial sites. The planners noted how the steady advance of urban development had crept up canyons into the mountains, followed hilltop ridges, and abutted the beaches (figures 4 and 5). Their report addresses the dangers of speculation and "injurious encroachment."[6] The focus is resolutely on systems—the robust but ultimately endangered systems of nature in the mountains, high desert, the basin, and the Pacific coastline—and the ways these might best be integrated with urban systems, especially the infrastructure necessary for an expanding metropolitan region. The plan sets out recommendations and strategies for achieving an alternative future for the county and can serve as a benchmark against which we can evaluate subsequent studies and the occasional public challenges to the politics of growth.

An image taken one year later (and a few hundred yards to the south) shows
street improvements and an elevated pedestrian crossing along the waterfront
as well as an initial crop of large-scale, high-price housing on winding streets
leading off the coast road. The report notes that this beach has been "fenced
in for the use of owners of property in Castellammare" and recommends this
"quasi-public use" be encouraged and maintained. "Any private land that may
exist should be publicly acquired."

This vision retains its power, and the issues that county residents
grappled with then are similar to those they are facing now. Coastal
development, public access to beaches, preserving wetlands, encroachment into ecologically sensitive habitats: each of these remains
on the front page and front burner. In the past decade we have wit-
nessed the ongoing controversy over plans to recast the remaining
segment of the Ballona Wetlands in West Los Angeles into Playa
Vista, a 1,000 acre, mixed-use development intended to provide housing for 28,000 residents and jobs for 20,000, as well as debates over
the construction of luxury housing along the coastline at Bolsa Chica
in northern Orange County (figure 6).[7] These and similar projects are
shaping the region now and for the immediate future. Other proposals will follow. Urgency, vision, and perseverance are still called for.

As a type, the Olmsted-Bartholomew report for Los Angeles
County can be placed in a lineage reaching back to Frederick Law
Olmsted Sr.'s work as well as that of his associates, such as George

Figure 6. Ballona Creek is a small water course that empties into Santa Monica Bay from the west side of Los Angeles. The creek winds through present-day Culver City and West Los Angeles. The Los Angeles River once flowed through the Ballona Creek waterway, moved there by early nineteenth-century earthquake activity. Ballona Creek offered an opportunity for Olmsted and Bartholomew to, as they saw it, enhance natural settings through concerted and integrated planning. Though in a flood plain (this photograph depicts the creek following heavy rains), Ballona was at the heart of the report's west side visions. By linking coastal facilities with a parkway here, Olmsted and Bartholomew imagined "one of the great recreation features of the world." A tremendously sensitive environment, Ballona Creek has become the focus of political battles over development in recent years.

Kessler, whose plan for Kansas City is a precursor for the Los Angeles study. Although qualitatively different in approach and intention, Daniel Burnham's 1909 plan for the Chicago region and the Regional Planning Association's decade-long investigation of New York and its environs during the 1920s shared with the Olmsted-Bartholomew project structural similarities in terms of organization, project funding, and the call for rethinking metropolitan governance.

At the same time, the study that culminated in the 1930 report for Los Angeles is the last of a type, one led by a business oligarchy constituted as an informal but powerful adjunct to formal, electoral politics. These business titans understood large-scale planning as a means for achieving the city profitable.[8] During the 1920s, the federal Department of Commerce, urged on by Secretary Herbert Hoover, was in the vanguard of efforts to require cities to prepare land use plans

and adopt model enabling acts as a means toward constituting departments or commissions of planning staffed by professionals. This turn
to putatively neutral experts and their ascension into the ranks of
formal government at the national, state, and local levels increased
dramatically during the New Deal era. The minutes of the Los Angeles Area Chamber of Commerce board of directors reveal a business
vantage on the city similar to that of the Merchants and Manufactur-
ers in Chicago, the Merchants' Association in San Francisco, and
their counterparts in other cities, a complex amalgam of aesthetics,
utility, and socially conservative notions of reform and uplift. The
men who controlled these exclusive institutions viewed municipal
recreation and the provision of beaches for the public as the performance of a civic duty. Professional consultants such as Frederick
Law Olmsted Jr. and Harland Bartholomew shared their sense of
purpose, a form of *noblesse oblige* for the professional elite. Where the
business elite and these designers differed was in their assessment of
how to achieve these objectives; in Los Angeles, this difference proved
to be critical.

THE PARK "PROBLEM"

The Olmsted-Bartholomew report has been called a window into a
forgotten City Beautiful past for the city and county of Los Angeles.[9]
However, a study of the report reveals that it is something different.
Los Angeles did exhibit a brief infatuation with the formal, aesthetic
City Beautiful tradition in the early twentieth century. However, the
1930 plan is the product of an urban vision in which the passage
through open landscape and scenic vistas plays a more prominent role
than the axial clarity of Baron Haussmann's Paris, L'Enfant's plan for
Washington, D.C., or the grand boulevards rendered for Burnham's
Plan of Chicago. In the latter examples, a continuous building line
along thoroughfares serves as a framing device for squares and plazas,
the occasional obelisk, a civic center, or similar landmark. Yet in certain important ways, the Olmsted-Bartholomew report does represent a latter-day iteration of earlier planning and reform precepts.
Parks, Playgrounds and Beaches fits well within American urban planning traditions concerning both nature and the city. Given the institutional players involved in the creation of the 1930 plan, that history
can be sketched back at least as far as the life and career of Frederick
Law Olmsted Sr.

This plan also fits into a specific Los Angeles context, one that even includes the Olmsted firm at a much earlier moment than the late 1920s. Much of this history and continuity has been forgotten. The kind of planning vision that produced the *Parks, Playgrounds and Beaches* report of 1930 has been supplanted in the intervening seventy years by the exigencies of urban expansion in Southern California. Even the sheer breadth of this report is itself testimony to the ideals of an earlier era, one arguably more optimistic about comprehensive plans and bold projections of the future.

The early-century arena of comprehensive planning in Los Angeles, or at least ideas about such planning, belongs to progressive reformers such as settlement house founder and Methodist minister Dana Bartlett. Bartlett also saw a triad that linked aspects of regional planning into parks, playgrounds and beaches. His 1907 book, *The Better City*, fused the moral order of social uplift with the seemingly unlimited access to nature that characterized life in urban Southern California. Bartlett's ideas sprang directly from an amalgam of social gospel and social hygiene thinking, the notion that nature offered the regenerative powers to help the poor battle the temptations and vices of the increasingly congested city. Nature would do the work of social control as well: "It is a fact made clear by years of experience," Bartlett wrote, "that the fairer the city, the nearer to Nature's heart the people are brought; the more easily they are governed."[10]

Bartlett expected that Los Angeles could become the paradigmatic better city, "the world's dream of the City Beautiful."[11] Parks, ornamental and not, were critical to the plan. Bartlett figured the Santa Monica and San Gabriel Mountains would continue to lure the weary city-dweller in search of rejuvenation—he viewed the mountains as the perimeter and critical frame of any comprehensive landscape plan (figure 7). "No scheme for beautifying the city can be complete that does not include a comprehensive plan for a metropolitan park system."[12] Bartlett echoed planners of previous generations who imagined parks as the "lungs" of the city. (Of course boosters had long advocated the air and climate in Southern California as a palliative for those suffering from pulmonary and other diseases, and Los Angeles was known for some time as a city for those with one lung.) The recent past boded well, but demand for space would soon outstrip supply. Bartlett rehearsed the by-then familiar demographic future: by 1920 or thereabouts, greater Los Angeles would have a million in-

Figure 7. In 1914 the Los Angeles Playground Commission secured a long-term lease from the United States Forest Service for a twenty-three acre municipal camp at Seeley Flat, fifteen miles north of San Bernardino. The city piped in water from a nearby spring, constructed a cement plunge, and graded areas for tennis, croquet and other sports. In its annual report, the commission noted that the municipal camp was accessible via a "good automobile road" and that "numberless trips may be taken from this point to other beautiful places in these magnificent mountains." In the Olmsted-Bartholomew plan, Camp Seeley is classified as a "large reservation." At the time of the report, the city maintained four camp grounds, Seeley, Radford (San Bernardino National Forest), High Sierra (Inyo National Forest), and Oak Flats (Angeles National Forest).

habitants. Where were their parks? More parks were needed, great and small, ornamental and rustic, mountainous and coastal. "Some part of the ocean front should be reserved for great seaside parks," he insisted, "for all time."[13]

The distinction between highly cultivated parks and those less formally landscaped was, for Dana Bartlett and others, an important one. Parks with elaborate landscaping, though an important component to planning and beautification, must be accompanied by park space that presented "the natural condition which the city dweller longs for; parks so large that there is room for the planting of all kinds of trees in their native soils and altitudes."[14]

Dana Bartlett was no prophet—he was a civic booster imbued with

Figure 8. Established in the mid-1880s, Elysian Park was the city's largest public open space until Griffith J. Griffith gave the city Griffith Park. Covering over five hundred acres, Elysian had been planted with thousands of trees by the turn of the century. Like Griffith Park, Elysian Park was designed to offer city residents a variety of recreational opportunities, from formal plantings and carefully designed gardens to more rural retreats. Fifty thousand eucalyptus saplings were planted in the park's early years. In 1896, Angelenos voted down bonds which would have brought $100,000 to the park for upkeep and improvement. By the early years of the twentieth century, planners faced the additional challenge of factoring the automobile into an older, even European, park ideal. Olmsted and Bartholomew wished to add 420 acres of adjacent Chavez Ravine to the park; they expected that the new acreage, carved out of an existing neighborhood, might be devoted to athletic fields or a golf course.

ideals of Progressive-era and social gospel reform. Each of the component pieces of his vision fit together as an idealized whole. The assembled plan would render "the better city," an urban environment privileged with natural amenities, a rational, workable arena in which beauty and efficiency triumphed over ugliness and sloth. Bartlett called for a systematic plan to match his narrative homily, a call that would go largely unanswered for nearly two decades. He wished for a planner, an architect, or one of the newly-professionalized "city beautifiers" to come to Los Angeles and gaze across the basin from high atop one of the adjacent mountains. Inspiration would then find this man, in the form of "the mighty vision of the 'City of our Lady of

Figure 9. Early twentieth century visions of the playground included a wider set of ideas than simple recreation for children. Here the fourth and fifth grades at a school in the San Fernando Valley attend to gardening chores on their schoolyard. Such tasks, when accompanied by play (see the gym equipment in the background), were thought to be critical to encouraging proper social and physical development of the children of the city. Olmsted and Bartholomew emphasized the siting of school playgrounds with other nearby recreational facilities (see chapter IV of the report). Such multi-use features as playground gardens had, by this time, largely dropped from view.

the Angels,' with mountain, foothills, river, hilltops, seashore, parks, boulevards, happy homes—with the prodigality of nature over-mantling all. When that vision should find embodiment in a definite plan, no true son of this Southland would fail to give the plan endorsement and support, even though it might cost millions to fulfill the dream."[15]

Despite the lag time between Reverend Bartlett's stirring wish and the Olmsted-Bartholomew report of 1930, such planning ideas did dovetail with on-the-ground realities and continuities in early twentieth-century Los Angeles. A city Park Commission, established in 1889, was charged with oversight of the park lands of Elysian Park, the downtown Plaza, and Central Park (now Pershing Square) (figure 8). A Playground Commission had been inaugurated in 1904, and the city had begun to construct a number of urban playgrounds (and a municipal recreation center) within a few short years (see figure 2).

These, too, reflected the era's interest in integrated purposes—most playgrounds had garden plots for children and adults to work in—the park and playground were tied together (figure 9).[16]

Bartlett's dream for a plan that could comprehensively embrace as many beautification, reform, and urban rationalization components as possible would take years. But his was not the only integrated vision of planning for Los Angeles that meshed reform with landscape. Griffith J. Griffith, who had given the city the five square miles of Griffith Park in the late nineteenth century, wrote a 1910 follow-up to Bartlett's *Better City* that is, in many ways, a direct precursor to the Olmsted-Bartholomew 1930 report. Titled *Parks, Boulevards and Playgrounds*, Griffith's tract reiterated, in more detail, many of Bartlett's claims about the necessity of integrated landscape planning as well as the social good that such planning would provide. Griffith's arguments were by then familiar: park space could be the lungs of the city; parks could relieve class tensions; parks could be tied directly to comprehensive city planning. What is more, Griffith defined another in a long list of Los Angeles "problems": the park problem. A reflex toward classificatory order was extremely common in the era; along with its park problem, Los Angeles presumably suffered from "the Mexican problem" and the "housing problem." Like these two, the parks issue was a social and political problem, which demanded attention lest inevitable urban growth be compromised by congestion and irrationality.

Griffith, like Bartlett (whom he must have known) was a Progressive reformer interested in issues of social hygiene and the influence of environment on the individual. Unlike some pundits of the era, generally drawn from the ranks of commercial or real estate elites, Griffith both knew and stated that Los Angeles had neighborhoods of sub-standard housing stock inhabited by the working poor. This realization only rendered the "park problem" all the more pressing: it "has been forced to the front as one of the first importance."[17] Structural reform of industrial Los Angeles was not Griffith's aim except insofar as accessible parks and integrated boulevards could do the work of deep reform. In a classic reformulation of the frontier thesis for twentieth-century America, Griffith argued that "Public parks are the safety-valves of cities."[18] Free land remained America's hope, or at least open land in public, if urban, spaces.

Griffith's vision was both pastoral and not. Transportation innova-

Figure 10. Beginning in the late nineteenth century, Adams Boulevard was developed as the principal east-west thoroughfare through the city's preeminent residential district. Contemporary accounts speak to the value Angelenos placed on the scale of this street, the gracious houses built by prominent citizens, and the lush grounds that made the entire street appear as if it were a linear garden. In this undated view the variety and density of plant and tree specimens in a maturing landscape reveals why Angelenos singled this street out with pride. Olmsted and Bartholomew dismissed boulevards such as Adams as "decorated highways." The focus in their report is on "pleasure parkways," thoroughfares a quarter mile or more in width, screened from urban surroundings, and planted to produce a sense of spaciousness and seclusion as well as scenic effect. The planners considered automobile travel over pleasure parkways a "new, popular, and valuable form of recreation" that was losing value in Los Angeles given the city's "great spread." This shortcoming could be remedied if the system they proposed were implemented.

tions and decreasing costs had rendered the countryside far more accessible to urbanites; "city and country tend to merge in one another," he wrote.[19] The corridors between city and country ought best be tied to parks, one as the literal extension of the other. "For what is a boulevard, with its double row of shade trees . . . and its border of plants and flowers, backed, as it should be, by emerald lawns, but an extension of the park; just as the park itself is merely an expanded boulevard? Each supplements the other, and without its proper supplement each is incomplete"[20] (figure 10).

Griffith was particularly concerned about boulevards—he wrote this tract in large measure as a protest against Los Angeles city officials for not making his great park benediction accessible enough to the people of the region. Nonetheless, his insistence on more porous boundaries between park and boulevard (and even between park and playground) was one of the many design features that Olmsted and Bartholomew incorporated into *Parks, Playgrounds and Beaches*.

Like Bartlett, Griffith made an effort to distinguish between highly cultured landscapes and unsculpted (or less sculpted) public recreation space. "I am not at all insensible to the charms of landscape gardening, to trim lawns and floral decorations. . . . But I understand clearly that these were not the picture but its frame; that while fitting for the entrance to the people's playground they were not the playground; that the accessory should not be confused with the thing itself."[21]

Integrated planning ideas and social reform ideals swirling through Progressive-era Los Angeles made their way east, to the Olmsted Brothers firm in Brookline. Angelenos had recognized for some time the advantages that might accrue to their city if they were to engage the Olmsted firm for the design of Southland parks and public open spaces and in the planning of elite residential districts in the manner of Riverside, Illinois; Llewellyn Park, New Jersey; and Druid Hills in Atlanta. Frederick Law Olmsted Sr. and the Olmsted firm were preeminent practitioners of landscape architecture and civic design in the romantic tradition. Olmsted was a national authority in the closely related social and environmental reform movements. In addition to the talent and expertise that the Olmsted firm might bring to issues of park and subdivision planning, Angelenos no doubt desired the prestige that an association with the nation's preeminent landscape designer would bestow on a status-conscious city. In a 1895 overture sent directly to Olmsted, Charles Forman explained that a number of the city's citizens of means had been "endeavoring to induce our City Council to secure your services as Landscape Architect to make a general plan for the improvement of [Elysian Park]," a prominent outcropping just north of the city center where the varied terrain of hills and valleys might be transformed into "one of the most beautiful parks in the world." To date, however, he and his colleagues had been unsuccessful in persuading the council "chiefly for the reason that they think your charges would be greater than they could afford to pay." Olmsted apparently agreed and declined the commission.[22]

Fifteen years later, the city's Board of Park Commissioners approached John C. Olmsted regarding a master plan for Agricultural (later Exposition) Park. Olmsted, in San Diego working with that city's Fair Committee, offered his services for $2,000 plus expenses, a fee the board rejected as "too high for the Park Department in their present financial condition."[23] One month later, Wilbur Cook, a former Olmsted employee, wrote John C. alerting him to the mayoral appointment of a City Planning Committee charged with coordinating a comprehensive plan for "Greater Los Angeles, running from the foothills to the seashore." Cook had advised commission members "that you are the man for the work . . . I am heading sentiment your way." Some members supported Charles Mulford Robinson, author of a 1907 study that called for a civic acropolis on Bunker Hill (a work Cook dismissed as having "little value"). Cook realized that funding would have to come from "private subscription," but he noted optimistically that "we have enough wealthy men in the community to see the project through." He invited Olmsted to give an address to the City Club, attend an informal meeting with the mayor, park commission members, and other "substantial citizens," and craft an estimate for such a report and plan.[24]

Olmsted's brief, handwritten response drew on his recent experience in Seattle. In it he called for a charter amendment "making adequate provision for the employment of a commission of experts" as voters in Seattle had recently done. But in contrast to the 1908 Seattle project, an exercise that resulted in limited implementation of the comprehensive plan, Olmsted now considered it imperative that the commission, once established, "should be continued indefinitely, so as to advise as to changes of plan such as experience may prove to be necessary or advisable." Without the formation and institutionalization of this political structure, he stated, "I am not sure that I care to take up the matter."[25]

A formal overture from committee member Charles Randall arrived in less than two weeks requesting a meeting to consider the preparation of an extensive planning scheme. In his reply, Olmsted suggested the committee organize an automobile tour so he and one or two committee members might assess the "conditions and limitations of the problem." He also set out the firm's billing structure and a tentative fee for a project of this magnitude.[26]

A terse, handwritten response from committee secretary Florence

H. Mills followed. Regretfully, she informed Olmsted, for various reasons but "chiefly because of the great expenditure that Los Angeles is making for its aqueduct and harbor," the committee had determined that the first step toward a comprehensive plan "be made by experts now in the employ of the city . . . [L]ater it may be deemed necessary to secure expert assistance from without."[27] It would take almost two decades for the city's leading citizens to determine once again the need for a comprehensive plan, to secure the necessary funding through a private subscription drive, and to employ the Olmsted firm as experts to assist in their effort.

With the completion of the Los Angeles aqueduct in 1913, the city embarked on its remarkable program of consolidation and annexation. In just a decade, the city's incorporated area would quadruple. This burst of amazing territorial energy would prompt new planning necessities. In the summer of 1914, Kate Bassett, a self-described "lay member" of the Los Angeles City Planning Association, wrote Frederick Law Olmsted Jr. to ask how he thought comprehensive city planning ought to proceed from survey to plan to practice. "You are more or less familiar with conditions here I think. We are a city growing tremendously in a haphazard fashion. A major plan, very good in some particulars, was once formulated. In two and a half years after its presentation, the city had acquired more area than the plan comprehended, proving its inadequacy. It was laid on the shelf." Bassett pointed out that much good had come of recent traffic, transit, and other studies; she pointed out as well the "valuable work" performed by Dana Bartlett "on the humanitarian side of things." But a pressing need existed for a comprehensive city plan.[28]

> Of course I know that an adequate city plan is a work of several years, and is a growing thing, but am I right in believing that an *expert survey* is what is needed first? . . . You planned Torrance, and the attorney for the Vanderlip purchase [Rancho Palos Verdes] confirmed a recent newspaper report that your services had been secured and that you would soon be with us doing that work. This filled me with great hope that we might also have your help at the same time in working on our problems, for it will all be one city a hundred years hence.[29]

Bassett, who had taken an eight-year world tour that sparked her interest in city planning, knew the obstacles she faced in trying to get

Olmsted and his firm to consider a comprehensive Los Angeles plan again. "Recognizing the futility of trying at present to get 'the powers that be' to appropriate the money to secure the right kind of workers for the plan, I appealed to a very wealthy woman here to stand back of the plan and make it a gift to her city, as the Commercial Club in Chicago did. She passed away before it was arranged. Now I am making the same appeal to her son, to do it as a memorial to both his parents. The gift should perhaps be in the nature of a foundation, with an endowment caring for the plan after its acceptance." Bassett wanted Olmsted to consider coming on board. "Comparing Los Angeles with other cities, I believe that it could become as wonderful as any of them, and that nothing short of the *very best* the world has to offer, is the demand of the present. This costs money and it should be paid for, without any loss of time." Could Olmsted tell her how much such a report might cost?[30]

Olmsted crafted a thoughtful response. "A critical survey of the existing conditions and prospects is of course an essential preliminary to any intelligent planning," he wrote, "but it is a very sterile academic thing if it is not accompanied by constructive planning. Logically the plan follows the survey. Practically they must be advanced almost together in successive stages." Olmsted then turned to non-technical matters with a prophetic assessment. "It is all so much a question of degree and of local circumstance. In any given case the size of the steps and their very nature, the entire course of a wise procedure, are matters not of logic or of science but of expediency and the art political." Olmsted went on to point out both the universal and particular challenges that together might compromise planning in any "big city" such as Los Angeles where the "air is full of large plans and projects, more or less conflicting (or if not conflicting, at least without proper correlation)." Each would have promoters and detractors. Therefore it would take a "much bigger and more serious piece of work in city planning to make an impression on the public" and generate support.[31]

In this sense, the situation in Los Angeles was particularly challenging. "I should say it would now take quite a big and serious and able and at the same time cleverly launched sample of city planning to make much of a 'splash', and capture a wide enthusiastic public support. That is really your problem isn't it?" The plan would get nowhere for $10,000; it might get going for $50,000. "$100,000 ought to get things moving well unless the adverse conditions require time to overcome them rather than the concentrated application of such services as money can secure." But this was only a guess, Olmsted cautioned, much like the guess of how much it would cost to wage war.[32]

Bassett wrote Olmsted immediately after receiving his commentary. In her appreciative letter, she suggested one of the city's more pressing and specific problems, traffic congestion in the downtown district. Despite her hopes that the Olmsted firm could yet become involved in comprehensive city planning, it would be this more discrete issue that would first engage the firm, beginning in the early 1920s.[33]

A Major Traffic Street Plan for Los Angeles, which the Olmsted firm produced in 1924 with the assistance of Harland Bartholomew and Associates, was a concerted effort to disentangle the various traffic and transit problems of the congested districts in Los Angeles, particularly in the heart of downtown. Although it was not the comprehensive (and expensive) planning document that Bassett and others had hoped for, it nonetheless provided the two firms with a great deal of firsthand knowledge about the basin.[34]

RATIONALE AND APPROACH

During the 1920s, the Chamber was vitally concerned about the flow of visitors and tourist dollars into Southern California. Similarly, they recognized the value of making the region attractive to people of means who might choose Los Angeles as a seasonal or year-round residence. Their discussions, recorded in the minutes of the Board of Directors meetings, contain references to internecine competition and rivalry with Santa Barbara and San Diego, two sites then gaining favor among the ultra-wealthy who had formerly trafficked the "gold coast" of Los Angeles County. The 1930 Olmsted-Bartholomew report takes up this concern directly. The authors routinely trot out the city profitable as a rationale for undertaking proposed improvements and to make favorable comparisons with other cities. A section titled "Justification for the Proposed Expenditures" begins with climate and recreational advantages attracting tourists "to the profit of the community" and sets Paris as the metric. "Here is a most interesting opportunity for comparison," the authors suggest, because Paris "transformed itself from an unsightly place to a beautiful city" and has "long been the center of world tourist trade."[35]

The reference is to the three-decade-long transformation of that city commencing in 1850 under Georges-Eugène Haussmann, Napoleon III's Prefect of the Seine. The great boulevards are the best-known product of an effort to open up the city's dense quarters, make movement through the city more efficient, rationalize and modernize water supply and sewerage, and demonstrate Paris's stature as the center of economic, cultural, and political power in France. Los Angeles, on the other hand, could become a capital of recreation with "six hundred miles of pleasant driveways" and "scenic values *unequaled elsewhere in the world*" [emphasis in original]. Parks and pleasureways comparable to those found in the French capital would assure a continued flow of tourists and "might *even alone* justify [the] total cost [which] will be less than the sum now spent annually in Paris by American tourists" [emphasis in original].[36]

For the Los Angeles study, Olmsted and Bartholomew relied to a considerable degree on comparison in making their case for a comprehensive and coordinated system of large parks with connecting parkways, neighborhood playgrounds, and regional recreation areas including public beaches (figures 11 and 12). On one hand, comparisons with cities that were acknowledged leaders in the movement to create metropolitan park systems such as Boston, Chicago, Kansas City, and Westchester County demonstrated the shortcomings in Los Angeles. Olmsted and Bartholomew used case studies to illuminate a process similar to the one they were proposing for Los Angeles and to illustrate the results that might be achieved if Angelenos were to implement their recommendations.

Some aspects of the comparisons highlight Southern California's distinctive qualities. Throughout the document, text (often italicized) and select illustrations are intended to distinguish Los Angeles, and cities in the West more generally, from metropolitan areas in the Midwest and East. "*The Los Angeles Region is the only great metropolis that has developed almost wholly since the invention of the automobile*" they tell us, and the "*recreation of its people is largely dependent*" on the mobility the auto provides [emphasis in original][37] (figure 13). Some readers will find similarity with work the Olmsted and Bartholomew firms proposed and implemented in other metropolitan regions. Analyzed according to this metric, the report reads as formulaic, as if an outline or template crafted for prior assignments has been cribbed and then applied whole to a demonstrably different setting.

Figure 11. The report's efforts to tie local mountains into a chain of recreation facilities and opportunities matched regional culture and history. People in Los Angeles County had been hiking and picnicking in the local mountains for generations prior to the late 1920s. The planners insisted that public access to local mountains would be enhanced by incorporating them into a regional system of linked transportation corridors and recreational spaces. In this photograph Los Angeles fitness and health guru Paul Bragg leads a group of outdoor enthusiasts into the Hollywood Hills.

We can see an Olmsted template in the report's structure. It was organized according to a set of divisions for "important types of public grounds" along lines that Olmsted Jr. spelled out in a 1906 article co-authored with John Nolen. At that time, the planners noted, "public spirited people" had come to appreciate the value of open spaces in towns and cities. But there was a general lack of "clear thinking." Although they approve of a large increase in the number of parks and playgrounds "in a vague way . . . even the more enlightened communities seem yet to understand that these open spaces are of great variety, that they should be selected and designed to serve radically different purposes, and that the failure to understand this principle . . . leads to gross waste and inefficiency."[38] (As the minutes of Chamber discussions reveal, this assessment rang true twenty years later.)

The authors identified six types of public grounds: streets, boulevards and parkways; city squares, commons, and public gardens; play-

Figure 12. In Chapter V, Olmsted and Bartholomew calculate that at times
of peak use, visitors to Los Angeles beaches had on average fifteen square feet of
space per person. They compare this, unfavorably, to the fifty-six square feet the
average spectator and bather has at Coney Island, New York, the "world's most
heavily used beach." This undated photograph of the beach and beach-goers at
Ocean Park in Santa Monica looking south toward Venice Pier corroborates the
planners' findings. It is comparable to Plate 29 (Report p. 62) captioned "too
crowded for comfort." Both the quantitative assessment of spectators and bathers
and the visual documentation of use are marshalled to support their claim that
the "most active demand . . . in the entire Los Angeles Region . . . is for more
and better beach and waterside facilities."

grounds for small, school age, and older children; small and neighborhood parks; large parks; and great outlying reservations. With
some doubling up, and the reasonable substitution of public beaches
for city squares and public grounds, these align with the five chapters
of specific recommendations in the Los Angeles report.

The parkway segment of the proposal illustrates the synthetic nature of this study. In February 1912, the Los Angeles Park Commission issued a "brief discussion of the proposed Silver Lake Parkway
and its relation to a park and boulevard system for Los Angeles." In
an illustrated pamphlet, commission members strove to align the initiatives that a local improvement association had tendered to the city
council with its own objective, namely, creating parkways. In this
case, property owners and residents petitioned for land condemnation

Figure 13. Adapting the automobile to the metropolis beyond its streets and arteries proved one of the biggest challenges to Olmsted and Bartholomew. In this photograph, a car fords the stream in the center of the Arroyo Seco, the large ravine running southwest from the San Gabriel Mountains towards downtown Los Angeles. Staged though it is, this image nonetheless hints at the enormity of the challenge. Should the Arroyo Seco be a natural reservation, a park, a parkway, or some combination of all three? What future did parks hold in the metropolis with the world's highest per capita automobile ownership? Would the automobile change the fundamental relationships between city-dwellers and their parks?

to create a park running from Sunset Boulevard to Temple Street. Drawings depict a narrow, linear, and irregularly shaped strip of open space. The Commission encouraged the local entrepreneurs to consider extending the proposal and connecting Silver Lake to the north with Fourth Street and the Wilshire district to the south. This modified scheme, a public-private initiative, would transform a "ravine or valley lying in the north-western section of the city . . . [into] a two and a half mile long parkway varying in width from two hundred to four hundred feet and contain[ing] approximately one hundred acres." Foot paths and "shady seats" would line a "winding boulevard" running the length of the development, with the necessary cross drives and entrances, the whole planted with trees and shrubs "so as to form a beautiful and natural valley parkway."[39]

An obvious connection between this plan and later proposals is

Figure 14. Like Elysian and Westlake (MacArthur) Park, Eastlake Park, now called Lincoln Park, was one of the first public parks in Los Angeles. The city acquired the park's nearly fifty acres, just east of downtown and across the river, for $5000 in 1874. Electric streetcar access, as well as the park department's greenhouses and nurseries, helped make Eastlake a popular destination. Boating facilities and a carousel for children increased the park's attractions. Olmsted and Bartholomew (see Report page 82) wished to incorporate an adjacent racetrack and auto park, both of which they viewed with suspicion, into the park by turning these facilities into athletic fields. They also urged that the city turn the Selig Zoo, just to the north, into a public facility tied to Lincoln Park's recreational purposes.

found in a diagram showing the relation of the Silver Lake Parkway to a parkway and boulevard system designed to "furnish a connection between the western and eastern sections of the city." This 1911 drawing, attributed to landscape architect Laurie Davidson Cox and with the imprimatur of the Los Angeles Park Department, showed the city's existing parks—Griffith, Westlake, Exposition, Echo, Central (Pershing) Square, the Plaza, Elysian, Sycamore Grove, Eastlake, and Hollenbeck—linked by a series of new or enhanced roadways (figure 14). River Drive followed the course of the Los Angeles River between Griffith and Elysian parks. Near the former, a short feeder led to Silver Lake and the proposed parkway effectively linking the city's largest public open space with emerging commercial and resi-

Figure 15. The Los Angeles Department of Parks developed Lafayette Park on land George H. Smith and George S. Patton deeded to the city in 1886. In this 1913 view, taken from the Bryson Apartments at 2701 Wilshire Boulevard and looking toward the north and west, we see a neighborhood park laid out in the prevailing "gardenesque" manner. A system of curvilinear paths is set in contrast to broad boulevards meeting at right angles. The walks are composed carefully and lead visitors to displays of showy trees and flowering shrubs. Earth work has transformed the site and created "natural" features such as the small, recessed glade adjacent to a raised quadrant on the northwest (far right) edge of the park. A streetcar is heading south on Commonwealth Avenue. In 1913, this section of the city was at the western edge of urban development. This portrait captures a district subdivided into building lots and supplied with city services but where building construction and improvements are still intermittent.

dential districts along Vermont Avenue and Wilshire Boulevard (figure 15). From there, an enhanced Wilshire Boulevard would take pleasure drivers and others through Westlake Park across the Los Angeles River and into the eastside where Boyle Avenue and St. Louis Street fronted Hollenbeck Park. Figueroa Street is shown as the thread connecting Exposition, Echo, and Elysian parks. At the northeast corner of the latter, drivers would have access to the southern reach of an Arroyo Seco Parkway, effectively linking Pasadena with what then constituted the southernmost reaches of the city.

What would this system provide? According to the commission, Los Angeles was "far behind" comparable cities in providing parks. In their quantitative assessment they discounted Griffith Park as a "natural scenic reservation," not a city park in the strict sense of the term. Elysian Park they considered "almost unused" for lack of street car and boulevard connections. Deducting this area left residents less than four hundred acres of parklands available for everyday use, a deficiency that was particularly pressing for youth living in the city's older residential districts. The authors trotted out the standard, yet revealing, comparisons with Kansas City's two thousand acres of parks and the more than thirty-three hundred acres of improved parks in Minneapolis. This despite the fact that "no city in America, or in fact in the world, has greater possibilities for civic beauty, as regards topography and climate, than Los Angeles."[40]

What would it take for the city to reach its potential? Taking a cue from Kansas City, Boston, and other park cities, the commissioners advanced a utilitarian argument based on land and a speculator's trust in the continual increase in property value. Land acquisition and improvements would be funded through the creation of an assessment district. Property owners would reap a return beyond their contribution through enhanced property values. Other residents would enjoy the out-of-doors since the Park Commission would maintain an existing trolley right-of-way and public transit would make this sliver of green space accessible to people "who do not own automobiles or carriages." Finally, the city would benefit; the creation of a pleasure parkway would eliminate an eyesore and ensure that the bottomland would not be filled in for building lots. Rather, it would become an amenity around which real estate entrepreneurs could develop "one of the finest residential districts in the city."[41]

In their scheme for regional parkways, the Olmsted-Bartholomew study identified the Arroyo Seco as an obvious route for a pleasure drive with associated parkland. This seasonal watercourse had long been recognized as one of the signature natural features in the region. Residents of Pasadena and other incorporated and unincorporated communities along the arroyo had supported the creation of a series of parks including Sycamore Grove, Lower Arroyo Park, Brookside Park, and Oak Grove Park. In Pasadena, Arroyo Seco Park formed an almost continuous band of public open space along the city's western boundary. In what seems from our vantage to be a paradox, from the 1910s forward, Angelenos looked to the creation of a parkway along the bottomlands of the arroyo as a way to maintain

Figure 16 and 17. In a section on "Parks and the Drainage Problem," Olmsted and Bartholomew encourage County purchase of flood-prone property to realize a "double return." Public control alone could mitigate against inappropriate development (and future outlays to defray the cost of flood damage) while securing the benefits garnered when low-lying land is converted to parks and parkways. In their call for a pleasure parkway running from the Los Angeles River at Elysian Park along the Arroyo Seco through Pasadena and out to Devil's Gate Canyon (an eleven-mile route with 1,420 acres of associated parkland), the planners were building on a series of prior studies connecting the commercial center of Los Angeles with Pasadena. The genius of the 1930 proposal is in its call for a "pleasureway park" along a route that could be inundated during periods of heavy rain and mountain runoff.

and enhance this landscape amenity and to ensure that it would remain in public control (figures 16 and 17).

The Olmsted and Bartholomew firms and their network of affiliated associates (often past employees) brought to the county planning effort a considerable portfolio of area projects. Two previous efforts were incorporated into the 1930 report wholesale. Their 1924 study, *A Major Traffic Street Plan*, that fixed the system of north-south, east-west boulevards at one-mile coordinates remains the primary surface street route for regional transportation to this day. Immediately following the completion of the citywide study, the county contracted with the Olmsted office to survey and prepare plans for the "south-

Although much of the land had been in the public domain since the turn of the century, no work was undertaken until 1938 when the Works Progress Administration oversaw construction of the Arroyo Seco Flood Control Channel. As constructed, the parkway, cum highway, is contrary to the proposals spelled out in the report. These two views looking south from the York Avenue bridge toward Avenue 64 document the sequence of construction. The official opening of the initial six mile stretch from Avenue 22 to Glenarm on December 30, 1940 was timed to coincide with the Tournament of Roses parade and the Rose Bowl.

west district," the area between Baldwin Hills and Palos Verdes east of the city boundary from the "shoestring" (the narrow strip of land running between the core of Los Angeles proper and the harbor at San Pedro-Wilmington) to the ocean. The firm produced detailed plans, specifications, and property descriptions for a parkway running north from Palos Verdes to Hollywood and a secondary route along a widened Sepulveda Avenue (renamed the Sepulveda Parkway) beginning at a new park in Gardena through Hawthorne and into the northern beach cities.[42]

In addition to the *Major Traffic Street Plan* and the Hollywood-Palos Verdes Parkway, regional projects designed by the two firms included the Bartholomew Associates' master plan for Glendale (1926) coordinated by L. Deming Tilton, a protégé whom Bartholomew encouraged to move to Southern California to administer the firm's projects and oversee implementation; the Olmsted Brothers plan for Torrance (1911), a model industrial satellite; ongoing work at the Palos Verdes Ranch (1914–31); subdivision plans for Alta San Raphael (Pasadena, 1922–26) and Benmar Hills (Burbank, 1924); and consulting for the Pacific Palisades Association (1927) and Walter Leimert, the developer of Leimert Park (1926).[43]

PRIVATE INITIATIVE, PUBLIC PLAN

In a 1925 address examining the "Relation of Park Planning to City and Regional Planning," Frederick Law Olmsted Jr. set out a three-part process for park planning: an assessment of need (including projections for population increase, economic outlook, and the city's present and future patterns of development), a selection of land appropriate for parks (with an emphasis on achieving "least cost," which Olmsted defined as the sum of first cost, improvements, and maintenance), and a detailed park plan, "pure and simple." Here and in other public statements of the firm's professional philosophy, Olmsted placed greatest emphasis on the first two phases, survey and site selection. These clearly fall within the domain of city and regional planning which Olmsted implicitly equates with authority and power—or, at the least, a position closer to those with power than will ever be achieved by park planners, whom he casts as underpaid technicians employed by weak municipal departments overseen by "amateurish boards of directors."[44]

In Los Angeles, those with power and authority controlled access to the capital necessary for undertaking comprehensive plans and securing land for parks, playgrounds, and public beaches. A great deal of money would be needed for planners' salaries and additional matters, and money became a central issue for the Chamber and its allies. As late as the spring of 1926, only a year before the establishment of the blue ribbon Citizens' Committee that sponsored the Olmsted-Bartholomew report, the Chamber's Board of Directors had noted the lack of city funds, especially for beach improvements and beachfront property.[45]

Money, and lots of it, could be had by tapping the finances of Los Angeles' commercial and industrial elites. Representatives of these worlds gathered together, as they had been doing for decades, within the restricted confines of the Los Angeles Chamber of Commerce, probably the most powerful commercial body of its kind in the American West, if not in the nation. It is to that entity that we must turn to follow the thread of comprehensive city planning as it moved from the pens of social reformers to the ambitions of businessmen and film stars.

Enter "America's sweetheart." On the 28th of October, 1926, the Chamber of Commerce Directors welcomed Mary Pickford to their regular meeting. Chamber Vice-President McGarry, perhaps a bit nervously, introduced the film star to his colleagues. The actress got right to the point, more or less. "I have come to the luncheon today not to attempt to tell you how to run your business . . . but rather to offer some suggestions, I hope some constructive criticism, and I would like you to enter into this discussion with me and argue with me if you disagree with the points I am going to present to you." Following a brief digression about current events abroad, Pickford made her major points.[46]

> When our visitors come from the East or from Europe instead of going down to the city to come in, we always get them to get off in Pasadena. It is never downtown, always Pasadena, and I am wondering if it would not be possible when they are discussing the new station to bring it into a attractive part of the town, surrounded by a park with fountains. The first impression of Los Angeles would be a beautiful one and the last one something that they can carry away instead of going through packing houses. . . . It is very important. That is part of the staging of a city.[47]

Mary Pickford wanted a beautiful city, or even a City Beautiful, and, for part of a day at least, she had the rapt attention of the most powerful body in Southern California. She wished for the region to retain its "Spanish" flavor (Spanish place names "tasted good in the mouth"), and she could seamlessly mingle ethnicity, nationality, and history while stating that wish.

Pickford recognized the power of cinema as an advertising and promotional tool, and she recognized that the film scenery shown the world over created illusions of an ever-beautiful Southern California landscape. But that illusion, although perhaps based in some reality, was threatened. Demographic and spatial growth seemed assured, "but it is too bad we cannot direct the energies now in building a really model city rather than building and having to tear down a little later on."[48]

The Board of Directors held a brief discussion following Pickford's remarks. Irving Hellman (a Beverly Hills neighbor of Mary Pickford and Douglas Fairbanks), chairman of the Chamber's "Highways—City and County Planning Committee," which had a parks subcommittee, offered that he and his colleagues would soon issue "an exhaustive report," which would call for additional "park centers" where city streets intersected. Chamber director Crandall agreed with the actress that "our approaches to the city are vile." And he believed that comprehensive planning was no doubt called for. "You must bear in mind that this is a fast growing community. We have come up like a mushroom. . . . We have taken thousands of acres and subdivided them and put them into houses because that gave up the greatest financial return. No one has had vision enough in building up these subdivisions into a city to think ahead for parks. As Mr. Hellman has said, that matter is before us right at the present time, but other than giving it our moral support it is questionable if this Chamber can go very much further in it."[49]

Chamber President Lacy seconded that view, offering that the Chamber, as a commercial body, could do only a little for city beautification; much of the responsibility lay with city officials.

In 1924, when I had the honor of becoming President of this Chamber, in my inaugural address, after reciting our material progress and all that, I wound up expressing the thought that this Chamber of Commerce would forget to some extent our material progress and put greater thought into the development of the soul and I went on to mention then the necessity of parks and breathing space in this growing city for the vast numbers of poor people who are unable to get out to such places as Mandeville Canyon. We have done all we could do about it, but unfortunately like in other cities our authorities are those whom we select to make our laws and plan our cities and they are small calibered men. We have not been able to secure the services of the type of men we should have.[50]

Despite the presence of a city planning commission, Lacy (and other Chamber directors) believed that not nearly enough was being

Figure 18. By 1930, Los Angeles had two automobiles for every three residents. In the mid-1920s, Olmsted, Bartholomew, and Charles Cheney had worked towards an integrated traffic system in their *Major Traffic Street Plan. Parks, Playgrounds and Beaches* attempted to push beyond this earlier work by planning recreation and automobility together, often as linked endeavors. The report reveals the tensions inherent to that proposition. In this photograph, Angelenos do what by the 1920s and 1930s had become common. Having driven to a local park, Elysian in this case, they camp or picnic for the day. By the early years of the Depression and attendant increase in homelessness, so called "auto camps" such as these would be viewed as urban problems unto themselves.

done to plan for, and to protect, Los Angeles park space. *Noblesse oblige* required concerted action: "What we want to take care of is the poor people, the working people. Build parks right in the center of the city like they have at the Plaza now. That is what we need and we hope to bring it about"[51] (figure 18).

Lacy's comments, building on Mary Pickford's, sparked futher conversation. Director Hill added that beachfront property required as much attention as renewed efforts of park conservation and planning—"At the present time going down to the beach you can't go any place without trespassing on somebody's private property"—and the director pulled several of the planning themes back together in integrated fashion.[52] "[T]he next proposition is getting behind this park proposition not only for the benefit of beautifying our city and placing it in such a position that it is not an eye sore [sic] but is a breathing space for those who are unfortunate in not having estates and homes of their own and also in forming a beautiful pathway for those entering our city."[53]

Mary Pickford concurred, adding that the beautification of the city promised commercial dividends as well. "It is a purely business proposition because we are unique I think as a city and we are really a garden spot, and in order to attract people . . . and to hold them when they come here, we must be beautiful and charming and all of that and that to me is a business proposition. Very much the same thing as making a picture."[54]

But would the city and its park and planning bureaucrats understand? Perhaps. Director Chase did not think so. He offered that the Chamber directors were "idealists." City officials were not. "I can't see that you are going to make much headway along these lines until you have a park commission that has initiative and vision and the capacity to go ahead and carry out the vision."[55]

Pickford's visit started a series of conversations about park and landscape planning that would continue for months. In the middle of December, Chamber director Irving Hellman offered a plan by which the officials who made up the Planning Commission could be more or less outflanked by the organization of a private body to push park planning forward. Chamber President Lacy concurred: "We need another committee of 200, another harbor committee of 200, imbued with the same spirit and a long visioned program ahead of them and moreover realizing that every day we lose makes any program much more expensive to us."[56]

This is the genesis of the private committee that helped produce the 1930 Olmsted-Bartholomew report. Already by the mid-1920s, such private associations of interested people were a tried and true concept in Los Angeles civic and public affairs. What the Chamber wanted was quite simple: a higher profile for its own internal committees (especially the Parks and Recreation Committee) which considered such issues as parks and regional landscape planning. And the best way to do that was to constitute a blue-ribbon committee to put forth big ideas, big plans, and big money.[57]

None of this planning (or thinking about planning) occurred in a vacuum. The Chamber wanted to make certain its committees and its programs were in the forefront, ahead of the city's departments, agencies, and commissions, and ahead of any state initiatives designed to centralize such things as park planning. As one member of the Board of Directors offered in the early spring of 1927, California had "too many bodies supposed to be developing parks."[58] The Chamber wished to set policy alone.

By June of 1927, just such a Citizens' Committee had a nucleus membership built around Chairman John Treanor, a wealthy cement company executive.[59] Members were being recruited from the city and county, people willing to spend at least $500 to join. Eighty members had been signed up, from the ranks of the film community as well as commercial, industrial, and real estate elites. Optimism ran high, arguably higher than it deserved to, as memberships were proving a hard sell.[60] "The work will be very fine for the community and the city of Los Angeles and we are very happy in the personnel of those who have accepted the responsibility. . . . The gates are not yet closed so that there is an opportunity for sinners to return."[61] By August, the Citizens' Committee had just over one hundred members and had planned their first full meeting.

By the fall, Treanor's committee was up and running, and it had approached and hired both Olmsted and Bartholomew, using the prospect of membership dues as the promise of major funding.[62] But the work of the group occasioned at least some concern within the Chamber of Commerce leadership that had created it. Did the committee have a degree of autonomy? Apparently the Citizens' Committee made a request to the Chamber for a commitment of funds, (up to $10,000), for lobbying and pushing their findings to and through the California legislature. Chamber directors, at least a few of them, admitted to not quite knowing what the Citizens' Committee was all about. "I am not very familiar with their object," said one. "Were they appointed to devise ways and means for a park system?" The president of the Chamber responded that the committee was "to make a survey of the conditions and make recommendations as to the amplification and to suggest methods of financing. That was all that was involved."[63]

The Chamber president went on to assure his colleagues of the blue-ribbon nature of the Citizens' Committee. "This committee is organized and Oscar Mueller is one of them, Sol Lesser is another, Mary Pickford, they have their committee organized of that calibre of men [sic!]. They are going at it in the way they think best according to their judgment after discussing it and they think there are the proper men to care for the requirements. They are not, however, assuming the responsibility for the detail." Chamber directors asked to maintain oversight capability, particularly as finances were concerned. ("We started it and they contend so far as they are concerned that they are going to do the work, but they don't feel they should assume any financial responsibility. . . . All are in favor of their making a monthly financial statement and report to us."[64]). Yet the Chamber directors could not seem to keep track of the Citizens' Committee. Chamber leaders continually had to explain to one another what the Citizens' Committee was, what its duties were, and who was paying for it.[65]

Throughout 1928, the committee made reports to the parent Chamber of Commerce, hinting all the while at the sheer comprehensiveness, not to mention expense, of the eventual report, for both its contractual allowances and its recommendations.[66] Board members began to express increasing frustrations that perhaps the committee might overrun its allowed expenditures of $100,000, the amount authorized to complete the report. More problematic was the dawning realization by many that the comprehensive nature of the plan would, by necessity, create the need for equally comprehensive jurisdictional and supervisory bodies; here lies one of the primary reasons why the report went flat.

By early 1929, the Chamber's Board of Directors, which had tried to keep the Citizens' Committee on a fairly tight leash throughout its several year existence, had begun to question what the report would mean for the balance of power in Los Angeles. The Citizens' Committee had gone so far as to propose legislation to the California legislature regarding the creation of special tax-collecting jurisdictional districts (for example, a park district for metropolitan Los Angeles) and governance bodies that would then perform park duties, such as laying out streets and roads in greater Los Angeles and undertaking condemnation proceedings.[67]

At this point the Chamber balked. Thinking about an integrated park system, one that incorporated beaches and playgrounds, was one thing. Making the agency that could oversee such a thing was an entirely different matter. John Treanor attempted to remind board members of their original charge: "the instructions of this committee from this Board were to prepare a comprehensive plan for the metro-

politan park system of Los Angeles and an adequate agency for carrying the plans out. You did not tell us to prepare a plan calling for a
small amount of money nor did you instruct us to limit the powers of
this agency in any particular way."[68]

Treanor wanted, and the plan needed, a governing board, a "metropolitan park board," and he brought both Harland Bartholomew
and F. L. Olmsted along with him on a visit to the Chamber to reiter-
ate and justify that claim. "It has been generally conceded and urged
by the attorneys, the engineers, consultants of all sorts and by the citizens who have appeared before us," Treanor stated, "that there is no
existing agency that can do this thing."[69]

In essence, the Chamber feared that the child had become the parent. The planned park board, with its jurisdictional authorities extending to the creation of its own police force, simply scared the
Chamber members, many of whom clearly feared that the new body
would exert powers over and above the Chamber itself. "For instance," noted Chamber director Hill (a proponent of at least some of
the Citizens' Committee work), "there is one provision there of al-
lowing the committee to really lay out roads and highways and such
as that. To institute flood protection work. The committee has in its
discretion power to make contributions of monies to any project of a
like nature which a city or other public body of a like nature might
put forward." Said one: "It is terrifying if you come down to look at it
with the powers given. . . . The powers are tremendous." Another
spoke of the planned board as "a radical measure."[70] Another fierce
opponent, William Lacy, the same Chamber director who had spoken
in support of park planning several years earlier, stated simply, "We
have all the parks we want down here now as I see it."[71]

Harland Bartholomew responded to the Chamber's fears. The proposed agency, or parks board, would have no powers inconsistent
with like boards in other cities and districts around the country. The
board, which would be appointed by the governor, would not be the
creature of local politics. Its bonding powers (at two percent of assessed county real estate values, or approximately $70,000,000 in the
late 1920s) were large but hardly unprecedented. "What is the use of
creating a board if they have no funds with which to work?" he asked.
Besides, Bartholomew suggested, the need for such work in Southern
California ought to be obvious to Chamber members, concerned as
they were with the regional tourist economy.

Of all the large cities Los Angeles probably needs to undertake such a system. Partly because this is an automobile city and your people take their enjoyment largely through the automobile and partly because it is a tourist city and one in which such a system is naturally expected by people who come here, a great many of whom do not come now because they have been disappointed in failure to have such opportunities.[72]

Perhaps a bit defensive, and likely a bit exasperated, Bartholomew minced few words. As for regional parks, he said, "you are totally deficient. You have almost ignored the park question. Griffith and one or two others you have but virtually no others whatsoever." *Parks, Playgrounds and Beaches* offered an integrated solution to the deficiency: public beaches linked with parkways, parkways linked to parks, playgrounds, and athletic fields, as well as driving proximity to desert spaces outside the metropolitan region (figure 19). Some suggested that the region's forests answered the park problem, to which Bartholomew responded that the San Gabriel and other mountains were far too steep to provide reasonable recreation for Angelenos by the thousands. "Your people try to get into these mountainous areas and into these valleys and you see every Sunday great crowds of machines where people get in."[73]

Certain Chamber members, some of whom were also members of the Citizens' Committee, voiced vociferous objections. As important as any was George Cochran of the Pacific Mutual Life Insurance Company. Cochran, though he apparently never attended an Executive Committee meeting of the Citizens' Committee, nonetheless attacked the plan as "a radical measure," adding that "as a member of that committee I never heard of it until yesterday."

I did not know they were working on an independent municipal corporation going to override and overlap a great many others and create a body with such unlimited authority as that and such an expensive authority. I think it would seriously interfere with the activity of all the other departments of our civic life. . . . I think they are wasting their time.[74]

Of course, some members of the Chamber backed the plan, even in the face of opposition. Director Holloway felt that the Chamber would be making a mistake not to support the Citizens' Committee

Figure 19. This photograph depicts the Antelope Valley northeast of Los Angeles in the early years of the twentieth century. Olmsted and Bartholomew hoped to enhance metropolitan proximity to such large non-park natural sites or "reservations," through a linked system of parkways. "[W]ith the great use of the automobile, the range for pleasure seekers even in large numbers has been greatly extended." Of particular attraction were the region's Joshua trees. But would such places remain environmental safety valves for urban life if they could be made so accessible to automobiles? In recent years the Antelope Valley has become the site for exurban development tied to greater Los Angeles at a distance Olmsted and Bartholomew would have thought impossible to sustain.

and its consultants. "[T]his committee is our own creation. They put their own money into it. They hired the best brains in the United States, Mr. Bartholomew and Mr. Olmstead [sic], and I think they are on the right track."[75]

In opposing the plan, some Chamber directors highlighted the existence of a regional "Taxpayer's Commission," a group that loudly declared its opposition to any new taxation plans such as that which would accompany the creation of the metropolitan park district. Chamber directors could thus wash their hands of the matter, pointing to constituent concerns over money that dovetailed with their own concerns over power. And without the Chamber's support, both publicly and behind the scenes, Los Angeles stood no chance of raising the regional and state funds necessary to enact the report's integrated plans.

By the end of February, 1929, it had become clear that the Chamber's Board of Directors was divided, perhaps so seriously as to be fatal to *Parks, Playgrounds and Beaches*. Treanor came before the board to ask that the Chamber go on record supporting the legislative enabling action in Sacramento; such action would allow a referendum to go before the citizens of Los Angeles County at some point in the future. The enabling legislation was, for all intents and purposes, simply a law-making green light to go forward with the plan. The county voters could still turn it (or its bonding capabilities) down at an election. But even this fairly tentative step worried Chamber members intent on letting the report die. "I think that in the long run," Treanor stated with forceful deliberation, "great loss to this community will result because I believe this community will have parks sooner or later. I think it will have them at whatever expense is necessary."[76] Olmsted again spoke of the need for such comprehensive planning. The region needed to protect its beaches from private hands. It needed to offer athletic fields to "youths of the dangerous age" (figure 20). Los Angeles needed "elongated parks through which it is possible to travel under pleasant conditions from one part of the district to another." And doing all this required "concentrated, executive responsibility and power."[77]

But the moment was slipping and Treanor knew it. His allies attempted to come to his—and the report's—aid. "The longer we put it off the more it is going to cost us," said one. "We are living here in a city that has grown so fast and we do not realize the opportunities until a man of great national reputation like Mr. Olmstead [sic] comes along and shows us what we should do," said another. "I do not believe there is a more crying need any place in the world for parks than right here in Los Angeles, especially in the city," said Chamber director Hill.[78] The Citizens Committee proved willing to tinker with at least the parts of the report having to do with agency creation and bonding authority. The two percent figure regarding bonding capabilities was cut to one, for instance, and the procedures regarding appointment to the park board were altered in favor of the County Board of Supervisors (as opposed to the governor).

Yet the opposition had gained a foothold. Director Lacy, one of the most strident, vented his frustrations at enabling acts in general, which he equated with permissive credit acquisition. "Riding about here you see long miles of streets, paved most expensively, brilliantly

Figure 20. This municipal pool, bathhouse, and community building complex, the El Sereno Plunge, located at 2501 Eastern Avenue was completed in 1930 at a cost of $50,000 to serve residents in the El Sereno district on the city's eastern boundary adjacent to Alhambra. Construction funds were drawn from a $1,000,000 bond initiative. In 1930 the city operated sixteen municipal pools where recreation and park staff offered classes in swimming, diving, and life saving. Day use fees were set at five cents for children ten and under, ten cents for those ten to eighteen, and twenty cents for adults.

lighted, where only horned toads and jack rabbits inhabit the section and that is all brought about by these enabling acts. . . . one of the great curses of the country today is the ability to secure credit." Others simply wondered if opposing such powerful men as George Cochran was a good idea.[79]

Given all the attention, the effort, and the verbal bromides regarding public need and the benefits to be achieved through physical reform, why did Chamber members who supported the program fail to push it through? The financial costs of implementing the plan would be an obvious factor, and the Chamber minutes record that the project budget, the bond payoff, and the tax burden for individual property holders were a continual concern. (At the time, the city of Los Angeles and other municipalities in the county financed parks and recreation either from their general fund or through a mil tax.)[80] From the day Hugh Pomeroy first presented an outline of the report to its final unveiling, directors routinely insinuated that the funding required to achieve this comprehensive, regional project would most likely exceed the consultant's estimates and make it virtually impossible to mount a successful bond campaign.

The funding strategy, one of the most contested aspects of the Olmsted-Bartholomew proposal, called for bond financing based on two percent of the county's assessed valuation, or approximately $70,000,000. Still, editors writing in the *Examiner* reminded readers that it was imperative to purchase land for parks and playgrounds now, before land values rose. Acting quickly made fiscal sense in another way since parks and playgrounds would be "economic in turning out good citizens."[81] The two-percent bond was lifted directly from a local precedent, a 1924 report crafted by the city superintendent of parks and spelled out in detail with comparative justification in the appendices. The latter included reference to the Los Angeles Metropolitan Water District as well as park legislation in Westchester County, Chicago, and Missouri. Here again we find synthesis drawn from local precedent and the firm's experience running a national practice.

A favored line of attack began with members posing rhetorical, and seemingly innocuous, queries concerning the number of county and city projects that had already received a plurality from voters and for which bonds had been issued. The standard follow-up question concerned the number of large-scale projects already in the pipeline. The implication was transparent: voters in Los Angeles were negligent and failed to appreciate the cumulative financial responsibility of a series of bond initiatives. Funds for water, schools, street widenings, and storm drains were each based on the city's assessed valuation. One director personalized this investment strategy when he suggested that "[i]f they added all these bonds [together] we would have dozens of first mortgages on all our property."[82]

Most critically, a number of chamber members questioned the felicity of sponsoring a major bond initiative for the purchase of public beaches, the creation of additional parks, parkway construction, and local recreation facilities at the precise moment when civic elites were attempting to orchestrate the public support necessary to assure passage of a $220,000,000 act to finance construction of an aqueduct that would bring Colorado River water to a coalition of municipalities in Los Angeles County.[83] Despite Chamber members concerns about bonding capacity and questions regarding voters willingness to assume debt, in 1931, residents in the city of Los Angeles did approve two million dollars in bond measures targeted for the acquisition and construction of parks and playgrounds. These brought the city's total outstanding indebtedness for general purpose, municipal improvement, and acquisition bonds to more than $172 million, to say nothing of deficit financing in the county's other municipalities.[84]

Nevertheless, it is critical to note that the committee and its consultants were pursuing this project during a period when Angelenos were engaged in contentious debates about public access to the beach and ocean and the desecration of this finite amenity through offshore and beachfront oil drilling and the sludge left by coastal shipping. There was increasing awareness that the available public beachfront property was declining as more and more land was transferred into private holdings. Although this trend presumably could have lent urgency and a measure of popular support to the Chamber's initiative, the battles over Southern California's beaches delineated varying conceptions of what the beaches signified, how they should be used, and who should benefit.

For a March 1928, *Examiner* article "Redondo Women Fight Sale of Ocean Front," reporter Otheman Stevens accompanied Hugh Pomeroy to meet with members of that city's Women's Club who had organized to protest the sale of a stretch of beach owned by the Pacific Electric Company to a real estate syndicate which planned to turn it into a "peanut and hurdy gurdy zone." According to past president Mrs. T. A. Gould, "The men, that is the associations of men, think the sale would stimulate business, but we feel certain that if the project is stopped forever, it would result in far more benefit to the town than could possibly result from a few buildings being put up and that the interests of the public at large demand that [access to the beach] be preserved." Mrs. Sam Austin added that the proposed scheme would "destroy the front of City Park, take away the ocean view, and mar the prospect with a lot of more or less sordid, if not squalid, features." As Stevens noted, in arguing against temporary gain and for saving the beach as a public asset, these activists were fighting against what they perceived as a "community injury." People of vision understood that "greater prosperity would result if that beach were saved from private exploitation."[85]

Chamber members saw themselves as philanthropic city leaders bestowing the opportunity and right to enjoy an amenity upon citizens. Residents of Huntington Beach, Redondo Beach, Santa Monica, and other municipalities were doing the right thing as citizens, engaging as participants in a political contest.

Although members of the Chamber's Board of Directors might have recognized the general direction of change in local affairs, state governance, and the national economy at the time they commissioned a report on parks, playgrounds, and beaches, the nature, extent, and magnitude of change that would develop over the next few years was most likely inconceivable. By the time the report had been printed, bound, and distributed to committee members, the national economy (and in fact the international economy) had collapsed. The resulting crisis was less severe in Los Angeles County than in other metropolitan regions, but there as elsewhere residents, workers, business leaders, and elected officials turned to the federal government and federal programs, particularly those associated with the New Deal, as sources for financing and for the institutional and political counterweight for social, fiscal, and programmatic uncertainty. Gradually, the fiscal and institutional restructuring associated with the Depression realigned the political and business networks that Chamber members had so assiduously crafted.

LEGACIES

[T]his thing has taken of my own time and the time of the committee to such an extent here that I can't afford to give more time to it. If you want to kill this thing, let's kill it. Let's not let it die a long death. . . . Let's kill it now and get it out of the way. . . . Let's kill it and get a vote on it.

Chamber director Hill (March 1929)

By the spring of 1929, the Citizens' Committee, which never did reach 200 members, had imploded, with some members pushing for the enabling act and others dissenting. The Chamber's Board of Directors began to exercise political damage control in the face of an embarrassing tangle of disagreements. John Treanor appeared before the Chamber Board of Directors to present the final report of his Citizens' Committee in the summer of 1929. He said that the report prepared by Olmsted and Bartholomew was substantially completed, in need of only a little editing and cross-referencing.

> The report deals with the present and future needs. . . . This is an area of 1500 square miles; 400 square miles has already been subdivided and [organized]. There are forty cities within that area. There is a population of approximately two million people. Under our instructions and under any rational interpretation of our instructions we were forced to recognize that by 1950 there may be four million people in this area [a very good guess, it turns out]. That practically this entire area will be urbanized. The report, therefore, deals with the expectations of the next 25, 30, 40 or 50 years. Doing so and planning reasonably for such growth, the sums of money involved are necessarily large. The public of Los Angeles is undoubtedly unprepared to countenance large schemes for park development at the present time.[86]

As the Chamber minutes reveal, "the public" was not the only group wary of such a plan. And yet Treanor held on to a belief that mere publication of the report might promote some good work. Over time, a published document, something you could hold, admire, and refer to, might act as a lever for legislation creating a body with jurisdictional and financial capabilities large enough to reach across the Los Angeles basin. "We think . . . that this report should preserve the important work of the committee and that if reference to that [enabling] legislation and if the arguments calling for such an agency as proposed are not preserved in this way, they are going to be forgotten and a bad start will be made some time when this report perhaps may be used as a basis for a program."[87] The Chamber balked again at including legislative materials in the report.

This Citizens' Committee, and its sponsorship of *Parks, Playgrounds and Beaches*, marks a critical juncture in the history of regional planning in Southern California. After 1930, the federal government, under the rubric of various New Deal programs, entered the landscape architecture field and increasingly orchestrated the kind of comprehensive planning contemplated by Olmsted and Bartholomew in this report. Thus a transition from social reform objectives to commercial/private partnerships to the arrival of federal money and federal engineering is evident on the regional landscape, particularly as regards such sites as the Los Angeles River.

At first glance, it is reasonable to assume that the immediate needs of the Depression eclipsed the comprehensive planning objectives embodied in the 1930 report. But closer scrutiny reveals the presence of what Olmsted Jr. referred to as "the art political" as an important actor; the report was killed off well before the arrival of the Great Depression. As one Chamber of Commerce Director asked, in the wake of the controversy over the report: "If the Chamber of Commerce ever starts up another Citizens' Committee do you think you will get any of that group to put up money for the harbor, parks or anything when you give them no consideration at all?"[88]

The Chamber's suppression of this county-wide plan for parks, playgrounds, and beaches did not diminish the cachet of the Olmsted or Bartholomew firms, nor did it alter either the flow of work that these firms and their associates secured in the region or the type of projects they were asked to undertake. In fact, as seasoned professionals, they capitalized on the knowledge and visibility they had acquired through two years of study, analysis, and presentations. In short order, the Olmsted firm produced plans for a beach park in Santa Monica (1931), completed a project for Huntington Beach and Newport Bay (1932), and did work for the Marblehead Land Company for a Malibu park (1932) as well as a subdivision for Bryant Bixby in Long Beach (1931–32). In addition, the firm completed a study for the Riverside Park System, Burbank's Pioneer Park, and playground plans for the City of Beverly Hills at Roxbury Drive and La Cienega. Three months after the release of the Los Angeles plan, the Olmsted firm agreed to serve as "impartial . . . park authorities" for a study of recreational needs and possible public purchase of water district lands "involving a large bond issue or the creation of new governmental agencies" then underway in the San Francisco East Bay cities. In this case funding came from the Kahn Foundation and the University of California's Bureau of Public Administration served as the project sponsor.[89]

More important for our purposes, the Los Angeles County study did come to serve as a point of reference for future planning efforts, much as Treanor anticipated. In a chapter on recreation penned for the L. Deming Tilton and George Robbins compilation *Preface to a*

Master Plan (1941), Los Angeles park director George Hjelte adopted wholesale the structure of the 1930 report and then rehearsed the earlier findings and recommendations, including the budget and financial mechanisms. A full decade after the release of the Olmsted-Bartholomew report, Hjelte's commentary underscored the fact that the general degradation of the shoreline and the loss of public beaches remained the most pressing issue for Southern Californians.[90]

Five years later, the Board of Supervisors organized a blue-ribbon "county citizens committee on parks, beaches, and recreational facilities" chaired by Charles W. Eliot, director of the John Randolph Haynes and Dora Haynes Foundation. The committee's report, submitted to the supervisors in August 1945, called for the organization of a county commission or district with power to coordinate planning and programs, acquire additional land for recreation, develop regional facilities, and assist the operations of local jurisdictions. Governance would rest in a five-member commission that would consolidate and integrate all existing county park and playground activities, and financing would be through the issuance of bonds.

In 1945, the "need" was still "obvious," the conditions even more pressing. County population had surpassed 3.4 million and additional newcomers arrived every day. Park land needed to be "acquired ahead of population growth," and recreation was an important attraction, "one of, if not [our] most important asset. We cannot afford to neglect the 'goose that lays our golden eggs.'" Pollution had led to quarantines along "miles of our finest beaches." The committee referred approvingly to the Olmsted-Bartholomew plan. Whereas that report reviewed "all the needs and proposed specific locations for new public recreation areas," they had not had sufficient time to analyze the sites proposed in the 1930 report nor had they surveyed those sites that had been suggested in the intervening years. This task should be "*undertaken immediately by the proposed County Park Commission*" in line with the land uses identified by the Regional Planning Commission (emphasis in original).[91]

In short, fifteen years following publication, the Olmsted-Bartholomew report remained the gold standard. And as Mike Davis points out in "How Eden Lost Its Garden," the analysis and recommendations first synthesized in the Olmsted-Bartholomew study formed the basis for a series of regional investigations into open space in the five-county metropolitan region undertaken by the landscape and planning firm EDAW (Eckbo, Dean, Austin, and Williams) and published in the 1960s and 1970s.[92]

Just as critically, the debate surrounding the 1930 Olmsted-Bartholomew report reveals the structure of oligarchy, or more appropriately, oligarchies, in twentieth-century Los Angeles. On the one hand, it is possible to read accounts in the popular press, to examine legislative propositions and the battles to pass or deny, and the array of formal and informal committees and institutions that brought some degree of authority to bear on aspects of the plan as further evidence of fragmentation, an obvious reference to Robert Fogelson's well-known thesis. In his 1967 study, Fogelson focused on the business community and traced the emergence of an ethos he characterized as "growth for growth's sake" while chronicling the formation of coalitions dedicated to this proposition in Southern California. John Logan and Harvey Molotch elaborated on the "growth machine" thesis and the imprint of the rentier class in their study *Urban Fortunes*. Although these interests are clearly important for analyzing development in cities such as Los Angeles, boosters, speculators, and rentiers were so ubiquitous and their interests so divergent and diffuse that we must consider these people in conjunction with other interests.[93]

Mike Davis has posited a regional oligopoly centered around the Otis-Chandler dynasty that funneled power and capital toward the central business district and fought aggressively to enhance their authority and retain value for their investments in downtown. Beginning in the 1950s, however, an ascendant Jewish and Democratic power bloc associated with the city's Westside made significant inroads and the downtown faction was forced to share its spoils. Then, during the 1980s, investment capitalists based in Tokyo, New York, and Toronto entered the fray and the resultant "Darwinian place wars" destabilized the preceding bi-polar order and created a less stable set of competing centers. Davis's evolutionary schema focuses exclusively on the private sector and is designed to trace the course of "power lines" in the region and to serve as a guide for mapping the geographies of investment and distribution that have shaped Southern California during the century. In "How the Urban West Was Won," Steve Erie noted that conventional accounts, including Davis's, underestimated the importance of the "local state and public actors" in shaping Los Angeles from the turn of the century forward.[94]

Tracing the planning process for the Olmsted-Bartholomew report provides insight into the institutions and organizations that worked deliberately to mold social and economic power and wield political authority in greater Los Angeles during the first decades of the century. On one hand, the findings confirm Erie's thesis regarding the significance of the local state and public sector financing and we have, therefore, "put the state back in," to borrow a phrase from a recent historically grounded reassessment of political economy.[95] But it is less apparent that Los Angeles made a definitive transition from an entrepreneurial growth regime to a state-centered one during the first decade of the century as Erie suggests. In fact, a study of planning for infrastructure improvements during the latter part of the 1920s demonstrates just how important business-dominated, pro-growth organizations such as the Chamber of Commerce were when it came to providing the physical necessities of urban development. These included the basics—water, sewerage, and roadways, as well as parks and playgrounds. Chamber members spoke of the latter explicitly as urban "necessities" rather than as "luxuries" since supervised recreation deterred youth from delinquency and parks and beaches attracted tourists while they purportedly increased the value of neighboring property.[96]

Nevertheless, the Chamber was not a monolith. On the contrary, internal dissension inaugurated a factional debate that led directors to reevaluate their support for the Olmsted-Bartholomew project and then to limit their promotion of the report severely, in effect condemning it to languish in the archives. Nor do we find the Chamber participating in a ruling cabal, a predictable player in the "Chandlerian power structure," that "great constellation of private capital" that acted as a "permanent government in local affairs."[97]

What we find instead is something along the lines of Davis's multiple power centers, although it is clear this configuration was in place long before Japanese capitalists and New York bankers imposed their will on local real estate during the 1980s. Certainly the Chamber played a significant role shaping development in the county up to the late 1920s. But it is incorrect to assume that other institutions and, notably, the voting public, were solely a supporting cast. The nature of these relationships is evident if we follow the money. Bonds and bonded indebtedness have generated the funding for large-scale improvements in Los Angeles from the turn of the century forward. The majority of bond financing required a "yes" vote from two-thirds

of the electorate. The Chamber, the *Times* clique, and real estate interests had to convince voters to support initiatives and assume a
mounting tax burden. These relationships were, in effect, coalitions,
and these are, in all cases, dynamic and subject to change. Thus our
study points toward a theoretical synthesis. A close reading of institutional records reveals that competing groups, each relatively well-
organized, coherent, and consistent regarding their objectives, wielded
considerable political power in 1920s Los Angeles. The civic elite
were neither fragmented nor a simple two-part monolith.

And yet, it is fair to ask: Why is the 1930 plan still relevant? An
obvious response is that after seventy years the report has intrinsic
historical value, it is an important, and almost unexamined, primary
document for students of Southern California landscape. Principals in
the Olmsted and Bartholomew firms were versed in the Geddesian
tradition of landscape studies. (Patrick Geddes, a Scots biologist, advocated close-grained investigations of landforms and prior interventions as a necessary first step before beginning any planning endeavor.)
Survey before planning was a basic axiom for these professionals, and
the report offers a quantitative and qualitative primer of the region at
the close of one of the most dynamic decades in its history. It also
serves as a testament to how a team of outside experts, working col-
laboratively with resident consultants, the staff and directors of local
and state agencies, and civic elites, understood conditions in the
county and imagined its future.[98]

Even a cursory review invites closer scrutiny. It is a compelling
document and readers might well be shocked to see the Los Angeles
that was, and then amazed as they begin to imagine the Los Angeles
that might have been had the plan been adopted and implemented.
The former, a detailed survey of existing conditions, is a valuable
record for designers and urbanists both professional and academic.
Practitioners, scholars, and a general public skeptical of their ability
to develop solutions for urban issues and frustrated by the complex,
seemingly intractable nature of these issues should find utility in the
latter, a "what if" projection into the region's possible future.

Recent press reports concerning the fragility of California's coastline and the seasonal cycle of fire and flood—the more dramatic featuring houses sliding off engineered and natural hillsides—remind us
that the legacy of functional nature, the unique geology, ecologies,
and climate of Southern California seen as a resource to be exploited,

remains a central tenet for development and planning in the region. At the same time, the county's beaches and mountains have remained prized amenities. Contests over public access and recent cautionary calls for regulations and limits on development in these dynamic settings continue; both draw on the planning lineage championed and advanced by Olmsted and Bartholomew in their 1930 report. And perhaps knowing how our predecessors defined and responded to similar challenges can provide insight for the present as we plan for the future. These "real world" machinations (Olmsted's "art political"), have particular relevance for design professionals and students of landscape architecture, architecture, planning, and public policy. In this sense, the 1930 report on parks, playgrounds, and beaches is a useful case study, a textbook example of the distance that separates a plan, a vision of the future, from its realization.

Scholars and others interested in cities and city building are well aware that we are in the midst of an Olmsted revival. During the past two decades, archivists have provided researchers access to a wealth of primary material and publishers have offered a steady stream of monographs examining the life and work of Frederick Law Olmsted Sr. and his successor firm, Olmsted Brothers.[99] Olmsted and his protégés also loom large in general studies of nineteenth-century urbanism. Olmsted, his successor firm, and Harland Bartholomew are prominent in collections devoted to the emergence of modern city planning.[100] Interest in landscape history and the Olmsted firm and its projects is growing, a considerable percentage of the drawings and documents remain at the archive, and it is conceivable that this interdisciplinary investigation is still emergent. Given this, it is imperative that we enhance our collective understanding of the firm, its practice, and the ways in which an inclusive focus on the Olmsted and Bartholomew and Associates legacy can illuminate questions of urban planning, politics, and power both historically and in our own time.

An essential first step is inserting the West into this discourse. A review of the literature provides a geographically narrow, regionally specific understanding of the Olmsted imprint with origins in New York City and Brooklyn, significant projects in the major mercantile and industrial centers of the eastern seaboard and their outlying areas, and a dominant presence, increasing over time, in Boston and environs. This bias is evident in the primary sources. Invariably the Olmsteds illustrated their lectures, talks, and writings with examples drawn from Boston, Brooklyn, Washington, D.C., Baltimore, and Chicago. This is not to say that western cities, or Olmsted projects in western states, are entirely absent in the relevant literatures.[101] Nevertheless, the generation of singular case studies considered in isolation is quite different from analyses and interpretations that are national in scope or at least regionally inclusive.[102]

A state and regional analysis of the Master List of Olmsted design projects reveals both the numerical significance of California (and the West) and a surprising temporal depth. In the three categories devoted to large-scale urban projects—Parkways and Recreation Areas, City and Regional Planning and Improvement Projects, and Subdivisions and Suburban Communities—California ranks fourth, following Massachusetts (predictably), New York, and either Pennsylvania or New Jersey. The state is fifth in three additional categories. Factor in Oregon, Washington, Colorado, and western Canada and the ranking for the West is even more impressive.[103] The Bartholomew office was equally prolific, had an equivalent percentage of projects in western states, and was well represented in Southern California.[104]

Finally, as we suggested at the outset, the report is a reminder of an era that has seemingly passed, a time in the not so distant past when large-scale, comprehensive plans were the norm rather than the exception. We are not naive enough to suggest that anyone should pin the future on big plans. Who would? Large-scale, comprehensive plans are terribly out of favor, and the evidence from past failures reveals bureaucracy and waste, politics (in the sense of "pork-barrel" politics), greed, interest groups manipulating "the system" for short-term gains, a centralization of power, and marginal returns. Yet big programs and big projects go forward and often these generate big changes. This is true in Los Angeles County as elsewhere. A short list for Southern California would include the Colorado River Aqueduct (which the Chamber endorsed), recasting the Los Angeles River as a flood control channel, and the interstate highway system. (The list could be expanded to even larger projects such as NASA and the Cold War which have altered the economy, the landscape, and the lives of residents in Los Angeles and Southern California.) But our point is both smaller and greater than this list would suggest. Politics, bureaucracy, and greed are always present, and there are many failures.

But as Laurie Olin reminds us, that is the fate awaiting big plans. These projects are fraught with risk and in many respects doomed to fail. Failure is intrinsic when you plan at this scale. Not only will things turn out other than intended, often there is a complete reversal of intention over time or the problem steadfastly remains. This hindsight has been considered insight; thus we are all schooled in the wisdom of incrementalism. If they are to succeed, we are told, urban interventions must be small-scale. Calls for big projects, like the Olmsted-Bartholomew proposal, are one measure of the divide that separates us from the generation that came of age during the first decades of the century. Burnham's plan for Chicago, Edward Bennett's proposals for Portland, the Regional Planning Association's study of greater New York—all these and their counterparts appear to us as relics, dinosaurs from another age of planning. Now everyone knows better, and process and procedure are the practitioners' mantra. In truth, the present challenge may lie in figuring out how we might do good in the midst of failure.[105]

Ultimately it is too simplistic to rehearse the standard narrative about Los Angeles as Eden lost. Too simplistic because these accounts typically ignore the manifest ways in which the Southern California landscape had already been transformed by the turn of the twentieth century. Too simplistic because the tellers of these tales seldom ask: Whose Eden?, and their analysis then denies the histories of many Southern Californians whose aspirations and efforts created the contemporary metropolis. And too simplistic because these narratives of decline cast the contemporary metropolitan region as the inevitable product of factors and forces outside the bounds of our everyday lives. In this interpretation Angelenos were and remain powerless to define and shape the regional landscape according to their interests.

The unintended but nonetheless critical legacy of the Olmsted-Bartholomew plan is how it reveals the form and meaning, the very definition, of urban space as the product of an ongoing contest. As in other contests, power is not distributed equally. Nor is it simple to calculate probable outcomes, costs and benefits, who gains and who loses, to say nothing of the uncertainty of predicting future implications. Given all this, how might we proceed? One certainty is that if you choose to abdicate, others are prepared to make decisions in your absence. Another is that much can be gained through active participation. It would have been understandable if Frederick Law Olmsted and Harland Bartholomew had, in frustration, vowed never to work in Los Angeles again. Rather, both firms continued to produce relatively large-scale plans for that region and other metropolitan areas. Eventually they saw results. Discrete segments of the 1930 report were implemented. More important, the study provided a framework for future interventions and a benchmark for comprehensive investigations into the region. It is a legacy that we can value and one that we further if we approach the 1930 report on parks, playgrounds, and beaches as a living document and apply it instrumentally to achieve our objectives.

NOTES TO THE INTRODUCTION

1. "Gigantic County Park and Beach Plan Urged," *Los Angeles Examiner* 16 March 1930, Examiner Clipping Files, Hearst Collection, Department of Special Collections, University of Southern California (hereafter Hearst Collection); "Recreational Program Vast," *Los Angeles Times* 16 March 1930 II., p.6; "Greatest of Recreational Developments Projected Here," *Los Angeles Times* 30 March 1930 II., p.1; Olmsted Brothers and Bartholomew and Associates, *Parks, Playgrounds and Beaches for the Los Angeles Region* (Los Angeles: Los Angeles Chamber of Commerce, 1930): 1. Hereafter *Parks, Playgrounds and Beaches*.

2. See Stenographic Report, Board of Directors, Los Angeles Chamber of Commerce, February 7, 1929 at the Regional History Center, University of Southern California; hereafter "Stenographic Report." The Chamber announced the project in its *Bulletin* 1/51: 22 August 1927, 1,3.

3. *Parks, Playgrounds and Beaches*: xiv.

4. *Parks, Playgrounds and Beaches*: 1.

5. Gilbert L. Skutt, "Need is Evidenced for County Parks—Form Link Between Municipal and State Park; Size Should be Proportionate to Expected Density of Population," *Western City* 7/5 (May 1931): 19–20.

6. See the discussion on page ten of the report, where the authors address the public costs associated with private development in hillside and mountain areas which they describe as "convert[ing] a good thing of one kind," in this case scenic recreation trails, "into a poor thing of another," serviced lots for single-family housing.

7. Both projects are often in the news of late. A subject search in the *Los Angeles Times* website ("Playa Vista" and "Bolsa Chica") reveals dozens of recent articles covering various aspects of the controversial development efforts. See, for instance, the *Times* home edition for August 28 and September 10, 11, 15, 22, 27 (1998) and the paper's Orange County edition for September 10, October 4, 15, 24, and 25 (1998).

8. See Maureen Flanagan, "The City Profitable, The City Livable: Environmental Policy, Gender, and Power in Chicago in the 1910s," *Journal of Urban History* 22/2 (Jan. 1996): 163–90.

9. Mike Davis, "How Eden Lost Its Garden: A Political History of the Los Angeles Landscape," in Allen Scott and Edward Soja, ed. *The City: Los Angeles and Urban Theory at the End of the Twentieth Century* (Berkeley: University of California Press, 1996): 160–185.

10. Dana Bartlett, *The Better City: A Sociological Study of a Modern City* (Los Angeles: Neuner Press, 1907), 27; hereafter Bartlett, *Better City*.

11. Bartlett, *Better City*, 29.

12. Bartlett, *Better City*, 44.

13. Bartlett, *Better City*, 45–46. Bartlett did not necessarily have history on his side of the argument. Towards the end of the nineteenth century, the mayor of Los Angeles had argued that the city's "10,000 acres of orchards and vineyards . . . answer for public parks." See United States Department of the Interior, Census Office, *Report of the Social Statistics of Cities*, Part II (Washington, D.C.: Government Printing Office, 1887): 781.

14. Bartlett, *Better City*, 46.

15. Bartlett, *Better City*, 50.

16. Early Playground Commission publications and annual reports often reproduce photographs of children planting flowers or working in playground garden plots similar to figure 9. See, for example, *Annual Report of the Playground Commission, City of Los Angeles for the year ending November 30, 1907* (Los Angeles: The Commission, 1907).

17. Griffith J. Griffith, *Parks, Boulevards, and Playgrounds* (Los Angeles: Prison Reform League, 1910), 5.

18. Griffith, *Parks, Boulevards, and Playgrounds*, 21–22.

19. Griffith, *Parks, Boulevards, and Playgrounds*, 5.

20. Griffith, *Parks, Boulevards, and Playgrounds*, 15.

21. Griffith, *Parks, Boulevards, and Playgrounds*, 24.

22. Charles Forman wrote Frederick Law Olmsted Sr. in March of 1895, hoping that he could be consulted regarding the new city park carved out of 750 acres of Elysian Park. Charles Forman to Frederick Law Olmsted, March 7, 1895; from Papers of Frederick Law Olmsted, Archives Division, Frederick Law Olmsted National Historic Site, Brookline, MA, Olmsted Series B, Reel 254, Job #5370. [All references to F. L. Olmsted, John C. Olmsted, and F. L. Olmsted Jr., will use "Olmsted" spelling.]

23. November 21, 1910 letter to Olmsted from Office of Park Dept, City of LA; Olmsted to C. T. Herbert 25 Nov. 1910; Herbert to Olmsted 25 Nov. 1910 all in Series B, Reel 254, Job #5371.

24. Wilbur Cook to Frederick Law Olmsted, December 2, 1910; Frederick Law Olmsted to Wilbur Cook, December 4, 1910 in Series B, Reel 254, Job #5372.

25. Ibid.

26. Frederick Law Olmsted to Charles Randall, December 22, 1910; Series B., Reel 254, Job #5372. In an essay first published in *Landscape Architecture* and reprinted as "What is 'Professional' Practice in Landscape Architecture?" (1929) Olmsted set out the firm's approach to structuring project fees. These amounted to salary reimbursement for hours spent plus "corresponding" overhead for everyone from draftsmen to principals. "Under this system we feel at liberty, and our clients are glad to have us feel at liberty, to send our assistants to a job and have them stay as long as necessary, and do whatever work is necessary in the client's interest to get the desired results." Note that this system is ideally suited for the creation and support of satellite operations.

27. Florence Mills to Frederick Law Olmsted, January 14 , 1911 in Series B, Reel 254, Job #5372.

28. Kate Bassett to Frederick Law Olmsted, June 5, 1914 in Series B, Reel 254, Job #5372.

29. Bassett to Olmsted, June 5, 1914, ibid.

30. Bassett to Olmsted, June 5, 1914, ibid.

31. Frederick Law Olmsted to Kate Bassett, July 15, 1914 in Series B, Reel 254, Job #5372.

32. Ibid.

33. "Would it not be possible if we work our forces rightly, to get together under your leadership, for the general survey, such men as Mulholland, Goodrich, Arnold, Bartlett & others who have done most valuable work already, which is essential to the plan[?]" Kate Bassett to Frederick Law Olmsted, July 23, 1914 in Series B, Reel 254, Job #5372.

34. Frederick Law Olmsted, Harland Bartholomew, and Charles Henry Cheney, *A Major Traffic Street Plan for Los Angeles* (Los Angeles: Traffic Commission of the City and County of Los Angeles, May 1924).

35. *Parks, Playgrounds and Beaches*, 39–40.

36. *Parks, Playgrounds and Beaches*, 40.

37. *Parks, Playgrounds and Beaches*, 39.

38. Frederick Law Olmsted Jr. and John Nolen, "The Normal Requirements of American Towns and Cities in Respect to Public Open Spaces," *Charities and The Commons* 16 (June 30, 1906): 411–26, quotes, 411.

39. Los Angeles Park Commission, "Silver Lake Parkway" (Los Angeles: The Commission, Feb., 1912), 1, 3. A revised version published in July shows a half-mile extension of the parkway running south to Sixth Street and then west to Alexandria Avenue paralleling Wilshire Boulevard.

40. Ibid., 6.
41. Ibid: 7–10.
42. South West District, Hollywood-Palos Verdes Parkway, Olmsted Correspondence, Reel 424, Job #8101.
43. Tilton was credited with the plan for Westwood Village, a Janss Company project for which FLO Jr. had originally consulted in 1922 (Job #8000). See also Gabriele Carey, "From Hinterland to Metropolis: Land-Use Planning in Orange County, California, 1925–1950," PhD diss, UC Riverside, 1997.
44. An address given at the joint conference of the American Institute of Park Executives and the American Civic Association, Washington, D.C. (Oct. 1924) reprinted from *Parks & Recreation* (January–February, 1925), quotes at p.5.
45. See "Stenographic Report," March 11, 1926. In regards to concerted efforts at putting beachfront property in public control, Chamber director Hill reported that the "county is doing everything they can, but the city is marking time, saying they don't know where they are going to get the money."
46. "The French and the English are not well. They are ill and we can forgive them if they seem to be a little cross and irritable with us, riding about in our Rolls Royces and looking so prosperous." "Stenographic Report," October 28, 1926.
47. Ibid.
48. Ibid.
49. Ibid.
50. Ibid.
51. Ibid.
52. Ibid.
53. Ibid.
54. Ibid.
55. Ibid.
56. "Stenographic Report," December 16, 1926. Director Lacy offered a warning shot reminiscent of the 1910 dilemma of water versus parks: "If we don't get the water from the Colorado River we won't want parks."
57. Already by February of 1927, the Parks and Recreation Committee within the Chamber was said to be "considering a large and comprehensive plan covering parks, playgrounds and beach resorts." See "Stenographic Report," February 10, 1927.
58. "Stenographic Report," March 10, 1927.
59. Treanor's son later wrote about his father's commitment to the plan. "This work appealed to him greatly. He prepared a detailed report on the possibilities that still remain practical for a large park system. He was convinced that the city had seriously hamstrung itself as a resort

center and place of retirement for the wealthy by not lining itself with greenery like Chicago. The beauty of adequate parks he considered essential to a city in a semi-arid country." Thomas C. Treanor, *John Treanor: A Sketch of His Life with Excerpts from His Letters* (Los Angeles: Zamarano Club, 1937), p. 70.

60. Even a plan to have Mary Pickford sign up members was proving difficult as late as the spring of 1928. As one member of the Chamber stated, the Committee "also had a plan lined up with Mary Pickford whereby she would invite fifty selected women to her home and when she got them there, explain this thing to them and they felt that they would be so flattered by her attention that they would sign up, but that has fallen through." See "Stenographic Report," May 3, 1928.

61. "Stenographic Report," June 30, 1927.

62. The Olmsted firm had been apprised of park and planning issues, given their role in the preparation of the traffic plan, throughout much of the early 1920s. Frederick Law Olmsted had given the matter, and its intricacies, serious thought already by early 1926 (thus revisiting, in some ways, his earlier correspondence with Kate Bassett). See, for instance, Frederick Law Olmsted to W. H. Pierce, January 14, 1926; Olmsted Papers, Job #5372.

63. See "Stenographic Report," October 20, 1927, especially remarks of Director Crandall and Chamber President Lacy.

64. Ibid.

65. See, for instance, the discussion in the "Stenographic Report" for February 2, 1928, when Chamber directors express confusion as to which parks committee is which (the Chamber's own internal Parks Committee or the Citizens' Committee).

66. "Stenographic Report," August 2, 1928.

67. "Stenographic Report," February 7, 1929.

68. Ibid.

69. Ibid.

70. Ibid.

71. "Stenographic Report," March 7, 1929.

72. "Stenographic Report," February 7, 1929.

73. Ibid.

74. Ibid.

75. Ibid.

76. Ibid.

77. Ibid.

78. Ibid.

79. According to Lacy, who had previously stated that Los Angeles already had enough park space, even the privatization of beaches was not a big problem. After all, a beach was a beach, and if the owner of the prop-

erty wanted to charge a bit for access, so be it. "I think we have plenty of beaches for all concerned," he suggested. As the Chamber president put it, regarding the powerful men opposed to the report, "I can see that it won't be sixty days when some of the officers of this Chamber will be called upon to see these very men who are opposing this and requesting some services from them. I don't know how they are going to receive us if we go contrary to their wishes." See "Stenographic Report," March 7, 1929.

80. See the budget discussion in "Public Recreation Directory and Figures from 182 Western Cities," *Western City* 7 (May 1931): 22–23, 55.

81. February 8, 1928; Hearst Collection, USC.

82. "Stenographic Report," April 22, 1926.

83. "Stenographic Report," February 7, 1929.

84. Office of the Controller, City of Los Angeles, *History of Bonded Indebtedness of the City of Los Angeles, California, 1895–1931* (Los Angeles: Controller, 1931).

85. March 12, 1928. Clipping in Olmsted Series B, reel 424, job #8101. It is worth noting that Hugh Pomeroy, an Olmsted affiliate, was an active participant in these struggles and that the Olmsted job files indicate that the firm was tracking these debates through a steady stream of newspaper clippings.

86. "Stenographic Report," August 8, 1929.

87. Ibid.

88. "Stenographic Report," March 14, 1929.

89. Olmsted Brothers and Ansel F. Hall (National Park Service), *Report on Proposed Park Reservations for East Bay Cities (California)* (Berkeley: Bureau of Public Administration, University of California, December, 1930). The East Bay Regional Park Association consulted as did a committee of fifty-one East Bay citizens including Robert G. Sproul, Oscar Sutro, realtor Duncan McDuffie, and architect Walter H. Ratcliff, jr.

90. See George Hjelte's essay, "Facilities for Recreation," in George W. Robbins and L. Deming Tilton, eds., *Los Angeles: Preface To a Master Plan* (Los Angeles: The Pacific Southwest Academy, 1941): 213–226.

91. County Citizens Committee, *Parks, Beaches, and Recreational Facilities for Los Angeles County* (Los Angeles: The Haynes Foundation, 1945), 3–4.

92. Edward A. Williams, *Open Space, the Choices Before California: The Urban Metropolitan Open Space Study* (San Francisco: Diablo Press, 1969), EDAW, *State Open Space and Resource Conservation Program for California*, prepared for the California Legislature Joint Committee on Open Space Lands (Sacramento: Assembly Publications, 1972), EDAW, *Ventura-Los Angeles Mountain and Coastal Study Commission, Final Report to the Legislature March 6, 1972* (Los Angeles, 1972).

93. Robert Fogelson, *The Fragmented Metropolis: Los Angeles 1850–1930*

(first published 1967, rpt. edition Berkeley: University of California Press, 1993); John Logan and Harvey Molotch, *Urban Fortunes: The Political Economy of Place* (Berkeley: University of California Press, 1987).

94. Mike Davis, *City of Quartz: Excavating the Future in Los Angeles* (London: Verso, 1990), esp. chapter two; Steve Erie, "How the Urban West was Won: The Local State and Economic Growth in Los Angeles, 1880–1920," *Urban Affairs Quarterly* 27 (June 1992): 519–554.

95. Peter B. Evans, Dietrich Rueschemeyer, Theda Skocpol, eds., *Bringing the State Back In* (Cambridge and New York: Cambridge University Press, 1985).

96. See *Parks, Playgrounds and Beaches*, esp. pp. 7–10; see also Chamber of Commerce Director Hill's comments at the February 7, 1929 meeting of the Board of Directors. Hill noted that nature had blessed Southern California and that entrepreneurs had in turn parlayed this blessing into a robust tourist economy; that equation was now threatened, Hill said, and the Chamber needed to act and act quickly. "Stenographic Report," February 7, 1929.

97. Davis, *City of Quartz*, pp. 101, 102.

98. It is important to point out another facet of this report's hidden qualities. After large outlays of time and money, the sponsoring Citizens' Committee (itself sponsored, indeed created, by the Los Angeles Chamber of Commerce) opted to print fewer than two hundred copies of the report, instead of meeting an initial goal of several thousand copies. The document is thus rare. Scattered copies are housed in regional archives and special collections libraries, and some have found their way onto planning and architectural book stacks at elite universities. A few museums hold a copy or two. Doubtless many copies remain in private hands, probably passed down through a couple of generations by members of the original Citizens' Committee. A search through a large computer database reveals copies in several University of California and California State University libraries; the public library in Beverly Hills; the Rancho Santa Ana Botanical Garden Library; Harvard University's Loeb Library; Columbia University; the University of Houston; and the University of Virginia.

99. See for example Witold Rybczynski, *A Clearing in the Distance: Frederick Law Olmsted and America in the Nineteenth Century* (New York: Scribner, 1999); Laura Wood Roper, *FLO: A Biography of Frederick Law Olmsted* (Baltimore: Johns Hopkins University Press, 1973); Elizabeth Stevenson, *Park Maker: A Life of Frederick Law Olmsted* (New York: Macmillan, 1977); Melvin Kalfus, *Frederick Law Olmsted: The Passion of a Public Artist* (New York: NYU Press, 1990); Susan Klaus, " 'Intelligent and comprehensive planning of a common sense kind': Frederick Law Olm-

sted, Junior, and the emergence of comprehensive planning in America, 1900–1920," Master's thesis, George Washington University, 1988; Dana F. White, "Frederick Law Olmsted, the Placemaker," in Daniel Schaffer, ed., *Two Centuries of American Planning* (Baltimore: Johns Hopkins University Press, 1988); Jon A. Peterson, "Frederick Law Olmsted Sr. and Frederick Law Olmsted Jr.: The Visionary and the Professional," in Mary Corbin Sies and Christopher Silver, eds., *Planning the Twentieth-Century American City* (Baltimore: Johns Hopkins University Press, 1996).

100. See Sies and Silver, Schaffer citations above.

101. Mansel G. Blackford, *The Lost Dream: Businessmen and City Planning on the Pacific Coast, 1890–1920* (Columbus: Ohio State, 1993); William H. Wilson, "The Seattle Park System and the Ideal of the City Beautiful," in Schaffer, ed., *Two Centuries of American Planning*.

102. Wilson, for example, treats the Seattle project as a stand-alone; Blackford casts Seattle, Portland, San Francisco, and Los Angeles as urban outliers, second-tier cities whose elected officials, business leaders, and residents were aware of their status and strove to emulate the great planning innovations that design experts such as the Olmsteds had applied in Chicago, Washington D.C., and the other east coast and midwest metropolises.

103. Charles E. Beveridge and Carolyn F. Hoffman, *The Master List of Design Projects of the Olmsted Firm, 1857–1950* (Washington, D.C.: National Association for Olmsted Parks, 1987).

104. Eldridge Lovelace, *Harland Bartholomew: His Contributions to American Urban Planning* (Urbana, IL: Department of Urban and Regional Planning, University of Illinois, Champagne-Urbana, 1993).

105. See Martin Krieger, "Big Decisions and a Culture of Decisionmaking," *Journal of Policy Analysis and Management* 5 (Summer 1986): 779–97 and Krieger, *Marginalism and Discontinuity: Tools for the Crafts of Knowledge and Decision* (New York: Russell Sage Foundation, 1989).

PARKS, PLAYGROUNDS
AND BEACHES
FOR THE LOS ANGELES REGION

PLATE I. View toward the mountains from the proposed parkway along the Puente Hills.

PARKS, PLAYGROUNDS

AND BEACHES

FOR THE LOS ANGELES REGION

*A Report submitted to the Citizens' Committee on Parks, Playgrounds,
and Beaches, by Olmsted Brothers and Bartholomew
and Associates, Consultants*

1930

LOS ANGELES, CALIFORNIA

TABLE OF CONTENTS

vii

viii

LIST OF PLATES

MAPS, PLANS AND PHOTOGRAPHS

ix

x

CITIZENS' COMMITTEE
ON PARKS, PLAYGROUNDS AND BEACHES

PHILP, HARRY
PICKFORD, MISS MARY
PINKHAM, J. R.
POWELL, F. H.
PRIDHAM, R. W.
QUINN, MR. AND MRS. CHARLES H.
RACHAL, C. E.
RAY, MRS. WALTER SELDEN
RIVERS, E. B.
· ROBINSON, HENRY M.
ROWLEY, E. S.
RUDDOCK, A. B.

RUSH, F. N.
SALE, L. D.
SCHENCK, JOS. M.
SEAVER, F. E.
SHERMAN, M. H.
SIEGEL, MYER
STANTON, LOUIS B.
STERN, HAROLD M.
STETSON, F. F.
STORY, F. Q.
TOBERMAN, C. E.
TREANOR, JOHN

· UNDERHILL, E. F.
· VANDERLIP, FRANK A.
VAN NUYS, J. B.
WARDMAN, A.
WARREN, J. G.
WHOLESALE GROCERS' ASSN.
WIGHTMAN, E. J.
WILCOX, FRED M.
WOODS, JAMES
WREN, CHAS. F.
YOUNG, MRS. MARY C.

EXECUTIVE COMMITTEE
CITIZENS' COMMITTEE ON PARKS, PLAYGROUNDS AND BEACHES

TREANOR, JOHN, *Los Angeles, Chairman*

BARNARD, W. K., *Pasadena*
BENT, ARTHUR S., *Los Angeles*
BRENT, W. L., *Los Angeles*
COCHRAN, GEORGE I., *Los Angeles*
COLLINS, JAMES F., *Long Beach*
DARLINGTON, N. D., *Los Angeles*
DUDLEXT, S. M., *South Gate*
GORHAM, H. M., *Pacific Palisades*

HELLMAN, IRVING H., *Los Angeles*
HOLLOWAY, B. R., *Van Nuys*
LEIMERT, WALTER H., *Los Angeles*
LESSER, SOL, *Hollywood*
LIPPINCOTT, J. B., *Los Angeles*
LYMAN, E. D., *Los Angeles*
MILLAR, J. D., *Los Angeles*
MUELLER, OSCAR C., *Beverly Hills*

O'MELVENY, JOHN, *Los Angeles*
O'NEIL, P. H., *Los Angeles*
PICKFORD, MARY, *Beverly Hills*
UNDERHILL, E. F., *Glendora*
WARDMAN, A., *Whittier*
WIGHTMAN, E. J., *Long Beach*

HUGH R. POMEROY, *Executive Secretary*

PUBLICATION COMMITTEE

MUELLER, OSCAR C., *Chairman*

BENT, ARTHUR S.
BARNARD, W. K.

LEIMERT, W. H.
UNDERHILL, E. F.

xii

76

LETTER OF TRANSMITTAL

To the Members of the
Citizens' Committee on Parks, Playgrounds and Beaches:

The Citizens' Committee on Parks, Playgrounds and Beaches was organized during 1927 at the instance of the Los Angeles Chamber of Commerce. It was charged with responsibility for the following tasks:

(a) To make a survey of existing conditions as to publicly owned parks, playgrounds and beaches throughout the County;

(b) To prepare a report as to needed amplification of these facilities;

(c) To submit recommendations as to ways and means of carrying out the foregoing program.

In fulfillment of these tasks the report herewith transmitted has been prepared by Olmsted Brothers and Bartholomew & Associates, Landscape Architects and City Planners, entitled *Parks, Playgrounds and Beaches for the Los Angeles Region*. It has been printed for distribution to the members of the Citizens' Committee.

The report contains a survey of the present parks and other grounds giving recreation service in the part of Los Angeles County chiefly lying south of the mountains and comprising about 1,500 square miles. It compares this service with that of other American regions of similar size and circumstances. It then describes the unique characteristics of the Los Angeles Region, in regard to which there can be no profitable comparison with other regions. Recommendations are made as to needed enlargement of recreation facilities, and as to ways and means of carrying out plans for enlargement.

The report finds the Los Angeles Region far short not only of the minimum recreation facilities of the average American city, but also of those that are especially needed here. Its recommendations for remedying this condition are made in detail; they are supported throughout by analogies from the experience of other great cities in this country; and the detailed recommendations are clearly summarized in each instance. The report contains an array of facts, statistics, and maps to illustrate the recommendations; and a much larger accumulation of these, too voluminous to print here, will be deposited with the Los Angeles Chamber of Commerce in further support of the policy advocated.

xiii

The situation revealed by the report is so disquieting as to make it highly expedient to impress upon the public as soon as possible the present crisis in the welfare of Los Angeles and the surrounding region. It shows that the park question is closely related to the community's health, and that the policy followed in the past is by no means a safe one from now on, since there is a radical difference between the needs of a small city and a great one in the matter of park and recreation facilities. The requirements of a great city of the motor-vehicle age are shown by the report to be sharply distinguished from those of the age in which older cities developed, and the distinction of the Los Angeles Region in this regard is clearly brought out in the report.

Your executive committee believes that the acquisition of lands specified in the report, the general policy it recommends, and the form of administration it proposes, are the best obtainable specifications and recommendations. And the committee is especially impressed with the need for proceeding immediately with an endeavor to arouse the public to the same sense of urgency that is felt by the experts and this committee.

The eventual requirements of the Region will be evident to those who seriously examine the situation, and no preconceptions should stand in the way of that examination. The fact that the Los Angeles Region is committed to other great outlays should not close our minds against a study of the outlay here proposed. The fact that it is a large outlay should not discourage action, for the need is large. Nor is the absolute amount for which the Region is already bonded the sole test of our capacity to satisfy this need. It is important to consider the question also from the standpoint of the relative or per capita cost and of the probable effect upon the tax rate.

The dilemma confronting us is the large expenditure involved in action, on the one hand, and the heavy penalty of delay, on the other. The way to reconcile our needs with our means is to assign the task to a competent body, charged with power and responsibility. The great program of park development contained in this report can be carried out in measured steps under firm and wise management without increasing taxes beyond 15 cents on the $100 of assessed valuation as a maximum in any year; normally a lower rate can be maintained, averaging about 10 cents. This is equivalent to the cost of operating each pleasure automobile in the County approximately eight miles per month. A city destined to be one of the great cities of the earth is justified in assuming such a burden for the well-being of its inhabitants and for its renown throughout the world.

Your executive committee takes this opportunity to thank the men who have prepared this report for their unwearied devotion to their task, which has been of a magnitude that few can appreciate who have not accomplished similar studies. The services of Mr. George Gibbs, assistant to the consultants, deserve especial mention, as

xiv

do also the excellent co-operation and assistance rendered by Mr. Hugh Pomeroy, Executive Secretary of the Citizens' Committee on Parks, Playgrounds and Beaches.

Acknowledgment is hereby made of the important services furnished to the committee without charge by O'Melveny, Tuller & Myers; Eberle Economic Service; Price, Waterhouse & Company; Rogers Aircraft, Inc. and others; and the invaluable aid rendered by the Automobile Club of Southern California; the Park Departments and Playground Departments and other officials of the County and its various cities.

At an early date a meeting of the Citizens' Committee on Parks, Playgrounds and Beaches will be called to discuss the program set forth here, and determine what steps shall be taken toward making it public.

Respectfully yours,

EXECUTIVE COMMITTEE,
*Citizens' Committee on Parks,
Playgrounds and Beaches.*
JOHN TREANOR, *Chairman.*

PART ONE
GENERAL REPORT

CHAPTER I

GENERAL CONSIDERATIONS AND SUMMARY OF CONCLUSIONS

THE metropolitan part of Los Angeles County, which may be called "the Los Angeles Region," is the site of more than forty prosperous cities, in addition to the City of Los Angeles. Here are over two million people in an area of fifteen hundred square miles. The Region is noted for its many natural charms and its varied human interests. The population is increasing very rapidly and changing somewhat in character. As it does so the Region is losing some of its most valued charms, for lack of a methodical plan for preserving them. Among the things that make it most attractive are the very ones that are the first to suffer from changes and deteriorate through neglect. Especially attractive, and especially subject to destruction, are the opportunities offered in the Region for enjoyment of out-of-door life.

But these invaluable assets, now on the verge of disappearing, can easily be preserved by concerted action. They can, indeed, be greatly increased by systematic care on a scale large enough to match the rapid growth of population.

Continued prosperity will depend on providing needed parks, because, with the growth of a great metropolis here, the absence of parks will make living conditions less and less attractive, less and less wholesome, though parks have been easily dispensed with under the conditions of the past. In so far, therefore, as the people *fail to show the understanding, courage, and organizing ability necessary at this crisis, the growth of the Region will tend to strangle itself.*

The present chapter deals with general considerations which should determine public policy concerning recreation facilities in the Los Angeles Region. These general considerations are based on a study of experience in other cities, a study of conditions peculiar to this Region, and on general principles derived from both studies. The chapter ends with a summary of conclusions drawn from these studies, the details of which will be set forth in later chapters. The immediate purpose is to show why more parks and other means of recreation *are now urgently needed;* to suggest the most effective ways of meeting this need; and to point out the evils that will follow further delay in adopting and executing a sound and comprehensive policy.

PARK-SYSTEM FUNCTIONS AND ALLIED FUNCTIONS

Private enterprise on private land offers, in every city, a limited opportunity for recreation; and it is good as far as it goes. But in the most populous regions the need for recreation is not normally met in such a manner and cannot be adequately provided for in that way. The problem must be faced as a public responsibility.

PLATE 2. Los Angeles as it was in 1894, from United States Geological survey, showing a relatively small urban region at that time.

In a large city or group of cities this responsibility attaches to the functions of a park system, and these functions are found to be related to certain other administrative functions, performed by various agencies. In the performance or administration of one group of functions, another group, or several other groups, will be found not merely to relate to it but to overlap it. Thus the group of park functions, ministering to the need for recreation, may be found to overlap the functions of the schools, the highways, or commercial enterprises, which also help to serve the same need. Whether the park agencies, or these others, furnish the opportunity for recreation is solely a matter of expediency, provided the services do not fall between two stools and fail altogether.

There is not and cannot be a sharp boundary line between the various responsibilities of public agencies. Practical experience under varying conditions is the only valuable guide as to how far a park system ought to ignore such boundaries. In some small communities, fortunately circumstanced, there may be no need for public parks at all. But in great urban areas bitter experience proves that, *without adequate parks, the bulk of the people are progressively cut off from many kinds of recreation of the utmost importance to their health, happiness, and moral welfare.* Public agencies, therefore, must progressively fill the more and more numerous gaps left by commercial and other private agencies.

Related Educational Functions.

Any educational undertaking for developing physical, mental, or spiritual capacities has also a recreational function, whether its agent is the school, playground, museum, park, private home, or what you will. The recreational function may be served by any such agency, in so far as emphasis is laid on the pleasure that accompanies and directly arises from the healthful exercise of such capacities.

Thus the schools, taking a broad view of their problem, reach beyond the traditional function of book-teaching and include play in their program. They provide for it both indoors and out, and even extend the service of their facilities to parents and other older people. Just in proportion as they do this will they meet recreational needs which might otherwise be met by agencies devoted specifically to park and recreation functions.

Related Highway Functions.

The prime function of the highway system is to facilitate the movement of people and goods, irrespective of the reasons for their movement. The prime use of the highways is economic, but in addition to the economic use there is an enormous use for recreation, especially for the pleasure of simply riding through more or less pleasant surroundings. Probably nowhere else in the world does highway recreation form so large an element in the lives of the people as in Southern California.

Now, in proportion as the highways *and* their surroundings are adapted to recreational uses, and remain so, the need for other recreational areas will be reduced. On the other hand, in proportion as the highway system is ill adapted to recreation, or tends to become so, the demand for specifically recreational areas is increased. Long stretches of congested streets, through mile after mile of monotonous urban surroundings must be offset somehow. The functions of the highway department are thus seen to overlap somewhat the functions of other agencies not chiefly interested in highways.

Related Commercial Enterprises.

Another important overlapping field is that of recreation furnished on a commercial basis, or by private clubs. This plainly overlaps some of the recreation furnished by the public park systems, either free or for pay, of kinds intended especially for those unable to secure such recreation elsewhere.

Proper Limit of Park-System Functions and Facilities.

The sensible limit of park-system functions is not a matter for theorizing or bias, either for or against their extension. On the contrary, it is a matter of expediency, that should be determined by common sense, applied to local present and prospective circumstances. Past experience, here in California and elsewhere under comparable conditions, is the best guide as to the proper scope of park functions.

So also as to park facilities. No one knows any scientifically correct ratio of facilities to population, or to land area. It is known, however, that under such and such circumstances certain cities have provided themselves with such and such park facilities; and that they appear satisfied with them, or have found them too costly for their value, or worth their cost but not extensive enough. Such experience is probably the best available guide for this Region.

PARK SHORTAGE IN THE LOS ANGELES REGION

The facts are so complicated that condensed statistical comparisons, without personal knowledge of local conditions, can be very misleading. But when the situation in the Los Angeles Region is measured carefully and patiently by the crude but common-sense method of comparison with experience elsewhere, four conclusions become unmistakably clear:

1. There is a serious shortage of park system facilities in this Region, even for the present population.

2. There has been a serious lack of increase of such facilities in comparison with the rapid increase of population.

3. These shortages seem quite unreasonable considering the agreeable climate, the economic prosperity, and the exceptionally favorable social conditions here.

4. They appear not only unreasonable but positively reprehensible, because of the very close and direct influence of agreeable living conditions on the continued health of the people and the prosperity of the community.

All this has been realized for years, as indicated in the interesting report of the Los Angeles Park Superintendent in 1924. (See Appendix No. VI.) The bad conditions shown to exist at that time are more acute today, of course, owing to the lack of increase in park facilities pointed out above in paragraph 2.

The nature of existing park shortage and its alarming character will be considered at length below.

The Peculiar Economic Status as a Reason for the Lack of Parks.

The most disconcerting fact about it all is that the rapid growth of population, which makes the rapid expansion of park-system facilities so urgent, also makes its financing peculiarly difficult. The rapid influx creates an exceptionally insistent need for capital to invest in those private and public improvements which are always the first requirements of a new population, such as buildings, streets, sewers, and water supply. The annual absorption of capital in these primary improvements is therefore exceptionally high—high in proportion to present population, high in proportion to the value of existing improvements, and high in proportion to the current rental value of all real estate.

In short, the demand for capital investment in other things than parks is far more urgent here than in slower-growing communities of comparable size. This makes it just so much more difficult here to obtain money for parks.

Furthermore, the rapid growth of population leads inevitably to a high speculative capitalization of *future* rental values, in the form of high present speculative market prices for land. Of course, this makes the cost of park land far greater than in slower-growing communities of comparable size.

The situation is in many respects like that of the swiftly expanding pioneer communities that made America for so long a debtor country. We were a debtor country not because we were unproductive or unthrifty, but because the speed of expansion and the urgency of the opportunities for immediately useful employment of capital far outran even the phenomenally great annual productiveness of the pioneers. They followed two courses in varying combinations. They borrowed capital from outside, in the aggregate prodigiously, often paying heavily for it. And they also stinted themselves of many things they needed by postponing what seemed to each of them the least urgent among his many urgent needs. To get more land quickly into crops, to increase their livestock more quickly to what the land would support, they themselves often lived for a time like cattle. They postponed many of the finer things of life, perforce, in the effort to build up rapidly the wherewithal to enjoy them. And sometimes they killed themselves or their women folk in the process.

Similarly the Los Angeles Region, in its feverish growth, has postponed and postponed such things as park facilities, because every dollar its people could save, or reasonably borrow, seemed to be more urgently needed at the moment for something else. "Parks could wait." Whenever it came to the point, the price of land for parks has seemed so high (as it inevitably must be high in a rapidly growing community, optimistic as to future values) that people have generally shied off from the proposal. They have felt something like this: "The benefit of parks bought now will accrue largely in future years and even to future generations. We can get along without them a while longer, anyhow. And if land at those prices is a good purchase, we would rather use our money to get lots on speculation for personal profit than give it up in taxes for our share of a park system." As a result of such reasoning, most park proposals have gone by the board.

The conditions underlying this state of mind are chronic in this Region, and will probably remain so as long as the rate of growth keeps ahead of or even close to the rate of accumulation of capital. But they are not necessarily prohibitive of effective community action.

The Crisis that Confronts the People.

The Los Angeles Region probably has a greater future need for parks, of certain kinds at least, than any other community of its size. And it is perhaps harder, financially and politically, for Los Angeles to get them than for any other such community.

The more closely the problem is compared with similar problems elsewhere the more serious appear to be the financial and psychological (or political) obstacles to development of an adequate park system. So, too, in the long run, the seriousness of failure to make that development, becomes more evident.

The real question is, how far will the people, so rapidly gathered here from all sorts of communities where they have had no occasion to face this peculiar problem, be able to meet the test? Will they overcome the difficulties and provide while it is still possible for things that will be necessary to continued prosperity and success?

PARK-SYSTEM FACILITIES

Various functions and facilities embraced in the park systems of large metropolitan communities are fully discussed in later chapters. Here they are summarily divided into two classes:

I. Those that serve mainly *local* needs and can be reduplicated in small and easily accessible units in every part of the Region, as is done with schools and fire-houses.

II. Those that serve mainly *regional* needs, which people can reasonably be expected to travel rather longer distances to reach, and which cannot be reduplicated locally; more or less comparable to public museums and auditoriums.

CLASS I: LOCAL RECREATION FACILITIES

Including Playgrounds, Recreation Parks, and Special Units

The most typical local recreation facilities are: children's playgrounds, in conjunction with schools or separately; and provision for certain kinds of adult recreation. Both of these must be readily accessible if they are to be of daily use. The value of such local facilities increases very rapidly as scattered suburban communities grow into a continuous metropolis of great extent and considerable density.

Facilities that should be provided in such localities vary greatly with local conditions, and should include provision for active exercise and games, alternating with rest, for all ages; for example, basket-ball, tennis, handball, quoits, swimming, or mere walking and sitting in pleasant and refreshing outdoor surroundings. They may include opportunities for both outdoor and indoor meetings, dances, concerts, and many other neighborhood activities of social importance, if these are not satisfactorily provided, for the masses of the people, on a commercial basis or on a private club basis. One of the most important purposes of a park, and yet one of the most difficult to describe, is that of providing the peculiarly refreshing quality which has such a restful and beneficent effect on the nervous system. This is a subtle and complex thing, which brings, along with a sense of beauty, a sense of spaciousness, of freedom, and of contrast with urban conditions.

The importance of the different kinds of local facilities varies greatly with the time and place. And the necessary land area per thousand of population varies far more. In the change from rural or suburban to urban conditions, the first need to emerge as seriously urgent is public provision for children's play. With increasing congestion and increasing metropolitan size, the other needs become increasingly insistent.

Most of the local functions above outlined clearly lie in that borderland belonging to both recreation and education. This is a fact which is everywhere finding expression in the extending community use of school facilities. But the school authorities generally find themselves unable to meet the want when it relates more distinctly to adult recreation than to education of the young, except in co-operation with well-financed agencies frankly and squarely addressing themselves to recreational rather than to specifically educational problems. This is especially true when the demand is for ample outdoor space amid agreeable and refreshing surroundings. And here arises the question: How many and how large should the recreation centers or units be?

Efficient Size and Range for a Recreation Unit.

The effective radius of service for a recreation unit varies widely with the function of the unit. It may vary from a radius of a quarter of a mile for little children's play, to several miles for some specialized services appealing mainly to adults. The efficient size of a unit depends chiefly on the number and kinds of functions to be included, and the prospective density of population within the effective service-radius. But it is also affected by the differentials in cost per acre of acquiring tracts of different sizes.

A single large and diversified unit gives better service and involves less overhead cost than several detached smaller units. For meeting the local recreation needs in a large metropolis, experience seems to emphasize the practical advantages of neighborhood recreation parks of about twenty acres, serving mainly the people in an area of about one square mile, associated where practicable with a school center but including many functions not normally assumed by school boards.

These major local units usually need to be supplemented by more closely spaced and much smaller playgrounds for little children who can not go so far, on or adjoining school grounds where practicable, but detached where necessary because of inadequate school-grounds and the impracticability of enlargement.

So far as these two kinds of units fall short of meeting the reasonable demands of the people, they should be supplemented by certain other types, such as ornamental squares and triangles, and local parks of scenic interest, the value of which is dissociated from the activities of a well-rounded neighborhood recreation park.

Administration of Local Facilities.

All such local recreation facilities should be closely adapted to local conditions and needs. There are disadvantages in centralizing the administration in a single organization which, since it covers so many units, tends to become unresponsive to local peculiarities. Such centralization is likely to hold back progressive and prosperous neighborhoods by standardizing at levels which are merely the best that can be attained by unprogressive or impoverished neighborhoods. On the other hand, as in the case of the schools, efficiency demands that management be centralized for districts very much larger than the territory served by a single neighborhood unit, as otherwise good management can be secured only at an excessive overhead cost. Roughly speaking, a good sized administrative unit for local recreation facilities is that of the ordinary municipality or school district.

Class II: Regional Recreation Facilities

The second, or primarily regional, class of recreation facilities involves very different problems from the local, even though no hard and fast line can be drawn between the two classes. Regional facilities include beaches, mountains, and such other recreation areas as it is impossible to provide by reduplication in small units in every part of a metropolis. While such facilities may, it is true, be made available by local enterprise, primarily for the use of those who live near them, and at local expense, experience shows that local enterprise *will not* alone provide in any adequate way for the great mass of people in a metropolitan community. For them there is needed a public agency specifically charged with this duty, supported by taxation falling upon a correspondingly large area, operating on a large scale, and consistently pursuing plans which involve very large expenditures and require many years to come to fruition.

The four types of regional recreation facilities needed by the Los Angeles Region are these:

1. Public beaches.
2. Regional athletic fields.
3. Large reservations in mountains, canyons, deserts, and islands.
4. Pleasureway parks or parkways, and related large parks.

Each of these will be considered separately.

Public Beaches

Public control of the ocean shore, especially where there are broad and satisfactory beaches, is one of the prime needs of the Region, chiefly for the use of throngs of people coming from inland, but also for those living near by.

Private control of a portion of the ocean shore is, it is true, a legitimate and fruitful way for enjoying the recreational possibilities of the shore, and the value people attach to such property is evidenced by the prices they will pay. But the great problem is to get from the beaches the maximum possible recreation values of *all* legitimate kinds, both local *and* regional, whether public or private, in reasonable proportion one to the other.

Desirable Features of Regional Beaches.

The two things most to be desired in a regional public beach are:

First, to meet the demand for bathing, strolling, and sitting down near the shore, and for occupation and amusement associated with

PLATE 3. New highway along the ocean front, showing narrow strip of private lands fenced in and cutting off all access to the publicly owned tidelands.

the coolness and refreshment of the sea breezes, the surf, and the view of the ocean, together with convenient and reasonably agreeable access, parking space for cars, toilet facilities, bathhouse facilities, and the like. This demand is very strong, and bids fair to increase indefinitely with the increase in population, and probably at a rate faster than the population because of the gradual cutting off of certain other opportunities for recreation. The demand is already very large at its peaks, although extremely fluctuating with weather conditions and the incidence of holidays.

Second, to meet a demand, also great and increasing, but considerably less fluctuating with weather conditions, for motoring along pleasantly while overlooking the ocean, the surf, the beach activities, and the picturesque coastwise views, with opportunity to stop and take part in beach activities as well.

What percentage of the limited available ocean frontage of the region could most advantageously be used for these purposes, as against other valuable uses (such as beach clubs, exclusive private use, and other non-regional uses), only the experience of years to come can definitely prove. But in the meantime the public holdings should be very materially increased.

The present difficulty, and a very critical aspect of the situation, is that the demand for private uses of the shore is promptly effective, and is leading to the investment of millions of dollars per annum in acquiring property rights above mean high water and in the installation of improvements which largely determine the use of the beaches in perpetuity; while the demand for public control of beaches has no corresponding effective means of making its real strength felt now, while the situation still remains largely flexible.

Conflict of Private and Public Beach Rights.

The public owns all tidelands and submerged lands, and has an unquestionable right to use that part of *all* beaches lying below mean high tide. The law is clear on this point, as will be seen by consulting the exhaustive opinion given in Appendix No. V. But this use is largely dependent on reasonably frequent and adequate access to the beach from the landward side. It is also dependent on the occurrence of sufficient lengths of unobstructed public beach *above* mean high tide, for use when the tide is up.

All this is coming to be widely understood; but what is not so clear, either to the general public or to those purchasing lots with what they suppose to be "private beach" rights, is that the value of shore sites is very largely dependent on the manner in which public control of *all* beaches below mean high water may be exercised.

The present tendency is toward a condition in which private and public ownership will be ranged against each other on opposite sides of mean high water on an indefinite line which cuts the beach in two longitudinally near its upper edge, dividing it so that neither faction can secure what it wants except by sufferance of the other. Each, in that condition, will be hostile and aggressive, and able to retaliate by developments greatly injurious to the values possessed by the other. This will result in lower total values of all kinds than the physical situation is perfectly capable of rendering.

In the long run the representatives of the general public will hold the whip-hand unless they forfeit their rights, because, since the public already owns the tidelands, it is only a question of construction cost (when the demand becomes great enough) to reclaim additional lands from the sea and proceed to their development for use by the public. *But a do-nothing policy at the present time is certain to result in greater total expenditures and in poorer total results than would otherwise be involved.* Furthermore, the evil results of delay will damage the private owners as well as the public.

Everyone agrees that opportunities for adequate regional beach reservations are slipping away very fast. And there is a general and well-founded belief that prompt action on a bold financial scale is needful to seize these opportunities. That belief is opposed mainly by two sorts of people: those who are moved by selfish considerations, and those who are so fearful of the mistakes and extravagances which might be committed by any public agency capable of acting promptly and boldly, that they would rather risk the loss of the beaches, by delay and debate and insistence on unworkably complicated checks and balances and red tape, than grant to any agency the power to act promptly and on a large scale. The proper view to take of the question is that, while the power to get results is inseparable from the power to make some mistakes, the need for results far outweighs the risk involved.

REGIONAL ATHLETIC FIELDS

The highly important social need for healthful outlets for the energies of youths of "the dangerous age" instead of forcing them into pernicious channels, makes it comparatively economical and immensely important to supply a few large athletic fields or "sports parks" serving large areas of population.

These youths cannot distribute their recreation throughout the week so uniformly as the younger boys and girls; and they can go long distances to get to athletic fields when the occasion arrives. But to secure local recreation grounds large enough for field sports and the gathering of large crowds is difficult, and few local districts can compass it. Where they cannot, it is clearly a regional function to provide such fields.

The most efficient unit for economical administration appears to be one hundred acres or more of nearly level land, large enough to provide space for baseball games, football, track events, tennis, swimming, and various other games and sports, with field houses, lockers, and other necessary conveniences.

Large Reservations in Mountains, Canyons, Deserts, and Islands

From a recreational standpoint the people of the Los Angeles Region are fortunate in having comparatively near at hand many hundreds of square miles of country so mountainous, or so arid and difficult to irrigate, or so intractable in other ways, that it has remained comparatively unsubdued by man. It is not so intractable, however, but that the pressure of population and of land speculation is constantly encroaching upon it and impairing its natural recreational value for city people.

The natural resistance of some of the mountain lands to uses destructive of their recreational value has been reinforced by the far-sighted action of the Federal Government in setting apart large areas as national forests for protection of watershed vegetation and related public purposes. These areas are in the main permanently open to use for public recreation.

The Angeles National Forest embraces about 640,000 acres of such land in the County, reaching to within twelve miles of the heart of Los Angeles. As a matter of bald statistics this makes the impressive showing of one acre of mountain reservation for each 3½ people. On that basis a careless statistician might claim that the people of this Region are more amply provided with public recreational areas than those of any other metropolis in the United States. One could make an even more striking statistical showing of a speciously great per capita extent of open spaces adjacent to Los Angeles by reckoning as such a few million

acres of the Pacific Ocean, which certainly has recreational value.

Permanent reservation of thousands of acres of steep, brush-covered mountain slopes such as characterize the Angeles National Forest (and most of Griffith Park) is of unquestionable recreational value to the Los Angeles people. It would be so, merely for the scenic effect of those mountains as viewed from elsewhere in the Region, even if they were administered exclusively for protection of watershed values and if the public were fenced off from setting foot upon them. But it would be utterly misleading to reckon them acre for acre as an adequate substitute for areas adapted to more intensive recreational uses.

Large continuous mountain areas, preserved substantially in a natural condition, have an important scenic value as viewed either from within or without, and in many cases a large economic value as a partial source of water supply.

Within the mountains occur occasional parcels of notable value per acre for direct recreational use but of limited extent. And there, also, occasional opportunities exist for delightful roads and trails, the value of which depends chiefly on the extent and scenic beauty of the practically untraversable mountain slopes around them.

It costs so much in the long run to adapt rough mountain lands satisfactorily to ordinary intensive private uses that their real net value as raw material for such use is generally far less than their value for watershed protection and for public recreation. Unfortunately in the local speculative land market this fact is often ignored and subdivision sales are made which commit the community to extravagantly wasteful private and public expenditures for converting a good thing of one kind into a poor thing of another kind.

The simple fact is that the raw land value of such intractable areas is relatively low, because it costs a disproportionately large amount per acre in improvements and in the carrying charges to get any very large return from the land. And the most significant fact about many large intractable areas is that, where recreational value can be obtained from them with so small an investment for altering their natural condition, recreational use will bring a larger return than private urban or suburban uses.

In such a large area all that is necessary for recreational use is the improvement of a few widely spaced roads, trails, and gathering places. These can be exceptionally valuable per man-hour of use simply because they are surrounded by protected landscapes, on land that may remain practically unimproved and unpenetrated by the public at all.

Considering the numbers of people of the Los Angeles Region who, under increasing difficulties, seek the kind of recreation to be obtained from trips into these wild districts, and considering the price per trip that people show themselves willing to pay for this recreation in terms of automobile mileage alone, it is clear that there is a very large and strong demand for such recreation. The permanent maintenance of an area of this kind which would enable an average of, say, 2,000 automobile-loads of people a week to reach what they want of this sort of thing, twenty miles nearer home than they would otherwise have to go for it, would show a saving of 2,000,000 car-miles a year, which at eight cents a car-mile is $160,-000 a year, or interest on $3,000,000. Returns of such magnitude, obtainable from a small investment in improvements, would be better business than to convert an intractable area to intensive suburban uses at a far greater cost.

If the market value of raw land were based solely on the ultimate possible returns, and on a well-informed and honest comparison of the total cost of improvements both public and private necessary to adapt it to various uses, the intractable lands best adapted to large scenic reservations would be more or less automatically assigned to that purpose. Unfortunately the decision to commit a given piece of

intractable land irretrievably to subdivision and intensive development at large cost for improvements, as against leaving it in substantially its natural condition for recreation, is normally based on the judgment of the promoter simply as to whether possible purchasers in a speculative market can be persuaded to take the project off his hands at a satisfactory profit to him above the costs which *he* will have to meet *before he is able to get out from under,* leaving a large amount of costs to be borne by the purchasers or the public. Until promoters are required to provide for the full development of the property, it will be only in extreme cases that large reservations of intractable lands, intrinsically best suited to public recreation, can be reserved for the public without paying excessive and fictitious prices for the raw land.

Because land-market conditions are so unfavorable, recommendations for additional public reservations of the type here discussed must be made much more conservatively than the physical conditions and the strictly economic conditions of this Region would warrant. Yet, because of such conditions, the development of this great metropolis must unnecessarily suffer. Its people will have to travel much farther from their homes to get the enjoyment of large areas of wild land than they would under better planning and public control of such lands.

PLEASUREWAY PARKS OR PARKWAYS AND RELATED LARGE PARKS

Under this heading are a series of problems which are peculiarly associated with great modern cities. The seriousness of these problems here no one can possibly realize who approaches the subject from the point of view of past conditions, or without a broad and alert understanding of what is occurring in other great urban areas of the world.

The experience of other metropolitan areas in respect to their park systems points certain lessons, which are emphasized by analysis of conditions and trends that are specially marked in the Los Angeles Region and are specially associated with the motor-vehicle age as distinguished from the age in which the older metropolitan regions grew.

So far as we can see, these conditions and problems are here to stay. Due mainly to improved transportation, especially to the wide use of the automobile, the population living in continuous metropolitan urban and suburban conditions spreads over an area much greater than was formerly possible. Due to the automobile, there exists an enormously increased range of average daily and holiday travel, limited not by the time and private means available, as in the past, but by the capacity and character of the public ways open to such travel. By means of automobile travel a large portion of the population therefore seeks out-

PLATE 5. Another parkway in Olmsted Park in Boston where adjacent houses have a pleasant outlook and where passing travel is surrounded by park conditions.

PLATE 4. Broad, quiet, attractive parkway in Delaware Avenue, Buffalo, where travel is a pleasure. Such ways are almost unknown in the Los Angeles Region.

door recreation to an enormous aggregate amount, and over long distances both within the metropolitan area and by passing through it to the country beyond.

As a result of the great spread of continuously occupied territory, this new, popular,

and valuable form of recreation is losing its value in the absence of a means for preserving it; and traveling on congested roads, through long, tedious stretches of unrefreshing, monotonously urbanized territory, is proving too great a waste of time and effort in proportion to the mileage of attractive country traversed.

The desirability therefore of a few specially agreeable routes of pleasure travel within cities has long been recognized, and experiments in great variety have been tried in the older, larger, and wealthier cities of the world. But most of those experiments were designed to meet the requirements of horse-drawn vehicles, low speed, and a short radius of travel. Therefore, they fall far short of meeting the needs of the automobile. More recently some progressive communities have been creating routes deliberately designed upon a regional scale and of a character intended to meet the metropolitan conditions of the automobile age.

Under modern conditions, with endless expedients for combining the regional pleasure travel functions with those of ordinary residential and business thoroughfares, *experience elsewhere points clearly to one of the most urgent park needs of the Los Angeles Region*

94

—the need for a system of interconnected pleasureway parks, regional in scope.

Such a system should be so distributed that no home will be more than a few miles from some part of it; and should be so designed that, having reached any part of it, one may drive within the system for pleasure, and *with* pleasure, for many miles under thoroughly agreeable conditions and in pleasant surroundings. Free from interruption of ordinary urban and suburban conditions, driving there may be either wholly for the pleasure of such driving or, more generally, it may be over the pleasantest if not always the shortest route to some other recreational objective.

"Pleasureway Parks" and Parkways Defined.

In order to provide for travel amid pleasant surroundings, parkways necessarily should be greatly elongated real *parks*. Except that they include roadways for automobile travel, they have almost nothing in common with "boulevards" as that term is generally used in America. Varying in width, and having few cross-traffic intersections, they should provide for traveling long distances by automobile, and should be well screened from the urban and suburban surroundings through which they pass. They should be wide enough and have trees enough to produce, along with the topographic conditions, some sense of spaciousness and seclusion, and a variety of scenic effects. Especially in the broader park enlargements that may be secured where land is cheaper or otherwise more available, much of the land may be used incidentally for many other park purposes.

The branches of such a system of pleasureway parks may be few, and many miles apart, but they must be ample and far reaching. In the old days only a small percentage of the people could enjoy park scenery from moving vehicles, and even they would not often travel many miles through city streets for that pleasure. As to the mass of the people, an isolated park that gave opportunity to drive or walk a mile or two in pleasant park scenery by going only a short distance through the streets satisfied them well. Today, almost everybody can, and frequently does without hesitation, get into a car and go five or ten miles through uninteresting streets to get to what he considers a really pleasant route of pleasure travel, perhaps in a park or public forest, but more likely just a region that isn't yet all built up. But the majority, when they get out of town, want to drive fifty or a hundred miles in pleasant surroundings, coming home by a different route.

All this is more true of the Los Angeles Region than of any other great metropolis. The people here can and do get an immense amount of outdoor recreation in just this manner, and voluntarily spend an amount of time and money in getting it (in car-mile costs, for example) which gives a rough indication of what they find it worth. It is certainly worth much more to them than the price in car-mile costs or they would not keep on doing it.

Present Cost of Recreation Travel.

There is no reliable basis for computing the aggregate car-mile costs which are thus voluntarily and gladly paid; but if anyone will figure for himself, on any reasonable car-mile basis, about how many dollars a year his own family and those of his acquaintances spend in pursuit of this kind of recreation, and then consider that 714,804 pleasure cars were registered in Los Angeles County up to June 30, 1929, he will get some real notion of how much the people think it is worth to them to ride long distances in pleasant surroundings. The proof of the pudding is in the eating. *The people are voluntarily spending millions of dollars every year for such recreation under conditions which are growing more and more imperfect and unsatisfactory.*

Unless the opportunity is preserved to newcomers and future generations in a system of continuous parks and parkways, inter-penetrating the Region and connecting it with the countryside, the immense value to the people of this kind of recreation is absolutely doomed to disappear. Urban growth will fill in one after another of the open spaces, and extend continuously for score after score of miles.

To people of today, how great would be the value of a home only a few miles from a parkway of ample road capacity and agreeable scenery, where one might drive through a chain of similar parkways to distant parts and enjoy the open country of Southern California! Contrast this with the far inferior worth of a home shut off from any considerable area of open land by twenty to fifty miles of practically uninterrupted cities and suburbs.

Cost of Land for a Park System

What would be the cost in land withdrawn from private occupancy? In a given region parkways, averaging a quarter mile in width, if spaced eight miles apart in each direction, would occupy six and a quarter per cent of the area. To compensate for this withdrawal, the community could be extended an equal amount into the surrounding unoccupied lands. In a region thirty miles in radius, an equal area added around the outside, to accommodate the people displaced by the parks, would make a band a little less than a mile in width. Travel to the center of the region would, at the farthest, therefore, be lengthened only three per cent, and for such extensions, here, plenty of land is available.

What would be the cost in taxes to pay for such reservations? It has been estimated that an increase in the annual tax rate of ten or fifteen cents should suffice to acquire and develop *a complete park system, including parkway reservations*. Land withdrawn from private use to form such parks should have less value than land for other uses because the parks should be located mainly in those interstices of the metropolitan district that have been left vacant precisely because they are for various reasons least valuable or least available for intensive private uses.

Parks and the Drainage Problem

To the experienced eye, the slopes of the land show approximately where water must concentrate in times of heavy rainfall. No matter how innocent it may look in dry weather, low land must always be far less valuable for building purposes than other land. But the lowlands may be just as good as any other for providing spaciousness of open scenery for parks and parkways; and it ought to be relatively cheap to acquire. Because of the innocent look it has in dry weather, it is not as cheap as it ought to be. Between floods it looks pretty good for building purposes to those who never saw what storm water can do in this country. Unsuspecting purchasers, victims of their own ignorance, will fall into the traps laid for them by the sharp practice of ruthless promoters, and such lands will be cut up, sold, and occupied. Unfortunately, the burden of such a wrong development does not fall on the purchaser alone, and scarcely ever on the vendor, but most heavily on the community at large. There is, of course, a remedy, but it requires vision and vigor to apply it. Remedial legislation might prevent further mistakes and correct those of the past.

To sum up this vexatious matter: The community is confronted with four possible courses:

First, and best, police regulation can be adopted to prevent costly improvements in floodways unless and until adequate spaces have been set apart for handling the maximum floods and the floods have been confined to them by permanent channels, reservoirs, and reserved areas for percolation into the ground. The cost would thus be fairly divided between the community at large and the owners of land more or less subject to flooding. Such a policy would not only be a direct financial benefit to the community, but would indirectly prevent the sharp practice above mentioned and stop the ill-directed spread of the population. It would also open the way to an economical purchase of park lands in the very areas where nothing else is so clearly practicable.

Second, the community can purchase such lands for park and flood-control purposes, while still vacant, but at speculative prices, that are high because based on the cupidity of speculators unrestrained by police regulations.

Third, the community can permit the lands to become built up, and periodically spend large sums to repair recurrent flood damage.

Fourth, after long delay, the community can, through heavy expenditure, permanently remove the flood menace by the purchase and destruction of costly improvements.

These are, of course, primarily flood-control and water-conservation problems; but there are many opportunities for combining with them, at little extra cost, parks along nat-

PLATE 6. Map showing channels and areas of interest to the flood-control problem that may have joint value for park and parkway uses. From 1917 report, with additional areas indicated.

ural drainage lines on lands relatively cheap, and extensive enough for recreation purposes. Such land would have to be acquired only once, yet would serve a double purpose—flood-control use and park use—not conflicting but positively beneficial to each other. Especially would this be true of the land acquired as a margin of safety; the open land skirting the chief flood-control area which prudence would include in the purchase.

Where flood control alone is dealt with in computing the size of anticipated floods, there is a natural tendency to curtail the area of land to be acquired in this speculative market. Such curtailment is likely to reduce the factor of safety beyond the danger point. Such a policy defeats itself. It compels large outlays for costly construction on narrow rights of way which would not be necessary on wider rights of way. The combination of parks with flood-control necessities is frequently possible, and wherever practiced it not only will yield a double return on the investment in land but also may lead to *an ampler and better solution of both problems at a much lower cost of construction than either would separately pay.* An example of such a problem is discussed in detail in a letter on Nigger Slough and other lands. (See Appendix No. III.)

SUMMARY OF CONCLUSIONS
(As Set Forth in Greater Detail in Succeeding Chapters)

Most of the population, of over two millions, now lives within a region of about 1,500 square miles. Population is increasing at a rapid rate. It is thinly spread over a large part of the central portion of this area. There is no great congested district, such as is found in other large cities. There is no evidence that congestion will become a serious problem in the future.

Development of a satisfactory park system requires a suitable agency. The park and recreation agencies of the cities, the county, the state, and the nation have definite functions

to perform in this Region, and any such agency may be somewhat expanded. But in the Los Angeles Region there is no authority now existing that could or should assume the full responsibility of acquiring and developing a complete regional recreation system. Such authority should be created, with power to raise funds in order to acquire and develop property, free from the disturbing influence of frequent political overturnings, and operating over a long period under a continuing policy.

Local recreation facilities are needed throughout the occupied sections. Local playgrounds and recreation grounds exist, but they are inequitably distributed in the Region. Much more than half the subdivided area is practically unsupplied. Only 73 of the 726 schools in the Region have five acres or more of play space. School areas, even at best, are not adequate to meet all local requirements, but they have great value which should be coordinated with other recreation features. The present available recreation *space per capita* decreases in proportion as population increases. Therefore, more space should be acquired promptly, by the municipalities or by the schools, or both. To provide each district in the subdivided area with reasonable local recreation facilities might cost, over an extended period, $40,000,000 or more, but would be well worth the cost.

The public needs and should have a larger proportion of the beaches. Fourteen miles of beach is now publicly owned, six miles is quasi-public, and thirty-two miles is clearly of sufficient public value to warrant immediate acquisition. The balance of the ocean frontage within and near the County lines is now used for other purposes or is less urgently needed by the public. The public holdings are in general very narrow. Much of the area that may be acquired is relatively narrow, lying between existing highways or built-up areas and the sea. To acquire the shore-front properties and a small amount of adjacent land would probably cost about fifteen million dollars; to make them fairly usable would require not less than two million more. This doubtless should be increased to include a pleasure bay at a cost, for its share of breakwaters and improvements, of another ten million dollars, making in all, $27,000,000.

To meet the requirements of general recreation, some regional athletic fields are needed. Ten of the large reservations recommended as enlargements in the general park system are now fairly accessible to the populous centers, and should be set apart for this purpose. As many more in districts more remote may be needed eventually for this purpose. A fair share of the cost of the ten now most accessible has been estimated to be about $7,000,000 for acquisition and improvements.

In the more remote tracts embracing the mountains, canyons, deserts, and islands, large reservations should be acquired and made accessible. The cost of acquirement is estimated at less than a million dollars, but the cost for improvements, primarily for roads, eventually may reach twelve to fourteen millions, a large share of which, however, can doubtless be obtained from existing sources such as road-construction funds and labor.

Pleasureway parks or parkways as herein described practically do not exist in the Los Angeles Region. Large parks, publicly owned water lands, and the like, to the extent of about 16,000 acres, lie along feasible routes for pleasureways of which they may serve to form a part; 440 miles of parks and parkways, with approximately 70,000 acres of land (54,000 more than now owned) are needed to provide park areas, reservations, roadways, border streets, drainage channels, and the like, to serve the various public needs that can thus be jointly served. To acquire the lands at present prices may cost a hundred million dollars; to improve them may cost forty-five million dollars more. A part of each cost, however, includes costs that should be chargeable (in part at least) to drainage, local streets, highways, and other public purposes that will be served.

The above estimates for a complete park and recreation system include a number of projects and involve large sums of money; but the total is not unreasonable; it is not disproportionate to the character, magnitude, and wealth of the Region; and it is not out of scale with the provision for recreation being made in other large metropolitan Regions. The recommended expenditures should not all be made at once, but *should extend over a period of possibly forty or fifty years*, and thus not involve a heavy burden at any time.

Beautiful foothills roadway near Pasadena, typical California scenery that should be preserved with its border plantations and views into the mountains, as part of proposed parkway. (See Chapter VIII.) *(Photo by Fiss.)*

CHAPTER II

CONDITIONS AFFECTING THE NEED FOR PARK AND RECREATION FACILITIES IN THE LOS ANGELES REGION

THE previous chapter has indicated the kinds of park and recreation facilities needed in the Los Angeles Region. Another study is now to be presented, examining the conditions which may affect the many problems of meeting the need. The first of these conditions is, of course, the character of the Region itself, and the first of the problems is thoroughly to understand the people for whom its solution is of such great importance. Incidental to these are studies of what has already been done, what the existing facilities are, and what is the wealth of the Region. The extent of the use of automobiles is considered, with the volume of tourist travel; movements of population are carefully estimated, also the possible effects of zoning and other restrictions. Regional or local conditions that now exist or that can be fairly predicted for a not distant future are considered; and the whole chapter is an effort to determine just what the people of the Region are, what they have, and what they can do and should do in the matter of parks and recreation in order to preserve and advance the prosperity of the Region.

CHARACTER OF THE REGION

The Los Angeles Region is a large one, including about one-third of the County. The other two-thirds are mountains and deserts. The Region lies south of the mountains, covering 1,500 square miles of coastal plain, low hills, and high agricultural development, into which the population has spread, very thinly,

and is still spreading. In this Region more than forty cities and a number of unincorporated communities form local centers, with separate jurisdictions, and deal with park development with no common or general policy, with no generally accepted uniform standards, and with no unity of control. There has been wide variation among them in park development. And, partly because of the newness of many of the communities, the need for such facilities has in some cases been almost wholly unrealized.

THE POPULATION

With a population of over 2,000,000 in the Region, but recently gathered from all quarters of the nation and constantly increasing, community life is not yet highly developed and recognition of local interests is limited. The population of the Region, having grown from a little over 100,000 thirty years ago to twenty times that number now, bids fair to double again by 1950.

With the growth of population the urban area is becoming greater; the large open spaces of the countryside are being pushed farther and farther from the center and are being made less and less accessible to the people, except in those lamentably few cases where land is acquired to be kept open for public uses. The area almost wholly cut into lots now extends out ten miles or more from the center and covers nearly 400 square miles, within which few large spaces are now available for park uses.

This area is extending still farther, and in it most of the population is now gathered.

From the spread of population for 1922 (shown in Plate 7) and that for 1928 (in Plate 8) and from the record of the change during that time (Plate 9) the trend of growth in recent years is fairly evident. There is a general spreading in all directions, a more intensive growth toward the west, south of the hills, and some added concentration on the west side of the center. Also, the change shows a loss of population in the south side of the city, where business and industries are driving out the small homes.

Low Density of Population.

These studies show a remarkable freedom from congestion of population as compared with any other great city. It is true that nearly half the population lives within five miles of the center of Los Angeles, in a space little more than five per cent of the 1,500 square miles south of the mountains, but even here the average densities are low, as follows:

Zone	Population	Area Sq.Mi.	Avge. Density per Acre
In a circle 1 mile in radius	54,800	3.14	27.3
In a ring 1-2 miles in radius	163,600	10.42	24.5
In a ring 2-3 miles in radius	220,700	14.70	23.5
In a ring 3-4 miles in radius	258,700	21.98	18.4
In a ring 4-5 miles in radius	292,200	28.26	16.2
Total within 5-mile radius	990,000	78.50	19.7

But such *average* densities over large areas may be very misleading. The entire New York Region, for example, with a population of nine millions, has an average density of only two and one-half persons to the acre, and even if the boundaries are contracted to include only six and one-half million people the average density is only twenty-nine per acre. But the majority in the New York Region are crowded into districts of much greater density than occurs anywhere in Los Angeles Region.

There is here no truly congested area and congestion is not developing. The following table and the spot-and-dot maps (Plates 7, 8 and 10) show densities for 1922 and 1928 respectively, throughout the entire region by small enumeration districts, few including over 4,000 people and others much smaller:

	1922	1928
Over 50 per acre	1 sq. mi.	1½ sq. mi.
Over 25 and under 50	11 sq. mi.	23½ sq. mi.
Over 10 and under 25	45½ sq. mi.	90 sq. mi.
Over 5 and under 10	55½ sq. mi.	75 sq. mi.
Under 5 in areas subdivided into building lots		202 sq. mi.

There are no densities of 200, 300 or 500 persons per acre, such as are found in eastern cities. There are only two enumeration districts, one of 52 acres and one of 57 acres, which have a density of over 100 persons per acre.

Effect of Low Density of Population on the Park Problem.

Los Angeles is unique among populous metropolitan regions in the fact that the great mass of its people live in detached bungalows and cottages with a high proportion of open space on their lots.

Low density of population means that fewer people live within easy walking distance of any one given unit of local recreation facilities. A permanently low density of population means either a larger radius of service for local recreation units, or smaller local areas, to avoid excessive per capita costs.

Furthermore, although private home yards of fair size partially satisfy the need for outdoor recreation, especially for little children and for old and inactive people, they do not provide at all for the growing number of those, both transient and permanent residents of the Region, who by preference or necessity live in apartments and hotels without such yards. Except for the very wealthy, who own

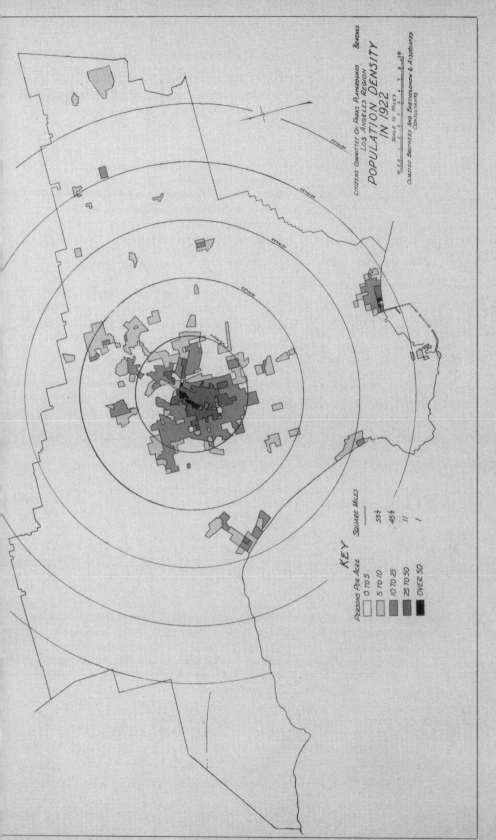

KEY

PERSONS PER ACRE		SQUARE MILES
0 TO 5		55⅔
5 TO 10		45⅔
10 TO 25		11
25 TO 50		1
OVER 50		

PLATE 7. Diagram showing density of population in the Los Angeles Region in 1922.

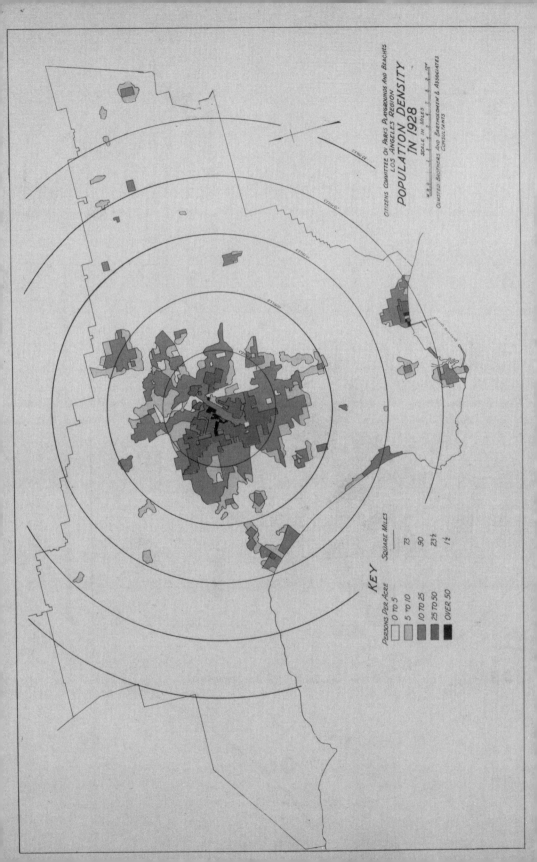

POPULATION DENSITY
IN 1928

CITIZENS COMMITTEE ON PARKS PLAYGROUNDS AND BEACHES
LOS ANGELES REGION

SCALE IN MILES

OLMSTED BROTHERS AND BARTHOLOMEW & ASSOCIATES
CONSULTANTS

KEY

PERSONS PER ACRE	SQUARE MILES
0 TO 5	73
5 TO 10	90
10 TO 25	23½
25 TO 50	1½
OVER 50	

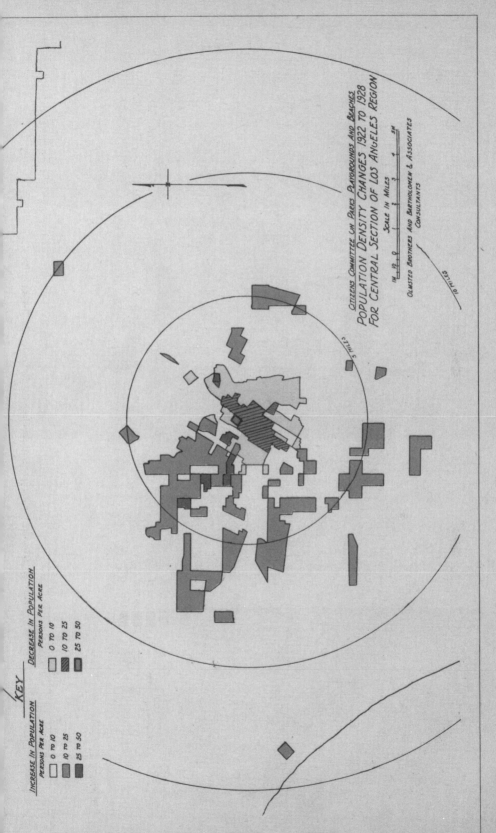

KEY

INCREASE IN POPULATION
PERSONS PER ACRE

	0 TO 10
	10 TO 25
	25 TO 50

DECREASE IN POPULATION
PERSONS PER ACRE

	0 TO 10
	10 TO 25
	25 TO 50

CITIZENS COMMITTEE ON PARKS PLAYGROUNDS AND BEACHES
POPULATION DENSITY CHANGES 1922 TO 1928
FOR CENTRAL SECTION OF LOS ANGELES REGION

SCALE IN MILES

OLMSTED BROTHERS AND BARTHOLOMEW & ASSOCIATES
CONSULTANTS

PLATE 9. Diagram showing increases and decreases in population in the Los Angeles Region 1922 to 1928.

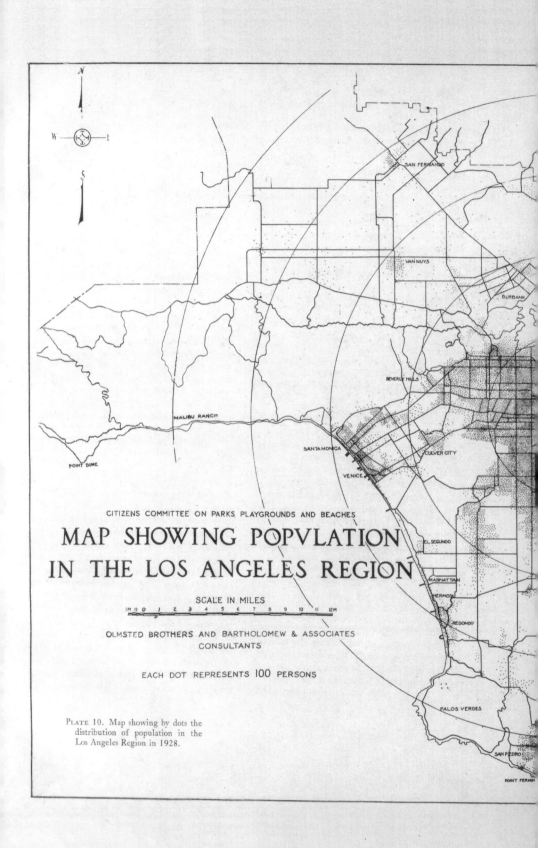

CITIZENS COMMITTEE ON PARKS PLAYGROUNDS AND BEACHES

MAP SHOWING POPVLATION
IN THE LOS ANGELES REGION

SCALE IN MILES

OLMSTED BROTHERS AND BARTHOLOMEW & ASSOCIATES
CONSULTANTS

EACH DOT REPRESENTS 100 PERSONS

PLATE 10. Map showing by dots the
distribution of population in the
Los Angeles Region in 1928.

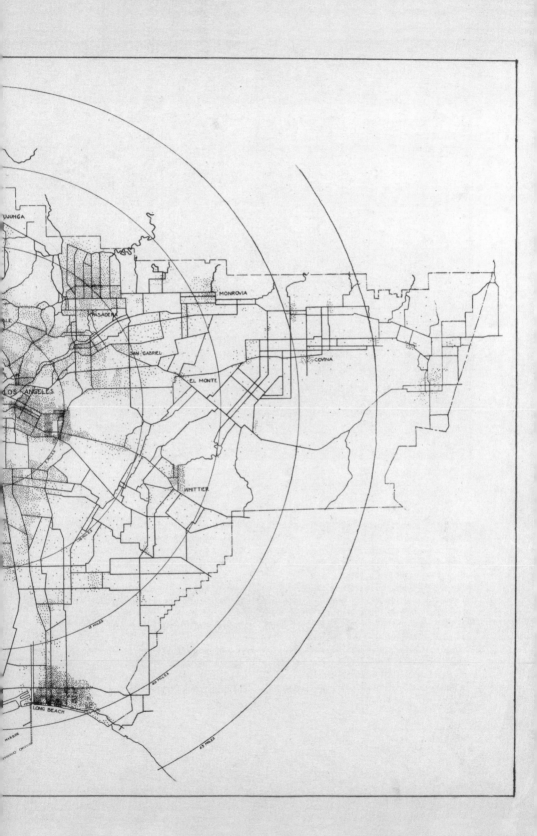

and maintain large private or club properties, such yards provide for none of those forms of recreation which require broad spaces, whether for active games and sports, and other gregarious activities, or for landscape enjoyment. Also, the spread of private house lots over a vast urban area tends to remove the open countryside to a far greater distance from the homes of most of the people than would denser types of development.

The relative sparsity and the wide spread of urban population is presumably due in the main to the combination of two factors: first, a general fondness for the single family detached house, peculiarly desirable in this favorable climate and especially attractive to the large number of elderly people who come here to live; and second, the general availability of the automobile during the period in which this Region has been growing to metropolitan size, making fairly long distances of travel in the common errands of every-day life a matter of slight importance. This trend will doubtless continue unless checked by traffic congestion and by the increasing lengths of travel through completely urbanized territory.

Evils of the "Friction of Distance."

Los Angeles may continue to grow as a metropolis of automobile users, living pleasantly in detached houses with plenty of room, with a minor percentage of apartment dwellers, but *only* if it provides motor ways (of which the pleasureway park is one type) on a truly modern scale undreamed of in the past. Otherwise the "friction of distance" will gradually press it back toward the familiar and deplorable metropolitan conditions obtaining in older cities, where population and land values are crowded into much smaller areas. Already in parts of Los Angeles, Long Beach, Pasadena, and other larger centers, there is a strong drift toward multiple dwellings which probably will increase in the future. So far as this drift

goes, the need for local parks and recreation grounds will be much greater than at present.

Age Groups.

A study of the population in Los Angeles by age groups shows a larger percentage of adults here than in most cities, due probably to the fact that climate and living conditions attract many adults to settle here, with a correspondingly lower percentage of children under twenty: 26 per cent here as against 36 per cent in most other large cities. Long Beach and Pasadena show a still smaller percentage of children than Los Angeles, and this would probably apply to some other parts of the Region as well.

This prevalence of adults indicates the need for a greater proportion than in other communities of those types of outdoor recreation, both local and regional, adapted to enjoyment by adults, as contrasted with playgrounds exclusively for children, essential though the latter are.

Income Groups.

The only satisfactory data on income groups in the Los Angeles Region is found in the records of organizations which have made economic surveys. Data, furnished by the Eberle Economic Service, based on a house-to-house survey of Los Angeles City and on rentals and building permits, show for a total of 328,685 families checked in the central urban area, the following ratios of incomes:

INCOME GROUPS BY FAMILIES FOR 1927, AND PERCENTAGE IN EACH

Class A—Income over $5000 per year	8.3%
Class B—Income of $2500 to $5000 a year	27.2%
Class C—Income of $1000 to $2500 a year	55.2%
Class D—Income under $1000 a year	9.3%

Corresponding ratios for the entire County are not now available but from random observations it appears probable that a complete record would show somewhat larger proportions of the two lower income groups.

These facts have a decided bearing upon the types of recreational facilities needed. People having large incomes (Classes A and B) are able to satisfy leisure-time desires and to live under whatever conditions seem most pleasant and enjoyable. Those of lower incomes (Classes C and D) generally live in small-lot, single-family home districts, and have more children and less leisure time in which to go to distant parks and recreational areas. These families comprise 65 per cent of the population, and they should be given first consideration, not only for their own good but for the welfare of the community.

HOUSING

Los Angeles is a city of single-family detached houses, but in certain urban areas apartments are gradually taking their place. The traffic volume on nearly all streets, the sharp rise of land values and consequent increase of taxes and assessments, are making large sections no longer suitable for ordinary single-family houses. The following table is a summary of the results of a house count made in 1925 by the Southern California Telephone Company for the urban area, having its outer limits approximately eight miles from the central business district, including portions of Beverly Hills, but excluding San Pedro, Long Beach and the west coast communities. The classification "residences" includes duplexes and bungalow courts, but is probably about one-half single-family residences.

TYPES OF HOUSING PROVIDED IN AN EIGHT-MILE RADIUS, WITH NUMBER AND PERCENTAGES OF FAMILIES LIVING IN EACH TYPE

Year	Residences	Flats	Apartments
1917	101,644	21,069	11,885
1922	157,045	37,722	14,725
1925	234,853	46,999	27,182

Year	Lodging Houses	Light Housekeeping	Total
1917	2,067	5,743	142,408
1922	4,608	7,653	221,753
1925	5,580	5,243	319,857

PERCENTAGES

Year	Residences	Flats	Apartments	Lodging Houses	Light Housekeeping	Total
1917	71.30%	14.70%	8.35%	1.45%	4.20%	100
1922	70.80	17.00	6.65	2.10	3.45	100
1925	73.40	14.70	8.50	1.75	1.65	100

These figures show only slight annual changes in the proportions of people living in the different types of dwellings. The increase of families living in multiple family dwellings is offset by the increased number of single-family houses in the outskirts of the city.

Los Angeles City building-permit records throw a somewhat different light upon the changing character of housing.

ACCOMMODATIONS FOR FAMILIES IN NEW BUILDINGS IN LOS ANGELES CITY

Year	Apartments	Flats	Single Dwellings	Double Dwellings	Total Families	Per Cent of Single Family to Total
1919	277	384	4,111	589	5,311	77.5
1920	561	475	8,850	956	10,842	81.5
1921	976	1,888	13,303	3,434	19,601	68.1
1922	4,458	2,184	15,373	6,018	28,033	54.8
1923	10,803	2,448	19,509	11,082	43,842	44.5
1924	7,652		14,669	7,543	29,894	49.0
1925	6,095		12,482	3,495	22,072	56.5
1926	7,459		9,999	2,559	20,017	50.0
1927	9,968		8,213	2,436	20,801	38.5

It will be seen that the percentage of single-family dwellings to total family accommodations has been almost steadily decreasing.

CLIMATE

It is needless here to praise the Los Angeles climate or to note the reduced cost of heating houses. Any real enjoyment of climate is *outdoor enjoyment*. Without facilities for outdoor recreation, climatic advantages might just as well be written down to a mere differential in heating bills. As an asset, the Los Angeles climate is worth far more than that; but it will be frittered away just as surely as outdoor means for enjoying it are not conserved.

Enjoyment of climate is in this region interwoven with all other forms of outdoor recreation and serves to heighten the pleasure they give. But the most conspicuous effect of climate and scenery is to increase very greatly the use of the automobile for recreation. On holidays and in leisure hours throughout the entire year thousands of motor vehicles are carrying young and old over the highways on pleasure trips. For increasingly frequent periods the primary highways are congested to a degree which makes the so-called pleasure trip anything but pleasurable, except to those who can enjoy any conditions so long as they sit in an automobile.

Obstacles to enjoyment of the climate deserve special consideration with reference to the tourist population. The widely-advertised attractions of climate and scenery bring thousands to the Los Angeles Region every year. They find the climate fully equal to expectations but the facilities by which the out-of-doors may be enjoyed often prove a surprise and disappointment. The pressure of growing masses upon the now available beaches, canyons, forests, and country roads is lessening their attractiveness and producing unfavorable reactions in newcomers. The beaches, which are pictured in the magazines to attract the eastern visitors, are suffering from the rapid encroachment of private use; the wild canyons are fast being subjected to subdivision and cheek-by-jowl cabin construction; the forests suffer annually from devastating fires; the roadsides are more and more disfigured by signboards, shacks, garages, filling stations, destruction of trees, and multiplication of poles and wires. So that driving for pleasure is often an exhausting and hazardous ordeal rather than a recreation.

SCENIC RESOURCES

A large number of those who have come to this section of California have been attracted to it by its scenic qualities. They have read that "no other part of the world offers such a diversity of scenery and climate in such a small area." These qualities contribute distinctly to the agreeable living conditions which induce visitors to become permanent residents. The natural beauties of the Los Angeles Region must, therefore, be considered among its primary assets, drawing new population and promoting contentment and satisfaction among those who choose to live here.

But scenic resources are dwindling. The beaches are being fenced off and withdrawn from general use with alarming rapidity. The opportunities now existing for the enjoyment of views out over the sea from the highways along the shore and from privately owned open spaces are being rapidly lost. A practically continuous row of buildings, walls and planting between motorists and the seacoast of Los Angeles County is in prospect. There are now only six miles of highway along the entire coast of Los Angeles County where views of the sea cannot be so cut off at the will of private landowners. There are no large parks or permanent public open spaces along the coast, such as the waterfront parts of Chicago, Belle Isle of Detroit, or Stanley Park, Vancouver. The few small squares, shore parks, and narrow beaches now existing are wholly out of scale with the present population and are deplorably inadequate for the future.

The mountains, which are dominant scenic assets, are slowly losing value because of the intensive urban growth. On the one hand such growth is steadily cutting off views of the mountains, views that can be effectively obtained only across open foregrounds sufficient in scale to complete and unify the landscape composition. The constant process of building upon open areas, the confinement of highways between rows of dwellings, stores, advertising

Plate 11. San Fernando Valley, looking toward the city, showing possible location for scenic routes along the hills and showing the washes where subdivision is spreading but has not yet absorbed all the areas needed for parks and parkways. *(Photo by Spence.)*

structures and other near-by obstructions is gradually eliminating enjoyment of the inspiring mountain scenery from the plains. This is a great loss which can be stopped only by reservation of occasional public open foregrounds. It is immaterial whether these be small local parks or parts of regional pleasureways.

Within the mountain areas certain characteristics of the mountains most enjoyed by intimate contact are being depreciated by misuse. Only certain canyons and ridges are readily accessible and easily usable, but these in some cases have been so occupied by motor roads, cabin construction, and commercial uses as to seem no longer distinctly mountain country, but merely reproductions of some of the poorer neighborhoods of the city.

The hills and sightly eminences in and around Los Angeles have never been properly worked into the expanding structure of the city in order to preserve their landscape value or save for public enjoyment the magnificent views from their summits. Land-platting and

PLATE 12. Signal Hill with its oil wells showing Long Beach on the plain to the right; along the ridge among the oil wells a parkway is needed. *(Photo by Spence.)*

road-building on steep hillsides generally result in scars and gashes which nature has great difficulty in healing. There are almost no continuous well-planned scenic drives in the hills behind Hollywood or Glendale or those on the east side. The drives and outlook points in Elysian Park are merely suggestive of the treatment that this great metropolis might reasonably be expected to give to many such elevated areas.

The value to tourists and residents alike of scenic routes *permanently protected against obstructive building on the side toward the view* in such situations as high on the Baldwin Hills, the Montebello and Puente Hills and just above the base of the mountains, would be enormous. Many thousands of visitors come to this Region expecting to find superb panoramas of the great city, the orange groves, the mountains and the sea from these high places, but month by month the opportunities to make them permanently available are slipping away. Even yet, however, many opportunities remain to carry out projects similar to such famous and popular drives as the skyline boulevards of Oakland and San Francisco, Mission Ridge Road and Lookout Mountain Highway in Chattanooga, the 25-mile scenic route on

PLATE 13. Plan for highways in the Los Angeles Region as prepared a few years ago by the Regional Planning Commission, showing a complete network of major highways.

the hills behind Duluth, Terwilliger Boulevard and the Columbia Highway at Portland, Oregon, and the hillside parkways at Seattle.

Native trees were never numerous in the Los Angeles Region, and every grove is precious. The introduction of an adequate water supply has banished desert conditions, and the planting of orchards and ornamental trees has of course enriched the view. Few concerted efforts, however, are made to save existing trees when in the path of subdivisions. They

are being destroyed by the spread of the city. In widening the highways, mature trees are cut down, thus removing the one effective relief to the monotony of commercial buildings. Many miles of once pleasant, tree-bordered rural roads are annually added to the already tremendous total of unsightly commercialized streets. Is this good business? It is through increasing lengths of such treeless streets that both citizens and visitors will be forced to travel in search of pleasure—unless the evil

PLATE 14. Plan for highways in the East Side as suggested by the East Side Organization in consultation with the Regional Planning Commission.

results of present highway construction are somehow counteracted and future improvements consider the good of the whole community.

STREETS AND HIGHWAYS

The streets and highways are developed primarily for other than recreational ends, but they play, or ought to play, an important part

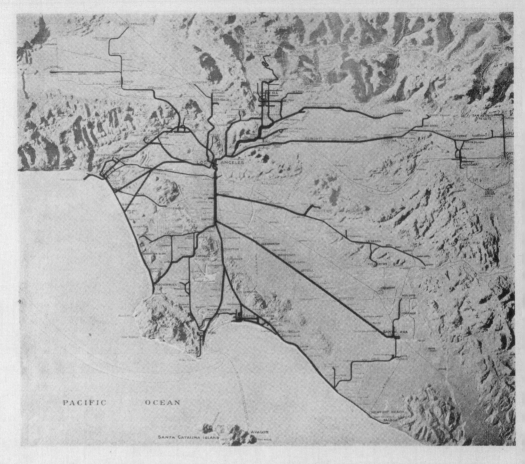

PLATE 15. Plan of the Pacific Electric Railway system showing a radiating system from the heart of the Region.

in recreation. Whether people find their out-door recreation mainly in parks or elsewhere, all pleasure travel originating in and returning to private houses must use the highways, possibly for many miles; and much of the joy of the day's outing will depend upon their condition. Yet all screens and opportunities for screens to form pleasant avenues, and also to protect adjacent property from the disturbing influence of traffic, have been lost in hundreds of miles of such highways. Such avenues as

Magnolia Avenue at Riverside, Euclid Avenue in Ontario, and the parkways and "boulevards" of other cities are wholly lacking in the Los Angeles Region.

CAR LINES AND RAILWAYS

In early days the street car was a much used pleasure conveyance and terminal parks were popular, but with the extensive use of the automobile the volume of street-car travel for pleasure has not kept pace with the growth of the city; the terminal park has become less profitable and street-car extensions into new areas have been limited. It is doubtful, in view of the wide use of the automobile for transportation and pleasure, whether any considerable extensions will be made in street-car facilities as other new recreation objectives are developed.

The most advantageous recreational feature of the present transit plan is the extensive service rendered the beaches and beach communities. There are now opportunities to approach by rail almost every stretch of usable ocean frontage from Santa Monica southward to Palos Verdes; lines extend to San Pedro, Wilmington and Long Beach and for miles along the coast farther south.

To the mountains there is very little street-car service and likely to be little in the future, as the total capacity of resorts there is necessarily limited and not likely to encourage costly railway building.

Steam railroads, other than as controlling factors in the location of industries and stations and as barriers between residential neighborhoods, do not materially affect the recreation problem.

ZONING TO CONTROL THE USE OF THE LAND

Los Angeles and other cities in the Region have adopted some regulations to control the use of the land, maintain standards in each section, prevent improper uses of the land, and keep the sizes of buildings in scale with conditions surrounding them. One-third of the municipalities have zoned for use, about one-fourth for height and area, and a few for side and rear yards. But there is no regulation of population densities, and most places zoned permit multiple dwellings almost everywhere and offer little protection to the small home owner. Hence there is little indication of where private residences are likely to continue in large numbers.

Where apartment-house construction is permitted practically all over a city, as is the case here, two evil consequences may result: first, the danger of the intrusion of apartments almost anywhere discourages the building of single-family houses, even though the fraction of the total area actually occupied by apartments will remain comparatively small. Second, apartments will be scattered and illogically bunched, and while their occupants will have far greater need for local park facilities than other people, it will have been impossible to provide for them adequately in advance of building operations.

Zoning for business frontage in most of the Los Angeles Region is far from reasonable. The speculative urge has almost everywhere led to permission of business on far more frontage than can ever be used, with resultant injury to property fronting on many streets that might otherwise form pleasant residential neighborhoods. In a study of property uses in twenty-three cities, by the Regional Plan of New York, the findings were as follows. Notice the business frontage:

PROPERTY USE IN TWENTY-THREE CITIES—FRONTAGES		
Use	Percentage in Residential Cities	Percentage in Industrial Cities
Residences	54.0 to 62.0	34 to 48
Business	1.4 to 2.8	5 to 10
Industry	3 to 5	21 to 26
Streets (fairly constant)	25 to 25	25 to 25
Parks (very wide variance)	2 to 17.5	2 to 17.5

SPECULATIVE LAND SUBDIVISION

Subdivision has been carried so far here that acreage parcels desirable for park purposes, because near in and of scenic interest, are rarely obtainable. And even when found they are often held at such high prices, set by lot sales in the vicinity, that it is difficult to prove that at such prices they will show satisfactory returns to the public as parks and recreation grounds.

117

PLATE 17. Map showing existing park areas and quasi-publ
grounds over five but under twenty-five acres in area. G
public golf and country club areas not on public lands. (

CITIZENS COMMITTEE ON PARKS PLAYGROUNDS AND BEACHES

MAP SHOWING

EXISTING PARK & RECREATION AREAS

IN LOS ANGELES REGION

OLMSTED BROTHERS & BARTHOLEMEW & ASSOCIATES
CONSULTANTS

★ PARKS & PLAYGROUNDS 5 TO 25 ACRES
▨ PARKS OVER 25 ACRES
▨ QUASI PUBLIC RECREATION AREAS

areas in the Los Angeles Region. Stars show parks and play-
park areas over twenty-five acres in extent. Red shows quasi-
y courtesy of Automobile Club of Southern California.)

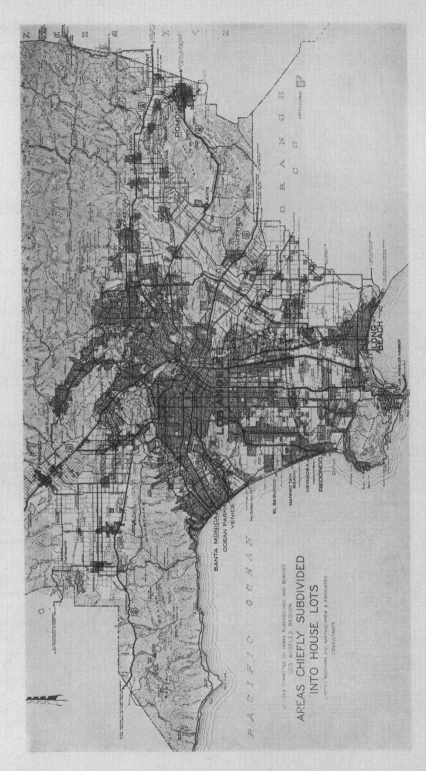

AREAS CHIEFLY SUBDIVIDED
INTO HOUSE LOTS

OLMSTED BROTHERS AND BARTHOLOMEW & ASSOCIATES
CONSULTANTS

CITIZENS COMMITTEE ON PARKS PLAYGROUNDS AND BEACHES
LOS ANGELES REGION

PLATE 16. Map showing areas now almost wholly subdivided into house lot units. (*Base map by courtesy of Automobile Club of Southern California.*)

There are few places in the world where land subdivision has been so constant and widespread as here. The habitable areas of the Region are very rapidly changing from pastures, orchards, farms, small farm lots, and brush land into streets and building lots. This takes place with only slight and very infrequent regard for the ultimate need for public open spaces by the increasing numbers who will occupy the subdivisions.

In the Los Angeles market, those who first buy lots from subdividers are largely intent on speculative resale—to anybody for any use. They are easily persuaded that almost any lot may turn out to be valuable for *business use;* they do not realize that only a very small percentage of lots ever will be so used; and perhaps they do not care; they are intent upon resale, nothing else. They do not appreciate the value of residential neighborhoods permanently satisfactory to live in because of having adequate local recreation grounds. They may be penny-wise and pound-foolish. Until the lot-buying public can be more generally educated to purchase discriminately, instead of on the basis of undifferentiated lottery tickets, subdividers cannot be expected to go very far in voluntarily setting apart local parks and recreation grounds. Can they be made to realize that in the long run such parks will make the remaining lots more valuable than the whole tract would be without them?

If people persist in buying lots that have not been provided with accessible parks and other ultimately necessary local public utilities, at almost the same price they will pay for lots that have those advantages, they or their successors will simply have to pay the heavy price for such shortsightedness.

SHORTAGE IN EXISTING PARK AND RECREATION FACILITIES

In the Los Angeles Region the existing parks and recreation facilities are very limited in extent and very irregularly distributed. The total acreage is not only below the standards of other cities, but below any reasonable minimum, either on an acreage or a population basis. Comparison on the basis of population is here illogical because population is increasing so rapidly and because such large sections still have an abnormal percentage of vacant lots. Comparison, as in the table below, on an acreage basis is more logical, as the total acreage will remain constant.

There is no satisfactory summary of statistical comparisons in regard to parks and related facilities in American cities, whether in relation to population or to area, and statistics are liable to serious misinterpretation without a personal knowledge of local conditions. The statistics used in the following table, whether originally made by the U. S. Census or other compilers, were mainly obtained from incorporated cities, though in some cases from special park districts, school districts, or counties. They show that the boundaries of administrative units relate in the most arbitrary and diverse ways to the distribution of urban territory and population. They frequently overlap each other so that the officials of any one of them may control and report on recreation areas within the jurisdiction of one or more other administrative bodies. Some of them own and operate recreation facilities outside their own boundaries. And there is much diversity in the types of recreation facilities classified under the same heading by different political units.

The most nearly complete and comparable data are those for the parks and recreation grounds of incorporated cities. From the figures for 1925-1926 of the Playground and Recreation Association of America a table has been made showing for Los Angeles and ten other cities (arranged by population) the existing park acreages, exclusive of school grounds, and comparing them with the total acreages of the cities, as follows:

TABLE SHOWING EXTENT OF PARKS IN ELEVEN CITIES*

City	Population in Thousands (1920)	Under Five Acres	Number of Parks by Sizes				Total Park Acreage	Acreage of City	Per Cent of Park Area to City Area
			5-25	25-100	100-1000	Over 1000 Acres			
Chicago	2702	18	36	10	9	0	4,487	131,190	3.41
Philadelphia	1824	4	10	7	4	2	7,802	80,017	9.75
Detroit	994	37	10	4	6	1	3,733	76,245	4.96
St. Louis	773	58	16	7	6	1	2,881	39,405	7.07
Boston	748	74	9	8	8	0	2,637	30,598	8.61
Los Angeles	576	42	16	4	2	1	4,906	262,893	1.87
San Francisco	507	20	31	7	4	1	2,536	81,280	3.12
Minneapolis	381	78	28	13	13	0	4,738	34,105	13.88
Kansas City	324	25	37	18	3	1	3,238	38,400	8.42
Seattle	315	36	67	8	6	0	2,145	45,760	4.70
Portland	258	25	41	8	6	0	2,182	42,240	5.18

*Exclusive, as in the other statistics, of school playgrounds, and exclusive of the National Forests.

Minneapolis has the most properties, the largest percentage of park acreage, the best distribution of areas, and the best develop-ment and maintenance. The data for Minneapolis, for Los Angeles City and for Los Angeles Region are in detail as follows:

COMPARISON OF PARKS IN MINNEAPOLIS AND LOS ANGELES
Number of Parks by Sizes

	Under 5 Acres	5-25	25-100	100-1000	Over 1000 Acres	Total Park Acreage	Acreage of City or Region	Population in 1920
MINNEAPOLIS:								
Number	78	28	13	13	-------	-------	-------	-------
Aggregate acreage	63	331	627	3,714	-------	4,737	34,105	380,582
LOS ANGELES CITY:								
Number	42	16	4	2	1	-------	-------	-------
Aggregate acreage	48	216	176	713	3,752	4,905	262,893	576,673
LOS ANGELES REGION:								
Number	95	69	19	12	1	-------	-------	-------
Aggregate acreage	247	839	934	3,896	3,752	9,668	960,000	936,000

Within the Los Angeles Region a wide variation is found in the percentages of park areas. In Pasadena, relatively large areas are now publicly owned. In Palos Verdes, 25 per cent of the entire residential district (800 acres out of 3200) is set aside for park and recreational uses. On the other hand, in many other districts the percentage of public open space is extremely low.

The total park area in the Los Angeles Region is 9,668 acres, or about 15 square miles.

That is to say, in a region of 960,000 acres, or 1500 square miles, there are only 15 square miles of park lands. This is only about *one per cent* of the total area. Compare this with the fact that there are now in the same region 42 areas in golf clubs and country clubs privately owned outside the park areas, and containing 6,179 acres, or about two-thirds as much as the total public park lands.

The following table shows what has been

done and is now being done in four large metropolitan regions. Los Angeles has a relatively large area in municipal parks, but it includes a number of mountainous areas having limited recreational value. In Metropolitan, County and State parks, Los Angeles is far behind other cities—in fact, has hardly made a beginning.

REGIONAL PARK AREAS—PUBLIC LANDS IN ACRES

METROPOLITAN REGION	Municipal Parks	Municipal Water-shed Properties	Metropolitan County and State Parks	Adjacent National Forest and Park Areas	Acreage of the Region	Population of the Region
CHICAGO:						
Cook County only, 1928	5,800	....	32,000	....	597,000	3,760,000
Chicago Region, 1928	12,000	....	38,900	....	5,000,000	4,800,000
Chicago Region official recommendations and estimates for 1950—						
(Minimum)	21,000	....	64,000	....	5,000,000	8,000,000
(Maximum)	74,000	....				
BOSTON:						
Metropolitan District, 1928	7,054	712	11,142	....	262,400	1,840,912
NEW YORK:						
New York Region, 1927	13,736	56,999	76,266	655,874	3,537,249	10,340,000
LOS ANGELES:						
Los Angeles Region, 1928	9,161	6,523	507	640,000	960,000	2,000,000

DISTRIBUTION OF SPACES NEEDED FOR LOCAL SERVICE

In order to indicate the extent to which existing public open spaces may serve local recreational and park needs in the Los Angeles Region, a diagram has been made (Plate No. 18) showing all public recreational areas: parks, playgrounds, school grounds, and others, together with the surrounding district for which they can logically be expected to provide local service. The diagram was drawn on the assumption that local service should extend over a district twenty times the size of the unit (the park area being 5 per cent of total area) but not more than half a mile distant from the unit.* On this diagram all such districts, and all large areas not requiring recreation facilities (industrial areas, hilltops, steep slopes, college grounds, and private recreation grounds) have been left in white;

within the region now almost wholly cut up into building lots all other areas have been shown in black; outside the intensively subdivided (black) areas all lands not served by existing parks and not withdrawn from residence uses have been shown cross-hatched. This diagram shows a lack of open spaces for local service in a large percentage of the Region.

Parkways or pleasureway parks in any adequate recreational sense, as they are known for example in New York, Boston, Chicago, Cleveland, Detroit, Minneapolis, and Kansas

*Five per cent of the total area would be a low standard for a region of great population densities. (The island of Manhattan has 12.4% of its total area in parks and, with a population density approximating 200 per acre, is very inadequately supplied. The Borough of the Bronx has 16.8% of its 26,524 acres in parks.) But 5% seems reasonable for the lower prevailing densities of the Los Angeles Region. The half-mile limit of effective service radius for local recreation facilities is based on observations and attendance counts in many eastern cities, but possibly the radius should be extended here because of the much more extensive use of automobile transportation.

VENTURA COUNTY

VERDUGO MTS

SANTA MONICA MOUNTAINS

KEY

◯ — Extent of Possible Recreational Service of Existing Facilities.

☐ — Industrial Areas and other Non-Residential Areas.

■ — Residential Areas Lying Outside Any Reasonable Range of Local Recreational Service or Existing Facilities.

▨ — Areas now partly built, into which intensive use for residential purposes is now spreading.

PALOS VERDES HILLS

PLATE 18. Diagram showing residential areas lying beyond the r

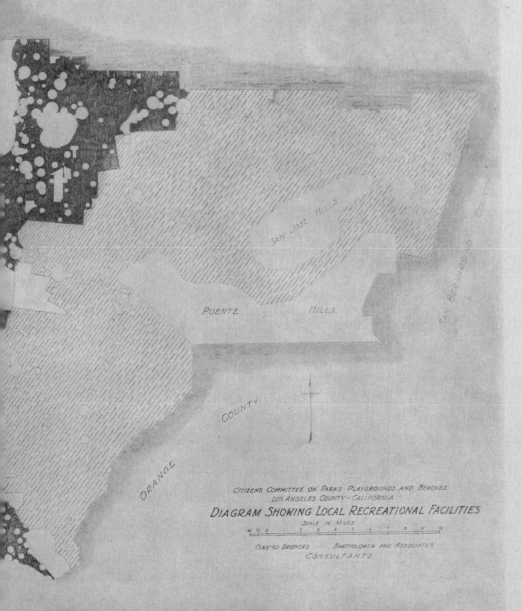

SAN GABRIEL MOUNTAINS

ANGELE'S NATIONAL FOREST

SAN JOSE HILLS

PUENTE HILLS

SAN BERNARDINO COUNTY

COUNTY

ORANGE

CITIZENS COMMITTEE ON PARKS PLAYGROUNDS AND BEACHES
LOS ANGELES COUNTY — CALIFORNIA
DIAGRAM SHOWING LOCAL RECREATIONAL FACILITIES
SCALE IN MILES

OLMSTED BROTHERS   BARTHOLOMEW AND ASSOCIATES
CONSULTANTS

...sible service by existing park, playground or school recreational areas.

City, are almost wholly lacking here. This lack cannot be due to a smaller need because of the peculiarities of the Region. The people of Los Angeles County have not less but more need and desire for outdoor enjoyment by automobile. Yet compare the almost complete lack here with the mileages in the following list:

LENGTHS OF PARKWAYS OR PLEASUREWAY PARKS

New York City	79 miles	Detroit	15 miles
Boston	20 miles	Minneapolis	55 miles
Chicago	84 miles	Kansas City	90 miles
Cleveland	43 miles	Los Angeles	
			No true parkways

Some of the mileage reported in this table does not come up to the standards for a true parkway as considered in this report.

CONCLUSION

It is realized that in a review of Los Angeles park needs, too much emphasis must not be put upon comparisons with other cities. The problem here must be solved almost entirely on the basis of local or at least California experience. In the last analysis the people of this Region must determine their own recreation needs and meet them in the same manner as they are working out the problems of water supply, flood protection, harbor improvement, transportation and other matters having significance beyond the boundaries of any single city.

The people of the Los Angeles Region have essentially the same normal desire to play and they derive the same benefits from exercise in the open as people elsewhere; youth here finds fully as keen enjoyment and healthful development in games and sports as youth in other cities; the climate constantly beckons outdoors, far more than elsewhere. Study has unearthed no factor which indicates that the people of this Region will be permanently satisfied with lower standards than those of other great communities, and many that point toward the expediency of higher standards. The big question is whether the people are socially and politically so slow, in comparison with the amazing rapidity of urban growth here, that they will dumbly let the procession go by and pay a heavy penalty in later years for their slowness and timidity today.

CHAPTER III

ADMINISTRATIVE, LEGAL AND FINANCIAL CONDITIONS AFFECTING THE CREATION OF AN ADEQUATE PARK AND RECREATION SYSTEM FOR THE LOS ANGELES REGION

AN adequate park and recreation system should recognize two distinct types of functions in order to meet needs that are primarily local and those that are regional. This difference of need and consequently of function profoundly affects the selection of sites, the design, and the legal, financial and administrative problems of control and maintenance. But there is no such sharp distinction between the kinds of parks that may serve such needs. Many park areas, primarily intended for the one purpose, may serve the other, or may serve both, and thus make for efficiency and for economy. Indeed, many a local recreation area such as a public city beach, created and operated by a single city primarily for its own people, is now effectively serving as a regional area drawing people from all parts of the region in even greater numbers than are other areas intended strictly for regional use.

A multitude of agencies, with responsibilities and powers overlapping in complicated ways, have in every metropolis developed serious deficiencies in practice and have left important needs uncared for. This is especially true of recreation, which is slighted far more than other branches of administration. As new needs have tardily been recognized, they have been imperfectly dealt with either by expanding the scope of existing departments or by creating subsidiary bureaus. This has been especially true of problems transcending jurisdictional boundaries.

Local Authorities and Co-operative Action.

Operating throughout every metropolitan region, and dealing with some of the problems here considered, are the school boards, which naturally deal with facilities that serve the people near at hand. At the same time and in the same area a number of other agencies, more or less independent, work upon recreation problems, some from a local point of view, others from a regional one. Among these some now act in co-operation with one another, and to this voluntary co-operation and interchange of views have been largely due such even moderately well-balanced and satisfactory results as have been obtained.

Existing methods have worked out best in those matters of local recreation where results have approximated standards which the local people demand and are willing to pay for. It is therefore believed that in such local matters the best results for the least money can be obtained by stimulating the activities of existing municipal agencies and school boards.

Regional Authority and Continuing Policies.

It may confidently be said that the more truly regional park and recreation needs have never been satisfied in a metropolis merely by adding to local agencies such regional functions as each municipality may see fit to undertake. Success requires an agency created for the regional purpose alone, and guided by the principle of unity—singleness of responsibility, authority, purpose, and policy.

Responsibility for and jurisdiction over a broad territory may be focused in one agency covering the entire metropolitan area. The agency may cover it as one unit or as more than one, but should in any case cover a section large enough to emphasize unmistakably its regional responsibility. For example, the Boston Region has one metropolitan park agency covering about forty municipalities, each with its own local agency. The New York Region extends into three states and has several park agencies of wide jurisdiction, mainly covering an entire county each; it also has two special commissions (one interstate and one for the State of New York) each having jurisdiction over several counties; there are in addition four hundred municipal agencies.

The success of such agencies depends on concentration of purpose. *Responsibility for park and recreation problems should not be made a side issue.* Continuity, stability of policy, and control of the budget are essential. This is true especially because the results of park expenditures are very slow to materialize, slower perhaps than those of any other expenditures.

Of the conditions most essential to success are: first, stability of tenure of personnel; second, a small deliberative body of large-minded persons, responsible for the policy but willing to delegate executive work in pursuance of the policy; and, third, a method of financing which permits budgeting systematically for considerable periods in advance.

Legislation Recommended.

Legislation embodying the principle above outlined exists in other states, and the principle is not unknown here in California. The East Bay Municipal Utilities District is an example of regional authority overlapping both city and county boundaries.*

*For a detailed comparison of powers, duties and resources of such agencies see Appendix No. IV.

Legislation is needed here to permit the creation of a regional park district. A large part of the needs of the Los Angeles Region is essentially regional, and can best be developed through the creation of a regional authority. To create such an authority will require legislation.

The Legislature should pass an enabling act providing for an initiative petition signed by a large enough number of persons, possibly five thousand, to show popular demand and to prevent hasty action. This provision would limit application of the act to populous districts where the recreational need really exists. The petition should be filed with the board of supervisors, who may reject or approve it, or reduce the boundaries of the proposed district. When the petition is approved, an election should be called in the proposed district to determine whether the district shall be formed.

Government of such a district should be vested in a board of five directors, to serve without compensation, with four-year overlapping terms, to be appointed by the Governor. In this respect the proposed act would follow closely the example of other successful park acts, such as that for Boston, or for the counties of New Jersey, where splendid personnels have been secured, consisting of leading citizens willing to give much time and thought to this question, capable of resisting political influence and attracted to the office by considerations of public service where no salary is involved.

The board of directors of the proposed district should have the following powers:

to control such affairs in the district as are necessary to carry out the purposes of the act. This power should be substantially the same as that of the flood-control, sanitation, and other districts now existing here, and that of similar park districts elsewhere, including the power to acquire and hold land and rights in land for the purpose of developing a system of parks and other recreation facilities.

to levy, in addition to taxes for service of bond issues, an annual tax for maintenance not to exceed five cents per hundred dollars of assessed valuation.

to issue bonds not to exceed two per cent of the assessed valuation of the district, by giving notice and holding hearings, with the provision that if a referendum petition is filed an election must be held, requiring a two-thirds vote to carry the bonds. Of such bonds, not more than one-half of one per cent of assessed valuation to be issued in the first year, nor more than one-quarter of one per cent in any one year thereafter.

to issue bonds thereafter, when approved by a two-thirds vote of the electorate of the district, above two per cent but not above five per cent of the assessed valuation.

The provisions above outlined are based upon a study of the probable financial requirements involved in acquiring and constructing a system of regional parks for the Los Angeles Region as fully described elsewhere in this report.

ESTIMATED COST OF THE PROPOSED PARK SYSTEM

To acquire and develop a comprehensive system of parks as here proposed will require a period of many years. It is difficult to approximate the probable cost very closely, but estimates have been made, as carefully as possible, under the three heads of acquisition, improvement, and maintenance.

Costs of acquisition will be high in the early years of the program. Improvement costs will vary with the rapidity with which acquired areas are brought to their fullest usefulness; but if sufficient funds are available the annual improvement costs will probably be highest from five to ten years after the greatest acquisition of property. Maintenance costs will be low in the early years and will gradually increase until the acquisition and improvement have been largely completed.

The total cost to acquire and develop the entire system of parks and recreation areas, inso-far as such development is herein recommended, including all local as well as regional features, is estimated at $224,000,000. But this estimate includes a number of features, such as highways and flood-control areas now being developed or now contemplated, for which funds will be wholly or partly available from various other sources, the total of which is large, possibly $100,000,000. This leaves $124,000,000 for which special financing is needed. This estimate is necessarily preliminary only and is subject to various modifications, but it is a fair measure of the size of the problem that confronts this Region. The cost of accomplishment will vary with time as well as with change in land values, for it will take many years even to approach a completion of the program.

Factors That May Modify Costs.

While spread of urban conditions and local improvements will tend to increase costs, there are several factors that should aid in reducing them.

The fact that a comprehensive plan exists for park development may encourage the donation of large areas by persons who might not otherwise be inspired to make such gifts. A public park makes a splendid memorial. Bequests of this sort have been popular in the older communities; and, already, here in this Region, several parks have been given, such as Griffith Park, Brand Park, and Stough Park. It is possible that further gifts, even on a large scale, may be made which will materially help to reduce the total costs.

The proposed park authorities should have sufficient power and leeway to make favorable purchases of lands, and it is possible that such favorable purchases may aid materially in keeping down the total costs.

There will undoubtedly be various instances where the creation of parks will lead to a very material increase in the value of adjacent lands. Such increase is a legitimate source for recovery in the assessment of benefits; and while it is not here proposed that the park board shall have authority to assess for benefits, it is possible that local communities may join in obtaining lands and use their power to assess benefits. Also, the fact of created benefits often serves to persuade owners of large tracts to give lands for parks in return for benefits the parks will create, and thus aid in reducing the total cost.

In the operation of the properties there will be certain features such as golf courses, bathhouses, boat landings, refectories, and possibly sites for amusement devices, that may produce some revenue to offset in part the cost of maintenance.

Large areas of proposed park lands in the rivers and drainage channels will have double value to the public because they will serve both park and drainage purposes. The cost of acquiring these areas has been included in the estimates for the park system, but part of the cost should be chargeable to drainage works, and thus reduce park costs. In either case the public will have to pay but once for the property, whether through park or flood-control authorities, and will gain in the greater usefulness of the areas under such a plan. As a matter of public record it would be more just if a portion of acquisition be borne by each of the departments, rather than by the parks alone.

Possible Source of Funds.

Bonds to the extent of two per cent of the assessed valuation of the district, based on the present valuation of approximately $3,500,-000,000 will produce approximately $70,000,-000. Assuming that the full amount of this sum may be issued in five per cent interest-bearing bonds in the first few years, with provision for $2,000,000 retirement annually, and that $2,000,000 of new bonds can then be issued annually, it will require from twenty-five to fifty years to secure sufficient funds to carry out the entire plan. The effect upon the present tax rate will then be as follows:

Charges	Tax rate on $100 Valuation
Interest of 5% on $70,000,000= $3,500,000	10.0 cent
Principal retirement $2,000,000	5.7 cent
Maintenance tax proposed	5.0 cent
MAXIMUM TOTAL	20.7 cent

As previously stated, there are numerous factors which may reduce this tax rate, such as gifts of land and money, favorable conditions of purchase, co-operation with the flood-control district and with local agencies, use of special assessments, and revenues from operation. There are still other factors that may assist in reducing the tax rate, the most important of which is the probable increase in the assessed valuations of the district. At the present rate of increase the total assessed valuations will approximately double in twenty years, which will automatically reduce the rate to approximately half the amount herein estimated at a maximum of 20.7 cents.

In the first few years after creating the park district it will of course be impossible to use any sum approaching the full amount of the bonds. Therefore, for several years, the tax rate will be considerably below the maximum. As these years pass, the assessed value will increase, and the tax rate will correspondingly decrease.

It is also possible that the total interest charges may be reduced by favorable methods of retirement of principal, or through special forms of serial bonds, or because of lower interest rates prevailing at the time of issue.

Against all the factors that may reduce the tax rate there is one that will tend to increase it: the higher cost of land likely to result from delay in acquisitions.

A balancing of all these factors leads to the conclusion that a maximum tax rate of fifteen cents may be required at certain times. *But it is believed that no more than eight or ten cents will be required for several years, with a prob-*

ble maximum average of ten cents over the orty or fifty years required to complete the ystem. But whatever the rate, the authority o incur expense should be established as here- a recommended.

JUSTIFICATION FOR THE PROPOSED EXPENDITURES

To compare the present plan with accom- plishments in other regions is difficult if not mpossible, because of numerous dissimilar factors. The Los Angeles Region has a far wider and thinner spread of population than any other metropolis, and a far greater use of automobiles.

The Los Angeles Region is the only great metropolis that has developed almost wholly since the invention of the automobile. The rec- reation of its people is largely dependent on the automobile. Favorable climate and recrea- tional advantages attract great numbers of tourists, to the profit of the community. To continue to attract such tourists or to increase the volume until it reaches an economic value comparable, for instance, with that of Paris, parks and pleasureways on about the scale here proposed are essential.

Here is a most interesting opportunity for comparison. Paris transformed itself from an unsightly place to a beautiful city. It has long been the center of world tourist traffic. The improvement plan that has so profitably re- sulted was undertaken in 1850, when Paris had a population of about a million and a half. During the next forty years about $400,000,- 000 was spent in carrying out the plan. Dur- ing that period, money was worth far more than it is today. Moreover, Paris had far fewer economic possibilities, a much less advantage- ous location, and a smaller population than Los Angeles; and a climate that compares unfavor- ably. Yet Paris is now the world's travel center.

If Paris, with all her handicaps, had enough confidence in her future to plan and execute a $400,000,000 program in 1850 at $267 per capita when money was actually of greater

value than it is today, has Los Angeles less confidence in herself and her future? Has she the courage to initiate an equally important program at an estimated cost of $62 per capita —less than a fourth of what Paris paid?

In America, the most recent and most com- parable metropolitan park plan is that of West- chester County, New York, where a $60,000,- 000 program was undertaken by a population of about 361,000, the total assessed valuation being about $670,000,000. The park system

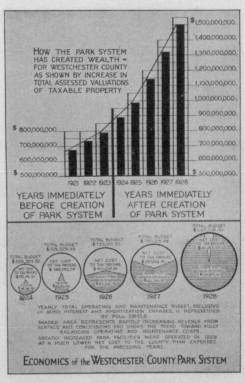

of Westchester County will comprise 16,000 acres of parks and 140 miles of parkways. It represented, at the time of initiation, a total cost of about $100 per capita, which should be compared with the $62 estimated for a complete park system for the Los Angeles Region. The Westchester system represented 10% of the total assessed valuation at the time of its initiation. The entire system here recommended for the Los Angeles Region represents 3½%. The accompanying chart, Plate No. 19, illustrates how, within six years, assessed valuations have doubled in Westchester County along with the development of the park system. Certainly such a system should serve to increase and maintain property values in the Los Angeles Region. Indeed, *in the absence of such a system urban growth will destroy conditions which have been among the important factors in creating and maintaining the present values.*

In addition to the enormous value the park system will have for the people of the Los Angeles Region, its very great value also as an attraction to tourists, might *even alone* justify its cost. Its total cost will be less than the sum now spent annually in Paris by American tourists. When completed, the Region will have here, in the beaches, mountains, and plains over six hundred miles of pleasant driveways a remarkable combination of scenic values *unequaled elsewhere in the world*—a great asset for the people, a stimulus for the value of home properties, and an attraction for tourist traffic heretofore undreamed of.

Industrial Growth.

A study of the economic resources of the Los Angeles Region, undertaken as a part of this report, shows that Los Angeles enjoys a unique position among large cities. In number of wage earners, in value of manufactured products, wages paid, and the like, Los Angeles now ranks industrially only about one-tenth of the size of New York; but Los Angeles is enjoying the greatest industrial growth of any of the large cities; and there is little reason to doubt the continuance of this growth, as suggested in the following table.

Comparison of Manufactures for 1923 and 1925
(Source: Census of Manufactures, U. S. Dept. of Commerce)

	Los Angeles	New York	Chicago	Philadelphia	Detroit	Boston	St. Louis	New Orleans
			NUMBER OF ESTABLISHMENTS					
1923	2,323	27,423	9,299	6,399	1,686	2,791	2,440	63
1925	2,691	23,714	9,112	5,636	1,614	2,620	2,367	66
Per cent change	+15.8	—13.5	—2.0	—13.5	—4.3	—6.5	—3.0	+4.
			AVERAGE NUMBER OF WAGE EARNERS					
1923	55,270	577,971	384,769	273,980	170,960	82,450	112,698	21,37
1925	58,086	538,845	370,041	246,680	172,742	77,334	105,022	22,11
Per cent change	+5.1	—6.8	—3.8	—11.1	+1.0	—6.6	—6.8	+3.
			WAGES PAID—UNIT: $1000					
1923	81,236	849,937	570,689	356,120	282,672	107,256	134,823	18,59
1925	85,736	844,648	563,635	332,415	293,896	103,812	130,857	20,29
Per cent change	+5.5	—0.6	—1.2	—7.1	+4.0	—3.3	—2.9	+9.
			COST OF MATERIALS—UNIT: $1,000,000					
1925*	275	2,719	1,882	1,049	906	290	513	9
			VALUE OF PRODUCTS—UNIT: $1,000,000					
1923	413	5,310	3,288	1,987	1,436	567	897	13
1925	532	5,324	3,439	1,937	1,599	586	875	13
Per cent change	+28.6	+0.3	+4.6	—2.6	+11.3	+3.3	—2.5	+2.
			VALUE ADDED BY MANUFACTURE UNIT: $1,000,000					
1925*	257	2,605	1,557	888	693	296	362	6

*No figures available for 1923.

PLATE 20. Map of the Region showing areas used for industries and oil fields and areas in agriculture for tree crops, hog farms and dairies, as prepared by the Regional Planning Commission.

Within the Region enormous deposits of oil yield a large income not enjoyed by other large cities. Agriculture forms another large source of revenue.

In 1923 Los Angeles suffered a period of exploitation that perhaps retarded its commer-cial prosperity, but the last few years have seen a steady and gratifying progress. The increase of population, unequaled by any other large city of the world, is a continuing evidence of the basic soundness and growing commercial strength of the Region.

The Burden of Speculative Land Values.

The magnitude of local real estate business, which has successfully withstood several periods of reaction, indicates that an enormous population throughout the country looks to this Region as a most desirable place for an ultimate residence. It has been estimated that the carrying charges on vacant lots in the Los Angeles Region must approximate $100,000,-000 per year. This is a very large sum for property not in use but held for future homes or as an investment waiting for a rise in value. Certainly the hopes of those who contemplate this as their future home and also of those who are anticipating favorable opportunities for resale would find a greater and earlier chance for realization if even a small portion of such a sum as this were devoted annually to the highly constructive purpose of creating an adequate park system.

Estimated Cost for Maintenance

The public recreation facilities now available are maintained by various agencies wholly or partly devoted to such service. The local park and local and county recreation departments are established for that purpose alone; the school departments furnish a definite recreation service, and spend considerable funds in maintenance; and to a lesser degree some other departments make expenditures for maintenance that serve recreation purposes. The total expenditures for maintenance from all sources amount probably to several million dollars a year, but are involved with improvements and other factors and are not readily ascertainable.

Such maintenance costs will doubtless continue to be met and additional costs for maintenance will arise: fairly heavy costs for the maintenance of local recreation facilities in built-up sections and for completed parkways and regional parks; and relatively low costs for the maintenance of large reservations.

The maintenance of local areas can probably best be met by local agencies in extension of or readjustment of their present activities. The maintenance of regional factors should be met by a general agency established for regional park development. The costs for such regional maintenance during the first few years will be relatively low as there will then be but little to maintain. But when the total system is developed as proposed the maintenance may cost approximately as follows:

1.	For large reservations and areas not intensively used	$ 200,000
2.	For 600 miles of park and parkway roads, planting, etc., at $2,000 a mile	1,200,000
3.	Regional athletic fields	200,000
		$1,600,000
4.	General overhead, engineering, accounting, Custodian and Guardian force, etc.	$ 500,000
		$2,100,000

This total exceeds the proposed budget of five cents maximum tax on the basis of present valuation, but is not greater than such a tax will produce by the time the system has been fully developed.

Cost of the Plan to the Average Home Owner.

Assuming that the maximum estimated tax rate of 15c should be necessary at the present time, the average cost to the owner of a home assessed at $10,000 would be $15.00 a year; to a workman whose home is assessed at $2,000, the average cost would be $3.00 a year. To them the benefits would be far greater than this small annual cost, and to other taxpayers and investors the benefits will come both directly and indirectly, through general increase in values in the community. Certainly this represents a small increase in present cost per family in order to produce more enjoyable neighborhood living conditions, and also more pleasurable opportunities for outings on Saturdays, Sundays and holidays, amid pleasant and agreeable surroundings—*an opportunity now fast disappearing in the Los Angeles Region.*

Early Action Needed
to Obtain Results.

A complete plan and program is here proposed based on conditions existing and anticipated in the Region. Much of the value of the plan will be lost, however, if work in accordance with it is not started soon. Changes are taking place and the chances for accomplishment will be seriously interfered with by delays. Local agencies can adopt and may be ready to adopt portions of the plan, and should be encouraged to do so promptly. Other agencies interested in portions of the plan may be ready to adapt their plans to the larger scheme for general public benefit and should

be urged to do so. Any other means should be encouraged which would stimulate public interest and keep open the possibilities for the finest park development in the world, so that when a regional authority is set up it may find a start already made and many existing fine features preserved.

Local existing agencies at their best cannot accomplish all that is needed. Legislation should be obtained and a board established to acquire and preserve the best features of the Region. The plan here presented should serve as a guide and an aid toward development. The present opportunity thus to improve the Region should not be lost. The public must be informed of the economic urgency of the enterprise as a means to protect and promote the health, welfare, and contentment of the people now here and the millions yet to come.

PART TWO
SPECIFIC RECOMMENDATIONS

CHAPTER IV

RECOMMENDATIONS FOR LOCAL RECREATION FACILITIES

PLAYGROUNDS, RECREATION PARKS, AND SPECIAL UNITS

THE chief means of serving local recreation functions are the municipal parks and playgrounds, and the school playgrounds.* Certain other functions, notably educational ones, are often to some extent combined with the recreational; and local functions may also be combined with regional ones.

The School Grounds.

Public schools with their playgrounds are probably the most equitably distributed institutions we have. Their distribution has come about through a systematic, unremitting, and largely successful effort to locate the schools at points accessible from the homes of all the children; locations being determined chiefly by the distances which pupils of various ages can reasonably be expected to go daily, by the present and prospective density of population, and by the economical and efficient sizes for school units.

These are practically the identical considerations that should control the placing of local recreation centers for children of elementary school age. And the considerations controlling location of high schools and junior high schools are substantially those that might control the placing of recreation facilities for adults. This practical identity of policy strongly counsels associating school playgrounds, as

far as practicable, with other local recreation grounds in combined neighborhood units. And it should be immaterial whether the lands are acquired and the facilities operated by the school or the recreation authorities, or by the two jointly.**

There are in this Region numerous examples of school grounds that provide adequate recreation for the children, and contribute not a little to other recreation needs of the neighborhood, especially by community use of school buildings, good architecture, and pleasant landscape settings. But there are few schools having ample areas for outdoor recreation, even for children of school age; and the great majority of school grounds are decidedly inadequate. Only 73 of the 726 public schools have five or more acres available for play. (See Appendix No. I.) The remaining 652 have an average of less than two acres each.

The total area—2,057 acres—available for active recreation on all the school grounds of the Region, is a comparatively small one for a growing population of over two million people.*** A map (Plate 18) shows the distribu-

---

*For general statements relating to local recreation facilities, see Chapter I.

**Interrelation and overlapping of school and recreation functions were discussed in Chapter I. Expediencey alone should decide how much should be done by schools and how much by the park agencies; practice varies widely. This report does not attempt to discuss the apportionment of responsibility; it is enough merely to urge the importance of co-operation.

***All other existing public and quasi-public open spaces directly or indirectly valuable for outdoor recreation are listed in Appendix No. II.

tion of all recreation areas and indicates, on the basis of assumed standards, all territory not conveniently accessible to any such area of adequate size.

Existing Public Parks and Playgrounds.

While under existing agencies public parks have been developed in various parts of the region and playgrounds have been established in some cases in such parks and in other cases upon independent grounds, they are, as explained in Chapter II, very inequitably distributed, being almost wholly lacking in large sections of the region while fairly complete in others. In the city of Los Angeles the Department of Playground and Recreation maintains fifty or more properties, including 160 acres in city playgrounds and recreation centers, 5 miles of beaches considered herein under the chapter on beaches, and 6 mountain camps, and, under the plans of the Department, increased facilities will be provided in other parts of the city also. These areas, together with those under the Park Department of the city, however, are still far below the needs as estimated on any reasonable stand-

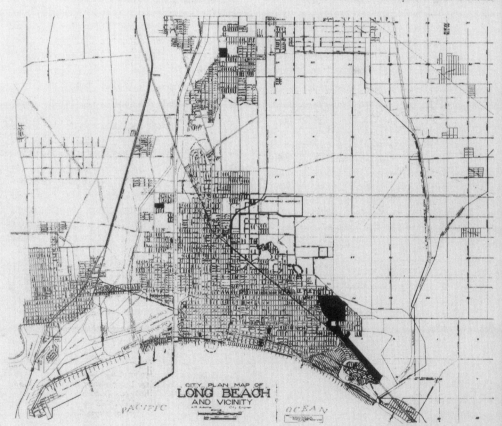

Plate 21. Map of Long Beach showing in black the existing park areas and in outline the water lands and the airport.

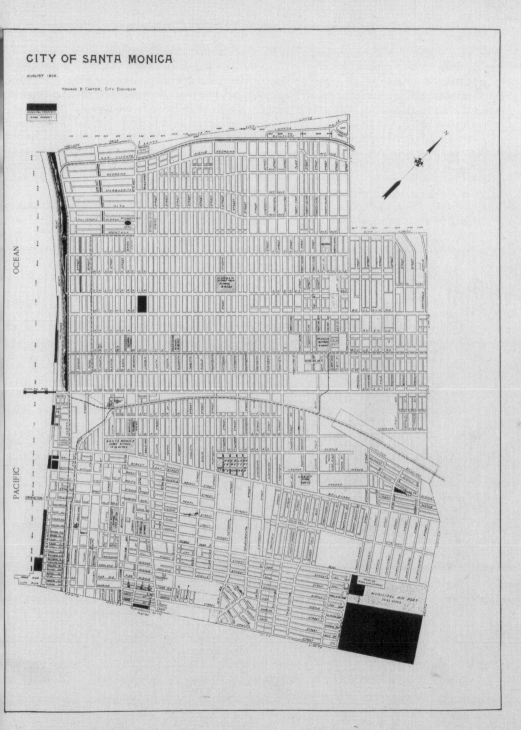

PLATE 22. Map of Santa Monica showing in black the existing park areas and cross hatched the school areas, and near the large park the airport.

141

ards, as are those also of many other cities of the Region.

Long Beach (Plate No. 21) has one large park, several smaller parks and has an airport and some water lands that have some recreational value, but as yet many districts in the city are not provided with local parks other than school grounds.

Santa Monica (Plate No. 22) like Long Beach, has several parks, but has many districts not yet provided with local facilities other than school grounds.

In Pasadena (Plate No. 23) there is one large string of city parks along the west boundary in Arroyo Seco with several smaller parks scattered more fully throughout the district. And there, as in Long Beach, the Department of Parks and Recreation has planned, under cooperative management, to develop the school grounds and playground areas in a way to serve as completely as possible for the entire city. (Plate No. 24.)

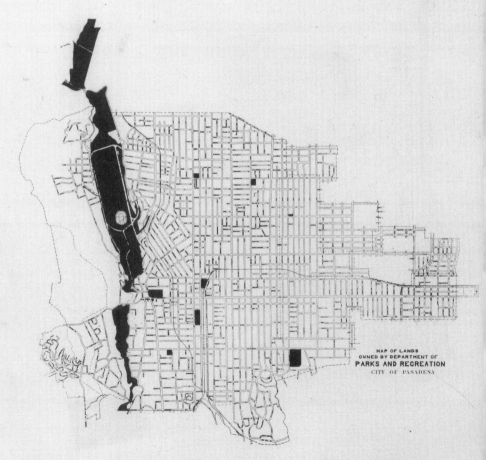

MAP OF LANDS
OWNED BY DEPARTMENT OF
PARKS AND RECREATION
CITY OF PASADENA

PLATE 23. Map of Pasadena showing large parks in the Arroyo Seco near the west boundary and showing smaller parks in other parts of the city.

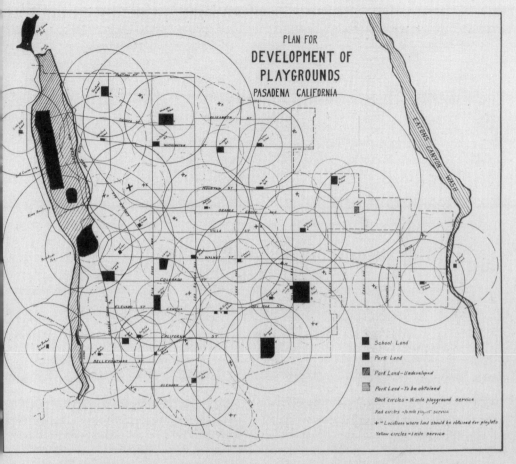

PLAN FOR
DEVELOPMENT OF
PLAYGROUNDS
PASADENA CALIFORNIA

School Land
Park Land
Park Land–Undeveloped
Park Land–To be obtained
Black circles–¼ mile playground service
Red circles–½ mile playlot service
+ = Locations where land should be obtained for playlots
Yellow circles–1 mile service

PLATE 24. Plan of the Department of Parks and Recreation of Pasadena for development of playground service.

Similar maps are available for some of the other cities and sections of the Los Angeles Region showing more or less similar conditions.

In the entire Los Angeles Region south of the mountains there are now 195 public park and playground areas, exclusive of the school grounds, of more than one acre each in extent, and having a total combined area of 9,559 acres, as listed in Appendix No. II.

Nearly all of the large existing park areas lie in the line of the proposed regional Park and Parkway System, except Stough Park, in Burbank, 120 acres; Malaga Park, in Palos Verdes, 249 acres; the Huntington Estate, in Pasadena, 200 acres; and the proposed California Botanical Gardens (to be 800 acres), near Sawtelle, each having some regional value as well as some local park value.

In the Region there are also private golf and country club grounds, amounting to 6,288 acres, or nearly two-thirds as much as the total

PLATE 25. Map showing the Region divided for convenience into classes of use, residential districts "A, B, C, D, E, and F," mountain and hill stricts "M," and industrial districts "Y," and each district or portion of district numbered for convenience of reference as listed in school and park lists in appendices No. I and No. II. *(Base map by courtesy of Automobile Club of Southern California.)*

public park and playground area, but not open to the general public and liable to be subdivided when most needed by the increasing population.

The entire Region has been divided for convenience of reference into classes: Residential (A, B, C, D, E and F); mountain and hill districts (M); and industrial and commercial districts (Y); and these in turn have been divided into units as numbered on Plate 25, to which the numbers in the appendices refer.

PROPER SIZE AND DISTRIBUTION FOR LOCAL RECREATION UNITS

Experience has shown that people living within less than one-half mile of any park or recreation unit adapted to their local needs tend to visit it frequently, use it extensively, take personal pride in it as a neighborhood pos-

session, and get large values from it; but that persons living much more than one-half mile from such an area are seldom able to visit it and are certain to gain less from it than those living nearer by.* It is probable, however, that the reasonable average service radius will prove somewhat greater here than in eastern cities, because of the lower population density, the more favorable climate, and the more nearly universal use of automobiles. The people of each locality will have to work out for them-

*As to the use of local parks and playgrounds, the Los Angeles City Department of Playground and Recreation in its 1926-27 report shows an average daily attendance for the twelve months for 25 playgrounds, containing 147.6 acres. This average is 8,144 persons, ranging from 84 persons per day on the 20-acre playground at Griffith Park, to 761 persons on the 2-acre playground at South Park. The average shows 326 persons per day per area, and 55 persons per day per acre. The extremes show from 84 to 761 persons per area per day, and 4 to 380 persons per acre per day. The extremes in the case of Griffith Park are probably due chiefly to its newness and its present remoteness from populous areas.

selves, gradually, how much they want and what they are willing to pay for. Suffice it here to indicate what seems a reasonable norm that should be approximated.

Local Recreation Districts and Recreation Centers.

To this end it is convenient to regard the Region as divided into residential neighborhood districts, each a square mile or more in extent, not infrequently considerably larger. Their boundaries are largely determined by natural or artificial barriers, such as hills, canyons, railway tracks, main thoroughfares, industrial districts, or business districts. They also may be determined by very marked and relatively permanent social differences, or differences in economic status. Recognition of these barriers may lead to a considerable variaiton in the size and shape of certain districts.

In each such district the most effective method of meeting local park and recreation needs, other than those met by the schools, is to establish a single, adequate neighborhood center, in co-operation with the schools wherever feasible. It should provide for people of all ages: sand piles and wading pools for the little tots; playground apparatus and small play areas for boys and girls; tennis courts, local ball fields, playground apparatus, and other facilities for active play; parklike areas for quiet and mental refreshment; field house and swimming facilities, also club rooms and other indoor facilities for community use. This list can be curtailed so far as the schools adequately provide for community use on school premises.

Such a center, serving many kinds of needs in a well-balanced and economical manner, is a development of comparatively recent years and is probably not familiar to many of the people in Los Angeles. In it there should be agreeable landscape features, such as are found in Westlake Park, Bixby Park in Long Beach, and Central Park in Pasadena, combined with playgrounds and athletic fields. And, further, the better school-community centers should have some at least of the elements found variously combined in Lincoln Park, Hazard Park, and Echo Park in Los Angeles, Brookside Park in Pasadena, and Monrovia Park in Monrovia. All of these more or less suggest the desirable type.

How far it is practicable to consolidate these functions in one center for one district, and do it efficiently and economically, is a matter of local expediency. And how far it may be unavoidable to distribute the functions to separate centers because of the first cost of getting enough land in one piece, or of starts already made, is also a matter of local expediency. But in the long run it is most likely that the convenience, efficiency, and economy of administration of a large, consolidated unit will more than offset a considerable initial outlay for the purchase of land.

In a district of one square mile entirely built up with single-family houses and having an average population density of 25 per acre, there would be accommodations for approximately 16,000 people,* and they would fall into the following age groups, according to Los Angeles ratios:

1. Children under 5 1,000
2. Children of 5-12 (elementary-school age) ... 1,500
3. Children of 12-15 (junior high-school age) ... 600
4. Children of 15-18 (high-school age) 600
5. Youths and active adults of 18-35 4,800
6. Adults of 35-65 6,400
7. Elderly group, of 65 and over 1,100

Of these the children under five can be and properly should be accommodated mainly on private grounds throughout practically all the Los Angeles Region, owing to the prevalence of single-family residences with good-sized yards. But already the multiple-dwelling problem has become insistent, since within eight miles of the central business district, from 25-30 per cent of the families live in multiple dwellings. Such dwellings are mostly

*Many districts may be much more extensive, the size being offset for a long time by a much sparser population. Others, of the normal square-mile size, may, in the more densely populated parts of Los Angeles, have as many as 40,000 inhabitants.

without yards, but doubtless a very much smaller percentage of young children live in them than elsewhere.

Children of school age always have some play space on school grounds. Nevertheless, school grounds are generally so inadequate that even if considerably enlarged they will still remain inadequate. Therefore, the most efficient and economical way to meet adequately the needs of these children would be to concentrate most of the possible additional space in one unit for the entire neighborhood, whether that includes one school or many.

Unless neighborhood centers are provided for them, the people above school age—12,-300 in all, or three-fourths of the entire district population—will have outdoor recreation only in private yards and in the streets, with possibly a partial use of school grounds.

Standards for Recreation Centers.

In considering the desirable acreage, and also the least that is at all adequate, three distinct kinds of area should be included:

1. Intensively used areas for organized or supervised play, such as outdoor gymnasia, minor local ball fields, tennis courts, swimming pools, and the like. These are normally from 5 to 10 acres in each unit.

2. Open meadows and playfields for general exercise and free undirected play, normally from 5 to 10 acres.

3. Park-like areas for quiet, rest, and mental relaxation, for picnic groves, and music courts. They should include planted borders and areas, in order to give to the open fields and playgrounds a satisfactory enclosure and setting. Normally they should contain not less than 10 to 15 acres for each unit.

These three kinds of areas, together, would therefore require a total of 20 to 35 acres, or from 3 to 5 per cent of a square-mile district, in order to form a neighborhood park and recreation center reasonably complete.

The Problem of Acquiring the Necessary Lands.

In districts where considerable land remains unimproved it is possible that park sites can be acquired at prices admitting the purchase of areas of this standard size, or even larger. And larger areas may be desirable, especially where the topography is irregular, and where regional interest can also be served.

Where land values are very high, or existing improvements must be destroyed to make space for a park, it may be impossible to justify the acquisition of as much as twenty acres. It is also probable that no area of that size could be found free of improvements of excessively high cost. Therefore, in such districts it may be necessary to consider a smaller total area, or even to use two or more separate units.

But no single area of less than 10 or 12 acres can be expected to approach adequate service to a square mile or more of residential district, even if developed to the highest possible efficiency. Furthermore, the district where the temptation to buy small parcels is strongest is nearly always the very place where it should be most strongly resisted, because such a district is usually a densely populated one, or becoming so, and the need for recreation space is correspondingly greater than elsewhere. Therefore, any wholesome departure from standard should be toward larger rather than smaller units.

On the other hand, in districts having a population density of less than 10 per acre, there is today relatively small need for or justification for fully improved neighborhood park and recreation grounds. But in such districts the opportunity in some cases now exists to obtain land at a cost far below the prices that will obtain after the community has been more fully built up. And it is possible also in those districts that needed park lands may be acquired now through dedication or gifts, at little or no cost to the community.

The Example of Palos Verdes.

Such standards have already been applied within this Region in connection with the establishment of combined school and neighborhood park sites in Palos Verdes, where in the process of subdivision of a large tract, sites averaging a mile apart were set aside, each with a space for a local playground and community park. The total area of each unit is in some cases less than the minimum above proposed because of the existence of other large parks nearby, but is larger than that required for schools alone. There the total number of pupils predicted on a basis of the total number of families possible in each district under the zoning regulations was available. These areas were as follows:

1. High school and local park and playground containing 46 acres in two terraces of 18 and 15 acres, and the balance in steep slopes to be planted as park land. School to serve 1,200 pupils.

2. Junior High School and local park and playground combined with one elementary school, containing 28 acres all nearly level land. Junior High to serve 1,700, elementary school to serve 800 pupils.

3. Six other elementary school and local park and playground areas, ranging in size from 6 to 11 acres each, that will be required to serve less than 1,500 pupils each.

Types of Districts in Which to Acquire Land Promptly.

Speculative value in land is an unusually serious problem in the Los Angeles Region, especially within subdivided areas, where market land values are generally higher than in other large cities. Future increases of rental value are here more highly capitalized than in other metropolitan regions. On the other hand, the value of improvements is lower, and the improvements are subject to more rapid depreciation. Consequently, in areas already subdivided, there is less to be lost financially through postponing the purchase of recreation grounds until the need for them is urgent and insistent, because the increment in land cost, less depreciation of improvements, is not likely to outrun the accumulation of compound interest on an earlier purchase.

Summing up this phase of the subject: the three types of districts in which it is most urgent to acquire land promptly for local units of recreation are:

Outlying unsubdivided areas where a sharp speculative rise in price has not yet taken place;

Older districts in which, after a dormant period of one type of occupancy, rebuilding for a denser population is reasonably to be expected; and

Well-established districts in which the present urgent need clearly justifies the present cost of securing the land.

In all three instances, again, the relation to the school situation and the possibility of correlative action should be considered.

In this connection a few places in the Los Angeles Region have been noted where the effective service of present playground and school facilities could be increased very materially by eliminating obstacles between nearly adjacent areas. For example, between the Manchester Playground and the Manchester School, where an alley and one row of buildings separate the two. Again, at the Euclid Avenue School, where Argonne Street might well be vacated to increase materially the usefulness of school grounds and buildings, which are now on both sides of the street. At Hazard Park a playground, two schools, two park areas, and some local streets could all be combined, extended, and redesigned to become a more complete unit and still serve all purposes. And at Roxbury Playground in Beverly Hills adjacent vacant land in the city of Los Angeles should be added to make a more complete neighborhood center.

Small Detached Local Parks

In many districts of the city there are now, beside the school grounds and neighborhood parks, various other park-like areas that have great value, such as small squares, triangles and circles at street intersections, small monument sites, and odd bits of public property and grounds around public buildings, no one of which will go far in itself toward meeting the recreation needs, but each of which has some recreational value as well as great potential value in adding to civic pride and the contentment and happiness of people. Some of these incidental areas may afford space that can be satisfactorily used for play facilities of limited character, such as sand piles, wading pools and park benches, provided those uses do not conflict with any higher value such areas may have for ornamental uses. Terrace Park, St. James Park, Pershing Square, and the Plaza in Los Angeles, Memorial Park in Pasadena, and Drake Park and Santa Cruz Park in Long Beach are areas of this sort.

Such small detached parcels of local park land of course add substantially to the general attractiveness of a neighborhood if well kept up, and their free dedication is far easier to secure in connection with subdivision than that of larger areas. Within rather close limitations the creation of such small local public park areas should be encouraged; but an analysis of costs of park maintenance, especially in Washington, D. C., where such parklets are exceptionally numerous, shows that the public burden of the annual cost of maintenance is excessively high per acre and that even if freely given to the public they are an expensive luxury, to be indulged in only with discretion.

There is one sort of district in which the maintenance cost of small decorative open spaces is practically negligible because of the number of people who benefit from them, provided they are so placed and improved as to give real benefit and to avoid interference with the prime functions of the district. This is an intensively used central district, where a space such as Pershing Square or City Hall Park is enjoyed by immense numbers of people daily. One such space that has been suggested and that might well be acquired, is the block between 12th and Pico and between Hill and Broadway.

Among other units of park-like character of public interest may well be included landmarks of historical interest, such as the old adobe houses of Southern California, some of which should be preserved as public monuments.

Local Parks for Industrial Districts

Industrial districts need spaces also for active recreation, some of which are already provided by larger industries on their own grounds. Just how and where additional areas can best be located is now difficult to determine, because of the rapid spread of the industrial districts and the lack of any definite knowledge as to what are going to be the requirements of the industries that may come to occupy the land. Even so, a few areas should be acquired as opportunity offers in the industrial sections.

A Study of Four Typical Neighborhoods

Four typical neighborhoods of approximately one square mile each in extent, in different parts of the Region, now lacking local recreation facilities, except on school grounds, have been studied in detail to determine the local needs and conditions and present possibilities. The neighborhoods chosen are of widely different character. One is in a small community fairly remote from the main city, one in a region closely built up with inexpensive houses, one in a partly built up section of more expensive character, and the fourth in a more densely populated section where improvements are of relatively high cost. The results of these studies are as follows:

TABLE SHOWING RESULTS OF STUDY OF FOUR TYPICAL RECREATION DISTRICTS

	A	B	C	D
Area of district in acres	936	762	592	640
Population in 1922	2,240		4,050	
Population in 1928	3,340	9,950	8,298	20,000
Annual rate of growth	8%		17%	
Density of population per acre in 1928	3½	13	14	31
Total assessed valuation, 1928	$2,104,030	$2,305,242	$5,592,430	$27,390,049
Area of existing school lands in district	26.65	11.96	19.47	2.10
Area of same available for recreation	8.48*	9.10	16.11†	1.00
Area to be acquired in acres	21.6	18.6	3.81	14.5
Assessed valuation of same	$23,500	$36,089	$47,800	$283,320
Estimated cost of same	$58,750	$90,223	$119,500	$608,300
Cost for preliminary development	$21,250	$30,000	$10,500	$141,700
40-year bond issue required	$80,000	$120,000	$130,000	$750,000
Total bonds per capita on present population	$23.95	$12.06	$15.67	$37.50
Annual bond retirement 2½%	$2,000 to 0	$3,000 to 0	$3,250 to 0	$18,750 to 0
5% interest on bonds outstanding	$4,000 to 0	$6,000 to 0	$6,500 to 0	$37,500 to 0
Maintenance and further development	$1,000 to $4,000	$1,500 to $6,000	$750 to $2,000	$3,750 to $20,000
TOTAL ANNUAL COST	$7,000 to $4,000	$10,500 to $6,000	$10,500 to $2,000	$60,000 to $20,000
Assessed value of remaining land	$2,080,530	$2,269,153	$5,544,630	$27,106,729
Assessed value in 40 years assumed double	$4,161,060	$4,538,306	$11,089,260	$54,213,458
Tax rate per year required	34c to 10c	46c to 13c	19c to 2c	22c to 4c
Annual cost per capita on present population	$2.10	$1.06	$1.27	$3.00

*Including High School. †Including small park area.

ESTIMATE OF TOTAL COSTS BASED ON THE FOREGOING STUDY

These figures show that fair space for park and recreation purposes in the four chosen districts would cost, if handled entirely as a local district improvement, from $80,000 to $750,000 each, would involve annual costs at the outset of from $7,000 to $60,000, would involve a local tax increase at the outset of from 19c to 46c and, at the end of 40 years, when bonds have been paid off, of from 2c to 13c. They would involve a cost per capita to the present population of from $1.06 to $3.00. At such rates, any family in the district could have access to a local park and playground at all times at an annual cost (even during the period of highest charges) of little more than the cost of taking the family out to the beach or mountains for one holiday trip.

A similar study of other neighborhoods throughout the Region would presumably show a similar range of conditions to prevail. While the cost for each district may appear from these figures to be higher than can be justified as a totally local charge, the fact should be recognized that various other districts now have local facilities that may have been provided for in whole or in part from general taxes; therefore, some aid from general taxation or from a general Metropolitan Park District can fairly be given to each such districts as may be ready to undertake such improvements.

The estimates for the four local parks and playgrounds show total bonds per capita required of from $12.06 to $37.50 and an average of $26.00 per capita. It seems fair to assume that these represent average conditions for three-quarters of the population of the Region. Since the total population of this Region living within urban and suburban areas approaches 2,000,000, this means that the total cost of providing additional complete *local* park and playground facilities for the 1,500,000 people in the entire occupied area of the Los Angeles Region would be about $39,000,000.

This total estimate is made up of two items that can be divided approximately as follows:

(1) Acquisition _____ $31,200,000
(2) Development _____ 7,800,000

Total _____ $39,000,000

The above figures are based on per capita estimates. On the other hand, on an area basis, the four units estimated involve a cost of practically one million dollars or at the rate of one-quarter million each, and if there are 160 districts that should now be so treated, the cost would amount to $40,000,000 or about the same figure. A part of this cost, if not all of it, can be borne by local districts or local municipal or other administrative units unless by mutual agreement the entire problem is to be handled as a regional one.

CHAPTER V

RECOMMENDATIONS FOR PUBLIC BEACHES

THE most active demand for more parks today in the entire Los Angeles Region, especially during the summer months, is for more and better beach and waterside facilities. The public now owns and controls for recreation along the ocean front above mean high tide line a number of strips varying in width from a few feet to a hundred feet or more, and in length amounting to 14 miles. The public owns also *all* the land below mean high-tide line and the land under water, but most of this land cannot be used except at low tide without trespassing on private land. (See Appendix No. V.)

With many miles of the finest ocean front in the world, where the climate is ideal—cool but never too cold for enjoyment—the public now finds about nine-tenths of the entire frontage destined to be screened from view from the nearest highways by private developments. The remaining tenth is divided into short disconnected stretches.

About six miles is taken up by the harbor district, which of course can be used for pleasure only temporarily and where not yet needed for commerce. Much of the frontage at Long Beach, Redondo, Venice, and Santa Monica is public, but other portions are occupied by costly improvements and are highly developed out to the water's edge or beyond in a way to preclude extensive public acquisitions in those stretches except at enormous cost. The 17 miles of coast between the harbor district and Redondo Beach is marked by high cliffs, generally with rocky foreshores subject to almost complete submergence at high tides, and has no

wide beaches suitable and safe for use by large bodies of people, although it has a notable scenic drive along the top of the cliffs.

West of Santa Monica the 27 miles of coast has, alternating with the sand beaches, intermittent rocky and bouldery stretches, about 8 miles of such stretches and about 19 miles of fine sandy beaches. While those beaches are public property below ordinary high tide, they

PLATE 26. Coast highway near Topanga Canyon showing line of cottages cutting off all view of the ocean from the highway. *(Photo by Stagg.)*

151

PLATE 27. The Harbor from Long Beach showing Long Beach in the foreground, the harbor district in the center, and the San Pedro hills in the distance. (*Photo by Spence.*)

PLATE 28. Rugged shores and high cliffs of Palos Verdes, attractive to pleasure travel, but not adapted to beach uses. (*Photo by Padilla.*)

are privately owned above high tide for *practically their entire length*.

For the year 1927 the total number of users of certain beaches was estimated by the Department of Playground and Recreation of the City of Los Angeles, to be as follows:

COUNT OF PERSONS AT BEACHES DURING 1927			
	Spectators	*Bathers*	*Total*
Sta. Monica Canyon	828,451	219,892	1,048,343
Venice	11,505,062	1,917,338	13,422,400
Playa Del Rey	314,811	108,682	423,493
Terminal Island	215,812	89,850	305,662
Cabrillo	744,411	104,078	848,489
	13,608,547	2,439,840	16,048,387

In order to determine the actual usage of beaches during one busy day, counts were made in 1928 for the Citizens Committee by the Department of Playground and Recreation of Los Angeles, the results of which are shown in the following table:

	Width in Feet	Length in Miles	11 A. M. Spectators	Bathers	3 P. M. Spectators	Bathers
COUNT OF PERSONS AT BEACHES ON JULY 4, 1928						
West County line to Las Flores Canyon	550	19	5,426	1,588	13,456	4,917
Las Flores Canyon to Topanga Canyon	50	3	1,671	620	3,826	1,820
Topanga Canyon to Castle Rock	50	1	1,250	281	3,105	1,230
Castle Rock to Lighthouse Cafe	50	2½	2,505	687	6,525	1,867
Lighthouse Cafe to Santa Monica	150	½	1,246	832	7,825	1,808
City of Santa Monica	50	3	10,694	3,235	36,975	10,695
Ocean Park Pier to Venice Pier	200	1	2,460	4,662	9,872	11,119
Venice Pier to Del Rey	100	2½	2,743	2,564	3,127	2,547
Del Rey to Picnic Grounds	25	½	150	100	475	283
Picnic Grounds to Hyperion Pier	50	2	250	115	725	275
Hyperion Pier to El Segundo Pier	100	1	101	45	225	54
El Segundo Pier to Manhattan Pier	200	2	639	207	1,356	300
Manhattan and Hermosa Beaches	100	2½	15,303 *Estimated*	9,280	23,657 *Estimated*	20,137
Cities of Redondo and Torrance	75	3	12,000	5,000	20,000	6,000
Torrance-Palos Verdes Estates	5	11	715	70	1,345	70
San Pedro City	100	2	4,160	1,920	11,640	4,600
Terminal Island, Los Angeles	200	4	2,050	600	2,250	100
Terminal Island, Long Beach	200	1½	1,800	1,400	2,800	2,300
Long Beach City	100	9	8,189	2,444	18,959	5,629
	71		73,352	35,650	168,147	75,751
			109,002		243,898	

	Spectators	Bathers	Total
Total counted	241,499	111,401	352,900
Assumed total for day	515,748	156,915	672,663

These tables both show that the number of spectators using the beaches was several times as great as the number of bathers, and indicate the consequent need for a large amount of upland area.

From these figures it appears that there were at one time 47,670 people on the beach at Santa Monica, estimated by the observer to be 3 miles long and to average 50 feet wide, or 750,000 square feet of space with an average of *only 15 square feet* of space per person at one time. Beach "widths" are variable and uncertain things to estimate, and the area which these 47,640 occupied may have been considerably larger or smaller than estimated.

Comparison with Beaches of Other Regions.

Even with a large allowance for possible error in the Los Angeles figures, it is significant to compare these figures with those at Coney Island, New York, the world's most heavily used beach, where airplane photographs showed an average of *56 square feet* of beach above water-line per person under conditions reported to be unduly crowded, and at Atlantic City, where photographs showed great crowds with an average of *78 square feet* per person, also reported as too crowded for comfort. In New York, where beach is at a high

PLATE 29. Public beach at Venice on July 4th, showing use to capacity, too crowded for comfort. (*Photo by Stagg.*)

premium, it is estimated that a beach having a width of 150 feet with 9 times as much additional upland space can accommodate comfortably about 50,000 people per mile at one time, but in no portion of Los Angeles frontage is such a width of upland now open to public use, or likely to be so.

There were at 3:00 P. M. on July 4th, 1928, 243,898 people along the Los Angeles beaches, and at points they were much crowded. Furthermore, many people of Los Angeles who know that beaches are so crowded either stay away or go elsewhere at a heavy personal expense, when they would prefer to enjoy their own water front, and would flock to the beaches if more public beaches existed.

From conditions actually observed it is fair to assume that all the usable beach frontage here that can be made available for the public

may now be taxed occasionally to capacity if not actually to overcrowding. The demand for public use of beaches will inevitably exceed the supply. Considerable adjoining areas in addition to the beach itself must be available if a beach is to accommodate large crowds. Such adjacent areas may accommodate more people than the beaches themselves, and space is required for parking of automobiles even greater than the space required on the beach for the people who come in them.

Use of Beach Lands.

There are now other demands for riparian lands along the beaches where private ownership extends down to ordinary high tide, and these have raised to very high levels the market price of such land.

One is for residences close to the beach, in

PLATE 30. Public beach at Atlantic City, New Jersey, showing wide boardwalk and wide, sandy beach beyond.

itself a socially desirable and highly beneficial use, but a use that tends to become less attractive in proportion as great crowds use the neighboring public portions of the beach. Where the public now uses such beaches in spite of some inconvenience, crowds will spread on to the lower parts of the private property above the high tide line, and the value of such land for residential lots may decline.

A second demand is for business lots because of transient crowds that are attracted to the beaches, and for hotel and club house sites. Business may range from services which are of the utmost importance and desirability to the most injurious parasitism. The value of such lots will depend on the amount of profit that can be made from them.

The average beach-goer because of his holiday spirit, is an "easy mark." Helping him at a fair price to derive the maximum benefit from a visit to the beach is fair business. Exploiting him is not and should be prevented. In case after case where large crowds have once begun to go to a beach for pleasures obtainable only there, commercial exploitation has gradually put the beach or a large part of it wholly out of existence, as by decking it over completely, and has corralled the crowd into indoor commercialized enterprises which might just as well have been elsewhere and which are on the whole distinctly deleterious in character. Those are extreme cases, but tendencies toward such a result accompany commercialization of the opportunity for exploiting beach crowds, just as the tendency exists for crowds of transient visitors to blight the use of beach-front property for residence.

To get the greatest value from the shore lands, the frontage should be segregated to serve either private or public purposes, and should be protected accordingly. Such segregation should recognize the fitness of the lands for each purpose and the proportionate importance of each.

To some extent, such protection would follow use of the police power in one or more of

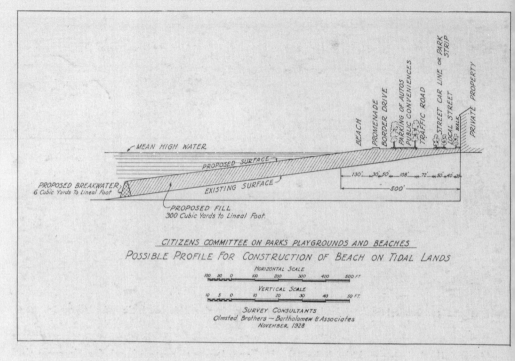

PLATE 31. Possible profile for construction of beach on tidelands.

its many forms, such as zoning of a highly specialized sort applied to properties peculiarly related to beaches. But the technique of this has not yet been developed and tested by experience. The main reliance wherever this problem has become serious has been public ownership and proprietary control of sufficient land to guard against the worst evils. Even such ownership alone may avail but little unless the control is entrusted to an agency specially and exclusively charged with the duty of protecting the recreational interests of the public, and having a job of sufficient size and importance to win and hold the interest of really first rate men.

SHORES ADAPTED TO PUBLIC USES

Before proceeding to the detailed enumeration of coast land to be acquired for regional public recreation, it seems desirable to outline two large problems affecting a long stretch of coast; the first from Santa Monica Canyon westward where conditions have not yet crystallized but soon will; the second from Santa Monica Canyon south to Playa Del Rey, where they have very rigidly crystallized in a manner which is in some respects highly unsatisfactory.

West from Santa Monica.

West of Santa Monica the public highway paralleling the shore for many miles is now a busy one and is destined to carry a vastly greater volume of traffic because it is the most direct, most level, and most agreeable route to Ventura and other coastal districts beyond. The time will soon come, as is now clearly recognized by the State Division of Highways, when

PLATE 32. Yacht harbor suggestion as presented by owners of property just above Santa Monica.

raffic will imperatively demand a much wider right of way than the present 80 feet. For about three miles the highway is built on a narrow strip between very high bluffs and a very narrow belt of privately-owned ocean-front property, where some buildings have already been erected. A continuous barrier of such buildings is likely soon to develop, cutting off from the road views of the sea and public access to the beaches. Farther west, the hills recede and the highway passes through wider areas, part of the way near the shore, where there is a narrow strip of private property outside the highway as in the preceding sections, and part of the way farther back from the shore and on higher levels with large blocks of private property outside the road.

A very fine stretch of beach adjoins the high-

way for nearly three miles just above Point Dume, and back of it lies a very fine seaside mesa.

All the way from Santa Monica to the county line the road must serve not only as a major state highway for all kinds of traffic, but also as a pleasure route of the utmost importance to the Region. It should have a right of way not merely wide enough to carry its destined traffic without serious congestion, but also wide enough to make travel upon it thoroughly agreeable, especially in the first stretch, where everyone driving westward first comes to the ocean and where the visual impression is of great importance. To get a glimpse of the sea and then file into a choked road behind a row of buildings is a calamity. With the opening of the State Highway and the invitation to

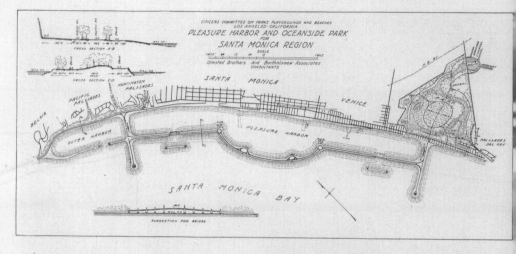

PLATE 33. Plan for an extensive Pleasure Harbor opposite Santa Monica and Venice, with a park in the Del Rey marshes and a parkway on a chain of islands around the outside of the harbor.

crowds to enjoy this coast, a new impetus has been given to the development of privately-owned lands between the highway and the sea. The beach here is generally good, and capable of being widened by groins, as experiments have shown. Already very high land values have been established in places along the shore; but land that is clearly most needed by the public should be acquired before further improvements and further subdivision of those areas make the difficulty of such acquisition still greater.

If the situation is not dealt with adequately now, if a narrow but heavily traveled and congested highway becomes walled in by rows of buildings, if only small openings here and there connect the highway with the beaches and if the crowds push in helter-skelter wherever they can get to the beaches below high tide, conditions will become so bad that reaction will set in and the recently boomed value of the shore lands will fall. Eventually such intolerable conditions will be relieved wholly or in part either by condemnation of the land and improvements, or perhaps by widening and extending the beach itself outside private

holdings and building a new road on the margin of the beach as thus advanced.

But unless immediate action is taken things will be in a mess for years and may never become just right. Any district that once goes wrong is very hard to rehabilitate.

South from Santa Monica.

South from Santa Monica Canyon to Playa Del Rey practically continuous buildings several blocks in depth separate the beach from the nearest practicable roadway along the coast. In certain places structures on private land extend to the line of mean high tide; in others structures on tidelands leased from the cities cover the beaches and extend on piles far out over the water. The public is now so much aroused, however, that further private encroachments on the tidelands are unlikely, and conditions still rather readily permit broadening the beach to seaward, where buildings on private land have curtailed the use of its upper edge.

In this entire region, three-quarters of a mile off shore, the water is only about 30 feet deep and projects have long been discussed for a

PLATE 34. Sketch for extensive Pleasure Harbor and park and parkway development as shown on Plate 33.

harbor primarily or exclusively for pleasure craft, to be formed by breakwaters about that distance off shore, starting considerably to the west of Santa Monica Canyon.

An off-shore breakwater can be built here so as to add great recreational value, whenever people want it enough to pay for it; and the cost will not increase with delay. It seems not unreasonable to look forward to the time when the Los Angeles Region will follow the example set by Chicago in its great park development out into Lake Michigan, and not merely build a jetty so as to form a harbor open to masted vessels at the head of Santa Monica Bay, but also a long breakwater or chain of narrow islands connected by bridges and carrying a park drive, from the State Highway at Santa Monica Canyon to Playa Del Rey. The sheltered water between there and the beach will be of great value for motor boats and small boating, and the beach bathing will be improved for most people, while a park drive along the chain of narrow islands, absolutely away from buildings and concessions, will be used and enjoyed by hundreds of automobilists to every user of boats.

SUMMARY OF SHORE FRONT RECOMMENDATIONS
(The classes lettered A to E are referred to in the last column of the next table.)

		Lands Along Shore Front Length in Miles	Land Back of Highway Area in Acres
A.	Now public (for recreation)	14	64
B.	Now quasi-public (for recreation)	6	188
C.	Proposed to be acquired for public recreation, in county, extending into Orange County	32	206*
D.	Specifically assigned to use for other purposes (including harbor)	9	—
E.	Other lands not included in recommended acquirements	19	650
	TOTAL	80	1,108

*In addition to the five other large reservations estimated and included in proposed park system.

Units of the Entire Shore Front
Classified as A, B, C, D, E, with numbers referring to locations on Plate 35 and to Descriptions following this List

Following the coast from Ventura County eastward into Orange County, the various units have been numbered for convenience of reference.

Reference No.	Name	Approx. length in feet	Approx. width in feet	Back land area in acres	Classification
1.	Sequit Beach	4000	200-300		C
2.	Arroyo Sequit Park			150	C
3.	Nicolas and Encinal Beaches and Bluffs	21000	500-600		E
4.	Zuma Beach	15000	150-250		C
5.	Dume Park	See Chapter VIII			C
6.	Ramirez Canyon Reservation	See Chapter VIII			B
7.	Dume Point Shore	13000	Narrow		D
8.	Ramirez Beach and Bluffs	6000	200-1000		E
9.	Escondido Beach	5400	10-150		C
10.	Escondido Canyon Mouth			35	C
11.	Corral Beach	16500	10-150		C
12.	Malibu Beach and Plain	4500	200-1200		E
13.	Possible Malibu Park			650	E
14.	Malibu Slough and Beach	2400	200-1200		C
15.	West Carbon Beach	2400	80-200		C
16.	East Carbon Beach	6200	100-300		E
17.	Carbon Beach and Las Flores Beach (small area now public)	3600	100-200		E
18.	Las Flores Delta	500	200-300		E
19.	East Las Flores Beach	2800	20-130		C
20.	Pena Canyon Beach	5400	20-130		C
21.	Tuna Canyon Beach	7200	20-130		C
22.	Topanga Canyon Park Upland	See Chapter VIII			C
23.	Topanga Beach to Los Angeles City Line	5300	20-130		C
24.	Topanga Beach in Los Angeles City	1600	20-1130		C
25.	Castellamare Beach	700	100-150		B
26.	Santa Ynez Beach	1900	10-500		C
27.	Bel-Air Pacific Palisades Beach	9000	10-200		E
28.	Lighthouse Cafe Point	300	200		E
29.	Huntington Palisades Beach	1800	10-200		E
30.	Santa Monica Canyon Beach	1110	200-300		A
31.	Santa Monica Canyon Park			9	C
32.	Santa Monica Palisades Park			46	A
33.	Beach Clubs in Los Angeles City	200			D
34.	Beach Clubs in Santa Monica City	900			D
35.	Georgina Avenue to California Avenue (few small public ways)	3900	10-150		E
36.	California Avenue to Arizona Avenue	1350	10-60		A
37.	Arizona Avenue to Broadway	1160	60-125		A
38.	Broadway to Santa Monica Pier	950	100-300		D
39.	Santa Monica Pier and beaches to Lick Pier at Santa Monica City line. Various parcels now public	3700	90-300		A
40.	Same—parcels not public	3000	90-150		E
41.	Lick Pier to Del Rey Pier all in city of Los Angeles in Venice. Various parcels now public	10520	20-200		A
42.	Same—Various parcels that should be acquired	5260	20-200		C
43.	Ballona Creek Marshes	See Chapter VIII			C
44.	Proposed outside mole and pleasure bay	See Chapter VIII			A
45.	Del Rey Pier to Hyperion Beach, areas now public	3500	20-400		A

134700

37350

Reference No.	Name	Approx. length in feet	Approx. width in feet	Back land area in acres	Classification
46.	Same—Areas to be acquired	8300	10-50	....	C
47.	Los Angeles Hyperion Beach	5350	20-100	....	A
48.	Los Angeles Hyperion uplands	....	....	180	B
49.	City of El Segundo (Standard Oil Co. frontage)	1900	70-100	....	C
50.	Same—Areas developed for other uses	300	....	....	D
51.	In Los Angeles County (Standard Oil Co. beach)	1900	70-100	....	C
52.	County Public Beach in Los Angeles County	1300	80-100	....	A
53.	Parcel owned by County in the City of Manhattan Beach	500	50-80	....	A
54.	Manhattan Beach, Various parcels city owned	900	50-80	....	A
55.	Manhattan Beach, Other beach to be acquired	7950	50-100	....	C
56.	Park in Manhattan Beach	....	....	2	A
57.	City of Hermosa Beach frontage now public	5500	20-100	....	A
58.	Same — Frontage developed for other uses	420	....	....	D
59.	Same — Beach frontage now public	3500	80-100	....	A
60.	Redondo North Beach	3950	10-100	....	A
61.	Redondo Amusement Zone	1350	....	....	D
62.	Redondo City Park	....	....	8	A
63.	Redondo South Beach	7030	10-150	....	C
64.	Redondo South Beach	1470	150	....	B
65.	Torrance Beach	4050	20-80	....	E
66.	Palos Verdes Estates L. A. County	26000	....	....	B
67-68.	Palos Verdes Ranch	35000	....	....	E
69.	Point Vicente Lighthouse	2000	....	....	B
70.	Palos Verdes Hill shore and bluffs	5000	....	....	C
71.	San Pedro Hills Reservation	See Chapter VIII			C
72.	Royal Palms shore and White's point to Los Angeles County Line	8400	200-500	....	C
73.	White's Point Beach in Los Angeles City	1900	150-200	....	C
74.	Point Fermin and the San Pedro shores	7875	100-400	....	A
75.	Point Fermin— Various parcels	1100	100	....	C
76.	San Pedro West Bluff	....	....	6 acres	C
77.	San Pedro East Bluff	....	....	6 acres	C
78.	Point Fermin Playgrounds	....	....	8 acres	B
79.	Harbor Section of Los Angeles and Long Beach on Terminal Island	30600	....	....	D
80.	Harbor Section at Long Beach	3800	100-600	....	A
81.	Flood Control Channel and West Beach	3200	100-200	....	A
82.	Amusement Zone	1260	....	....	D
83.	Long Beach Pier and Auditorium	2000	....	....	A
84.	Long Beach from Auditorium to East County Line now public (incl. 1800 county owned)	12800	10-50	....	A
85.	Same—Area that should be acquired	8100	20-250	....	C
86.	Long Beach Bluff Park	....	....	8 acres	A
87.	Alamitos Bay Shores	....	....	3 miles of inland shores	C
88.	Bolsa Chica Beach outside city	....	....	5 miles	C

Detailed Recommendations

1. Sequit Beach (4,000 Feet).

From the west county line for several thousand feet eastward is a good sandy beach. The old road followed this beach, but the new State Highway follows a line farther back. Any existing rights in the old highway should be retained and the strip between it and high tide should be acquired for public use. This might well be a State Park project in connection with Sequit Canyon, Zuma Beach, and Dume Park (No. 2, No. 4, and No. 5 below) and in connection with shores in Ventura County.

2. Arroyo Sequit Park (150 Acres).

At the mouth of the Arroyo Sequit are some fine trees and a bit of open relatively flat land having great value for a park in connection with the beach. The hillsides up as far as they form conspicuous parts of the valley scenery should be included with the floor of the valley and the reservation should extend back from the ocean half a mile or so, as far as beach picnic parties are likely to go.

3. Nicolas and Encinal Beaches and Bluffs.

From Sequit Beach to Zuma Beach for a distance of four miles the new highway follows the foot of the hills on a mesa 500 feet or so back from the sea and high above sea level. In this section the beaches are fair, but are remote from the highway. The chance for private development of the upland is excellent and it is believed that this stretch should be left for private use, subject, of course, to the existing right of the public in the tidelands.

The need for widening the right of way must doubtless arise soon and through this section it may be possible to develop a second roadway near the top of the bluffs, as has been done on Palos Verdes, for pleasure travel only, leaving the present highway for commercial uses and heavy travel.

4. Zuma Beach.

One of the finest beaches along the coast an one that would serve an enormous number o pleasure seekers is that above Dume Poir known as Zuma Beach, three miles in length This has been included in the recommendatior for parks and parkways as an integral par of that plan with the Dume Canyon and mes and the hills above. If the entire area is ac quired as recommended it will be possibl eventually to construct an upper level roa parallel to the present shore road and to divid and control traffic through this stretch in a wa to permit the largest possible use of the shor front for recreation. This beach has alread been in part subdivided and some costly privat developments have been made, but the entir beach should be acquired and the houses shoul be removed or remodeled for public uses.

5. Dume Park.

Dume Park, back of Zuma Beach, has bee included also in the park plan as one of th most valuable, healthful and attractive par features for that part of the general plan, an it is also intimately connected with the beac problem. This area with those to the west o it certainly should be considered in the pla for State Parks as well.

6. Ramirez Canyon Reservations.

Four hundred and sixty-four acres now U S. Lighthouse property that should be mad useful for public recreation with Dume Par in the general park and parkway plan.

7. Dume Point Shore.

For two miles eastward from Zuma Beac the highway lies a long way back from th shore, and the shore is mostly rocky and nar row, bordered by high bluffs, and is not adapte for use by large numbers of people. This are is well adapted to high-class private develop ment for which it is probably more valuabl than for public use. Therefore, it is not recom mended for public acquisition. Back of th hore the highway problem will be similar to hat farther west, and either a wider right of vay or two routes for travel will be needed ventually, and should be included in any plan or subdivision and local development.

8. Ramirez Beach and Bluffs.

East from Dume Point for a mile or so the ighway is still above and back from the shore >n high bluffs, and the shore itself is rugged nd of limited recreational value and therefore s not recommended for acquisition.

9. Escondido Beach.

From near Escondido Canyon where the ighway drops to the shore level eastward for . mile to Latigo Road and Point, the highway s very near the shore. The beach is good and ill intervening lands should be acquired.

10. Escondido Canyon Mouth.

Back of the highway in Escondido Canyon here is an area of 35 acres or so, large enough for a small shore front park that should be ac¬ quired to serve as a sheltered picnic ground ad¬ jacent to the beach.

11. Corral Beaches.

Three miles of beaches very near the new State Highway. All land between the highway ind the shore should be publicly owned, and he beach should be kept open to the public.

12. Malibu Beaches and Plains.

Opposite the mouth of Malibu Canyon there s a strip of flat land 200′ to 1,200′ or more in width and nearly a mile in length between the highway and the sea that is now lined with cot¬ ages and held at high prices and is well adapted to private uses and likely eventually to be used for larger buildings if the area back of it is developed as a small community center. This beach is not recommended now for acquisition.

13. Possible Malibu Park.

Back of the Malibu Beach and extending into Malibu Canyon there is a very attractive

area of one square mile or so, including the ranch headquarters, that could be made a beau¬ tiful park with the beach, if acquired, but is not included in the list as of prime importance.

14. Malibu Slough and East Beach.

East of Malibu Creek and at the mouth of the creek the beach and slough from 1,200′ to 2,000′ or so in width and half a mile long be¬ tween the highway and the shore should be acquired for public use, and in the slough a small space for water sports can be developed. Through the land back of this area and through Malibu Park the County now owns the right of way of the old highway that might reason¬ ably be exchanged for a portion of this ocean front property for public use.

15. West Carbon Beach.

From Malibu east beach to the Malibu Pot¬ teries for about half a mile the highway is again near the shore and all intervening lands should be publicly owned.

16. East Carbon Beach.

Along the potteries and lands to the east¬ ward for a little more than a mile to Coal Can¬ yon Point the space between the highway and the shore is somewhat wider and back of the highway there is considerable land that can be developed for residential uses. This section would doubtless be very costly to acquire and therefore is not included in the recommenda¬ tion for immediate acquisition, even though it would have great value for the public.

17. Carbon Bay and
   Las Flores Beach (3,600 Feet).

From Carbon Point eastward for a number of feet in Carbon Bay, the highway is now actually against the shore and no private land intervenes, and there public access to the shore can be kept open. Farther eastward costly im¬ provements have been made, and high land values have already been established. There¬ fore, this beach is not listed for acquisition,

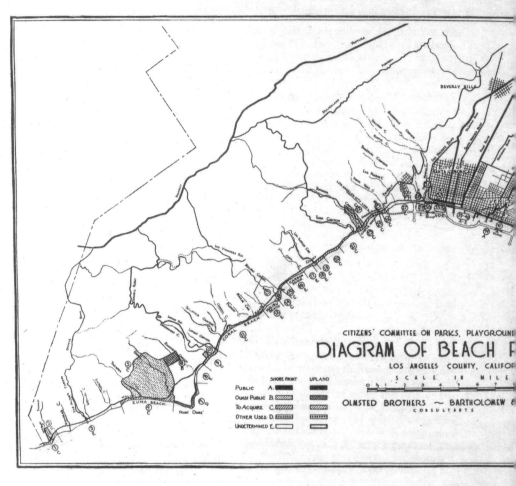

CITIZENS' COMMITTEE ON PARKS, PLAYGROUND

DIAGRAM OF BEACH F

LOS ANGELES COUNTY, CALIFOR

SCALE IN MILE

	SHORE FRONT	UPLAND
PUBLIC	A.	
QUASI PUBLIC	B.	
TO ACQUIRE	C.	
OTHER USES	D.	
UNDETERMINED	E.	

OLMSTED BROTHERS ~ BARTHOLOMEW &
CONSULTANTS

PLATE 35. Diagram showing public a

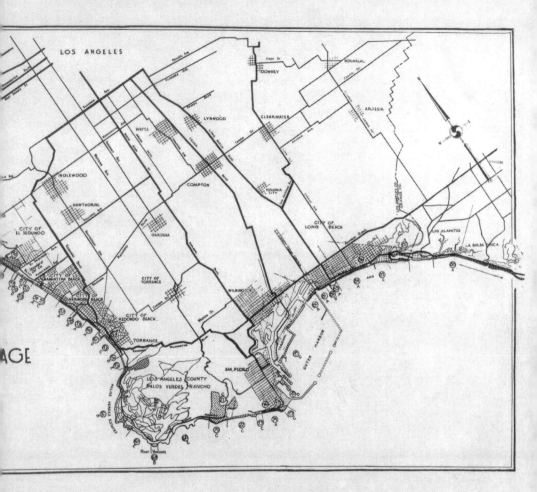

ch frontages and key to recommendations.

PLATE 36. Mouth of Topanga Canyon, showing areas that should be publicly owned to care for the vast crowds that gather there, and showing an endless chain of autos extending down the beach, cutting off all view of the ocean from the passing travelers. (*Photo by Stagg.*)

even though it also would have great value for the public.

18. *Las Flores Delta.*

Opposite the mouth of Las Flores Canyon for a relatively short distance of 500' or so, there is a small delta being developed with roadside buildings, cabins and conveniences, that would be costly to acquire and therefore is omitted.

19. *East Las Flores Beach.*

From Las Flores Canyon eastward for half a mile or so to the next point of land, the highway is near the shore below a high bluff all the way and there are 55 small cabins on the seaward side. The land on that side should be acquired for public use and all the cabins should be removed.

20. *Pena Canyon Beach.*

For a mile the highway is very close to the sea, supported most of the way by riprap. Private ownership, if any, in this section should be acquired.

21. *Tuna Canyon Beach.*

At the point opposite the Hearst Private Road, there is a small area outside the highway with a tent, and eastward from there to Topanga Canyon for a mile and a half there are 65 small buildings on the narrow strip between the highway and the ocean. Some of these buildings on high timbers may be standing on public tidelands. All should be removed and all land should be publicly acquired.

PLATE 37. Beach above Santa Monica that would be inside proposed harbor, showing groins built far out on the beach to protect the shore and catch the drifting sands. *(Photo by Spence.)*

22. *Topanga Canyon Park Uplands.*

At the mouth of Topanga Canyon the small flat area now occupied by a number of small cottages is all needed for a park and picnic area and to hold a large number of automobiles that come to the shore. Here the value to the public would be very much greater as a public park than can be realized on the same area under private ownership.

23. *Topanga Beach.*

From Topanga Canyon to the Los Angeles City line at the Parker Ranch Road for a distance of one mile there are 30 small buildings on the seaward side of the highway, with high cliffs on the other. The entire strip between the highway and the sea should be publicly owned, as it will have a far greater value for large numbers of people under public ownership.

24. *Topanga Beach in Los Angeles City.*

From the city line to Castellammare Beach, about 1600 feet, Topanga Beach is very narrow. The highway is filled out onto the beach and there is little if any private land on that side except at Castle Rock in the middle of this stretch. Any private land that may exist should be publicly acquired.

PLATE 38. Beach at mouth of Santa Monica Canyon, showing public beach in the center with private club and parking area in the left foreground. (*Photo by Stagg.*)

25. Castellammare Beach.

At the arch over the street and eastward a stretch of beach 700′ long has been fenced in for the use of owners of property in Castellammare, thus withdrawn from private ownership and dedicated to quasi-public uses, for which purpose it is recommended that it should be left.

26. Santa Ynez Beach.

For a distance of 1,900 feet between the highway and the shore opposite Santa Ynez Canyon there is one old building and some land that should be acquired.

27, 28 and 29. Bel-Air, Pacific Palisades Beach, Lighthouse Cafe and Huntington Palisades Beach to the County Public Beach.

Two miles of narrow frontage, a part of which has been built out recently by artificial means upon publicly owned tidelands. Through this section a plan is being considered for constructing a new State road, on a wider right of way, partly on the tidelands just outside the private lands and partly on those lands, and for abandoning the present highway in exchange for property rights along the shore. Either some such exchanges should be worked out or the strips of privately owned shore front lands should be acquired outright.

30. Santa Monica Canyon Beach.

The public now has the use of nearly a quarter of a mile of beach at the mouth of Santa Monica Canyon. This is a very valuable beach, fairly broad and now very popular.

31. Santa Monica Canyon Park (9 Acres).

At the mouth of Santa Monica Canyon a portion of the partly vacant land back of the highway should be acquired to make a small waterside park for intensive use by automobile parties near the beach, and to provide some of the needed parking space for automobiles and space for a public bath-house to be connected with the beach by a foot subway.

32. Santa Monica Palisades Park.

Santa Monica City owns a fine coast park of 46 acres, though it is almost entirely cut off from contact with the ocean, and is high above sea level.

33 and 34. Beach Clubs in Los Angeles City and in Santa Monica.

Eleven hundred feet of beach front is now largely taken up for intensive use by a number of beach clubs and houses on the shore. The value of this area and areas farther eastward has mounted so high that it will prove much less costly to leave this land in private ownership; to allow the present shore road to serve for ordinary traffic, and to plan for pleasure travel ultimately to pass outside these properties either on new lands to be filled out on the tidelands or on a chain of islands farther out.

35. From Georgina Avenue to California Avenue.

East from the clubs for three-quarters of a mile a very narrow strip of the shore outside existing lots might be acquired, but the lots run almost to high tide and in places may reach it, and the strip is so narrow that it would add little to the area of tidelands already publicly owned. Therefore, this strip is not listed for acquisition.

36 and 37. From California Avenue to Broadway.

From Broadway west to Arizona Avenue the city of Santa Monica now owns a fairly broad strip of beach frontage outside the walk, and west of Arizona Avenue for a quarter of a mile to California Avenue there is a narrow strip where the walk is built up above the tidelands. This land can be widened eventually to seaward by building groins to increase its recreational area.

38. Broadway to Santa Monica Pier.

Nine hundred and fifty feet of high value privately owned property is not included in proposed acquisitions.

39 and 40. Santa Monica Pier and Beaches to Lick Pier.

From Santa Monica Pier to Lick Pier at the city line there are now a number of narrow parcels of publicly owned beach outside the existing walk, and there is one small park of an acre and a half on the slope above the walk. In this stretch for about half the distance the narrow beach outside the walk is privately owned to tideland and possibly can be acquired at reasonable prices, but here again the cost of acquisition is likely to be greater than the narrow width added to the width of the walk would justify, and it is probably better policy from the public point of view to leave the beach here to be developed eventually farther out by filling on existing public lands rather than by recovery of the private holdings.

At Santa Monica Pier, and again at the Lick Pier, amusement parks have been built far out over the water on flimsy pile construction to attract large crowds with no special provision of space for parking of automobiles. Such facilities should eventually be superseded by more appropriate and adequate ones under public control.

PLATE 39. Shores of Venice and the Del Rey marshes, where a large park and harbor can be developed if the land is soon acquired. *(Photo by Spence.)*

41 and 42. From Lick Pier to Del Rey Pier through Venice.

Nearly two miles of beach front in Venice outside the walk is now publicly owned in various parcels, and all of the remaining frontage amounting to another mile should be acquired, subject to such arrangement as may be deemed best with owners of existing piers. This private property lies mostly at the easterly end of the beach. Some of the land claimed to be private property is probably really public now, having resulted from filling out upon public lands, and is now under litigation. Along most of this frontage the beach is now too narrow to render full value to the public and the entire beach doubtless should be greatly widened eventually by proper use of groins or breakwaters, but whatever is done should form part of a plan for the best possible ultimate use of this entire section of shore, probably as a pleasure bay of large proportions as suggested by the Venice Branch of the Los Angeles Chamber of Commerce and as shown in the sketch plan herewith presented.

43 and 44. *Ballona Creek Marshes and Lagoon and Proposed Outside Mole and Pleasure Bay.*

As described and recommended for the park and parkway system there is opportunity for creating one of the great recreation features of the world at the shore to include the Ballona Creek Marshes, a mole outside Venice and Santa Monica and the enclosed Pleasure Bay. (See Plates 33 and 34.)

At the Del Rey Marshes there is now a large area of low land which can be made into a broad waterside park to supplement the beaches that are elsewhere bordered for so many miles by commercial and residential buildings. Between the marshes and the sandy beaches there is a long, narrow lagoon now popular for still-water bathing.

45, 46 and 47. *Del Rey Pier and the Los Angeles Hyperion Beach, 3½ Miles Long.*

South of the Del Rey Pier for some distance the beach is now fenced in and subdivided; east of there the Pacific Electric car line follows the base of the bluff on the shore itself, in some places so close that a high tide washes the rocks along the tracks. Above the railroad, the newly constructed highway follows the edge of the bluff to Hyperion and there turns a short distance farther inland. The public now owns about 3,500 feet of this frontage south of the subdivision and also a mile of frontage at Hyperion, with a mile of narrow private property of limited value between the two. This private property and a narrow strip at least along the outer side of the subdivided area at Del Rey should be acquired to complete the shore holdings. The beach at Hyperion is now public property and insofar as it is not needed for sewer outfall purposes, it should be made available for recreation under proper interdepartmental arrangements.

48. *Hyperion Uplands.*

About 180 acres of upland is also publicly owned, stretching for a mile along the bluffs and sand dunes. It will eventually have very great recreational value and should be kept for such purposes, insofar as it is not needed by the Sewer Department.

49, 50 and 51. *El Segundo and Los Angeles County Shores Owned by Standard Oil Company.*

The Standard Oil Company owns nearly a mile of shore front at El Segundo and farther east. This shore from the car line and the highway down to high tide is almost all vacant, and is kept free from buildings as a protection to their property above. A short stretch is used for the pier and accessory uses. The balance of the beach should be publicly owned, and it is possible that under certain restrictions for their own protection the company might reasonably turn this over to the public.

52 and 53. *County Owned Beach at Manhattan.*

The County under favorable opportunity recently acquired about 1,800′ of beach frontage at the west edge of Manhattan, as another unit in the public holdings between the railroad and the shore.

54 and 55. *Manhattan Beach Shores.*

The city of Manhattan Beach now owns about half the shore along its frontage and the remainder in long, narrow parcels of limited commercial value should be publicly acquired as opportunity offers. The beach through the city is bordered by the railway and by a walk, but not by the highway.

56. *Manhattan Beach Park.*

Just back of the shore the city owns a small parcel of land overlooking the sea in which a pleasing local park and gathering place can be developed.

57, 58 and 59. *City of Hermosa Beach Frontage.*

Almost all of the beach frontage of Hermosa is now public, in a long, narrow strip outside the walk. 420 feet is privately owned at the City Pier, and the question of acquiring that was recently decided adversely by the city owing to high value placed upon it. This short parcel has not been included in the recommendations for acquisition. The entire shore is followed by a walk on which private properties face, but the highway and car lines are farther inland.

60, 61, 62, 63 and 64. Redondo Beach Shores.

The North Beach, three-quarters of a mile long (No. 60), is now publicly owned outside the beach walk. For a quarter of a mile, through the center of the city, the beach is occupied by an amusement zone (No. 61), outside a portion of which the city has built a public pier. This frontage is not recommended for acquisition. South of the pier to Avenue I, the beach and bluffs should be publicly acquired for a mile and a half, the easterly portion to extend up to the nearby public highway, the Esplanade.

The city has an 8-acre park (No. 62) near the pier that is used intensively at times for picnics and large gatherings near the beach, for which it is admirably suited.

At the south end of the city for about a quarter of a mile (No. 64) the beach below the Esplanade has recently been dedicated as a quasi-public community beach, and this is not included in the recommendations for public acquisition.

65. Torrance Beach.

The extreme southerly end of the sandy beaches of the South Bay District where they merge into the rocky shores of Palos Verdes is in the city of Torrance. It is about three-quarters of a mile long and is bordered by bluffs and very high cliffs, above which the privately owned lands are now being subdivided for residences. The beach, bluffs and cliffs should be, and probably in any case will be, re-served for recreation and scenic effect, but are of more local than regional value.

66, 67, 68, 69, 70 and 71. Palos Verdes Estates and Ranch and Lighthouse.

These areas lie in the unincorporated territory of Los Angeles County, including over 13 miles of coast line. Along the coast at Palos Verdes and all the way to Point Fermin in San Pedro there is very little sandy beach, the shore is generally rocky, and the shoal water for a long distance out is filled with kelp. Above the shore cliffs rise abruptly, 50′ to 150′ in height, leaving almost no open ground near sea level. Along the top of the bluffs for much of the way a shore front road, the Palos Verdes Coast Road, has been built, from which fine views over the ocean are obtained.

For the first five miles from the Torrance Beach the shore and bluffs and a large amount of canyon and hill land back of the shore, in all several hundred acres, are quasi-public held in trust for park purposes for the benefit of the local community (No. 66). The parkway above the cliffs follows the shore reservation most of the way and commands fine views that are protected by the existence of the reservation along the shore.

Farther east the coast highway follows a fifty-foot right of way owned by the County (Nos. 67 and 68) along or near the top of the bluff, with fair assurance that the Coast Road will be dedicated eventually 170′ wide, restricted to pleasure travel only, and that another through road farther back will be dedicated to carry heavy traffic.

At the Point Vicente Lighthouse the U. S. Government owns about 2,000 feet of frontage (No. 69).

Near the easterly end of Palos Verdes Ranch the road was not built along the coast owing to the abandonment of the former connection with Pacific Avenue and Paseo Del Mar in San Pedro, and plans for possible extension will depend on the possibility of reopening that section. A parkway should eventually coninue eastward along the bluffs, possibly to drop down to the seashore along Royal Palms and White's Point, then to rise again to connect with Paseo Del Mar in San Pedro east of White's Point.

The shores along Palos Verdes are of limited value for general public recreation, and no acquisition of shores is recommended, except for one mile at the easterly end (No. 70) where a large reservation is proposed in connection with the park system, to serve as a terminal feature (No. 71) for a large volume of traffic that will come to the shore.

72 and 73. *Royal Palms Shore and White's Point to Paseo Del Mar in San Pedro.*

From the Palos Verdes Ranch east line, eastward along the base of the bluffs and White's Point the shore and the face of the bluffs should be acquired, including a suitable road location following the shore past White's Point (No. 72), then rising to connect with the Paseo Del Mar in San Pedro (No. 73). The construction of a road along the shore will involve costly shore protection and costly inclines at either end, but will make a feature of shore front parkway of great value to the public. It will serve as a local outlet for San Pedro rather than as a through road in the park system, and will turn much traffic into San Pedro from the west to find its way through city streets where an extension of the parkway is impracticable, or to turn back to the San Pedro Hill Reservation.

74, 75, 76, 77 and 78. *Point Fermin and the San Pedro Shores.*

Of the nearly 2 miles of San Pedro Shore over 80% is now publicly owned, of varying width, including much of the bluffs (Nos. 74 and 78). The remaining private property near the shore (No. 75) and two parcels on the bluffs (Nos. 76 and 77) should be acquired to complete this park and beach area, where already a large number of people go, and where many more may be expected as the city grows.

79. *The Harbor Section and Terminal Island.*

Nearly 6 miles of ocean front from San Pedro across the bay to the old Los Angeles River, including Terminal Island, is practically all taken up for Harbor and Commercial purposes, and aside from minor local recreation grounds for persons employed in the district, this area should be kept free from pleasure seekers and devoted to the commercial and industrial uses for which it is primarily intended.

80. *Harbor Section at Long Beach.*

Thirty-eight hundred feet of the harbor lands lying within the breakwaters is now a public beach belonging to Long Beach. This section now has considerable recreational value, but will doubtless be used in time to meet commercial requirements, for which it is well suited; its recreational use will then be largely or wholly lost to the public.

81. *Flood Control Channel and West Beach.*

Three-fourths of a mile of intensively used beach in Long Beach, now publicly owned.

82 and 83. *Amusement Zone and Municipal Pier and Auditorium.*

Over half a mile of the frontage opposite the main part of the city is occupied by the amusement zone (No. 82), the city pier, and the fill now being made by the city for an Auditorium and other public uses (No. 83).

84, 85 and 86. *Long Beach from the Auditorium to East County Line.*

Four miles of shore east of the Auditorium in Long Beach, having a fine sandy beach and a very broad sandy tideland strip, should all be publicly owned. Three-fifths is now publicly owned (No. 84), much of that being only a narrow strip below the high bluffs, with a sea wall at the base of the bluff practically at flood tide level. The city owns the strip of Bluff Park for a distance of three-quarters of a mile (No. 86), over which a fair view can be had from the swarms of passing automobiles on Ocean Avenue.

East of the park the bluffs become less and gradually disappear, and from Termino Avenue eastward to Fifty-second Street all private holdings between the highway with its car line and the sea should eventually be publicly acquired and are now being acquired by the city (No. 85). East from Fifty-second Street the narrow strip south of the walk should be acquired to connect with the public beach now owned by the County. At the east County line and just beyond, the entire point east of Seventy-second Street should be publicly acquired. From this point a bridge will eventually be built across Alamitos Channel to connect with the shore road farther eastward, and then the highway along the Long Beach Peninsula will be used by large numbers of pleasure seekers.

87. *Alamitos Bay Shores.*

Alamitos Bay is the only large inland salt-water area in the County now used for recreation. It is of limited extent, having about 3 miles of shores and is only fairly well developed for public use. All the available area in the narrow strips between roads or walks and the shore line should be publicly acquired and some additional public recreation facilities should be established at points where automobiles may park in larger numbers without congesting the shores. For this purpose it seems possible that some of the vacant land northeast of the bay may yet be available.

88. *Bolsa Chica Beach.*

Five miles long, but immediately outside Los Angeles County, the beach between the highway and the tide-line is followed by the Pacific Electric Railway and in places small cottages have been built and the beach has been subdivided, but this entire stretch should be acquired in connection with the Bolsa Chica Marshes. There will be need for a bathhouse and a limited amount of shelter, but no extensive construction need be contemplated at present. There should be two bridges over the railroad with some automobile parking space along the shore side of the tracks.

ESTIMATE OF COSTS

Based on prices now prevailing in the several sections.

I. Land along shore front:	Length in Miles	Acquisition	Improvement
A. Now public	14		
B. Now quasi-public	6		
C. To be acquired	32	$13,700,000	$ 1,900,000
II. Lands back of the highway:	Areas in Acres		
A. Now public	64		
B. Now quasi-public	188		
C. To be acquired	206	$ 710,000	$ 240,000
		$14,410,000	$ 2,140,000
III. Pleasure Bay Improvements:			
(Partly charged under park and parkway plan) Beach share			$10,000,000
TOTAL		$14,410,000	$12,140,000

CHAPTER VI

RECOMMENDATIONS FOR REGIONAL ATHLETIC FIELDS

EVEN where local parks and playgrounds and school grounds may now adequately provide for ordinary daily use, and where parks and beaches are accessible for holidays and occasional visits, the important requirements of boys and girls just above school age, but not yet established in active employment, full of energy and strength and rapidly passing from the control of parents and teachers, but not yet held down by responsibilities of business, call for some special consideration. For these children, who are just at the "dangerous age" when they will establish their places in the community for good or for bad, there is need for wholesome encouragement and a free outlet for a large amount of energy, space for games of active competition too rough and too widespreading to be played on the local playgrounds. They need such areas as are provided in Franklin Field in Boston, with its many acres of open meadow on which a dozen baseball games are played at the same time, or the great fields in Prospect Park in Brooklyn, and similar fields in Jackson Park and other parks in Chicago.

To provide space for baseball games, football, track events, tennis, swimming and various other games and sports, with field houses, lockers, and other necessary conveniences, and to be able to serve large crowds that will gather at times, each such area should contain 100 acres or more of fairly level land.

Such areas, if they are to meet the particular purpose for which they are proposed, should be within easy reach of a large number of young people at a minimum cost for transportation. They should, therefore, be easily accessible by the street cars for a single carfare. There should be one or more such areas on each side of the center of the city.

Several areas have been included and numbered in the general plan for parks and parkways (See Plate No. 46) in some or all of which large fields can be developed, such as:

31. Culver Recreation Field.
35. Rancho Cienega Recreation Field.
48. Long Beach Water Lands.
55. South Gate Recreation Grounds.
57. Whittier Narrows.
59. Lincoln Park and Recreation Grounds.
61. Brookside Park, Pasadena.
62. Elysian Park (Chavez Ravine Section)
64. Griffith Park Playgrounds.
92. Eaton Canyon Wash.

In each of these areas, a space large enough for an effective large athletic field in agreeable park-like surroundings can be found and in several at least, if not all, the land should be made available, if not already so, for such uses. While some of these areas do not now meet the requirements as to accessibility, they can doubtless all be made easily accessible in time. Still other areas farther out may also be needed in time in the San Fernando Valley, the San Gabriel Valley and the Ballona Creek Basin, for which other large reservations can then be developed to meet this need, such as Alondra Park, the drainage basins, and the reservoir parks.

DETAILED RECOMMENDATIONS

31. *Culver Recreation Field.*

Culver Recreation Field as proposed, including the triangle between La Cienega Avenue and Venice Boulevard with 160 to 190 acres, is a low flat area suitable for such uses. It is, however, a little over a mile from the end of the city car line at Rimpau Boulevard, but is on the Pacific Electric car line.

35. *Rancho Cienega Recreation Field.*

Lying east of Angeles Mesa Drive and south of the line of Exposition Boulevard and lying north of proposed parkway into the city. About 125 acres of flat land is there available, or more if the proposed parkway be included. This area is accessible for a single fare by the yellow car line on Santa Barbara Avenue less than half a mile to the south, and by the Thirty-ninth Street car line one-quarter mile to the east, and by the Jefferson Street line at Ninth Avenue.

48. *The Long Beach Water Lands.*

The Long Beach water lands to serve Long Beach and its extension northward include a large area that can be and should be made available for such uses as the city demands become greater. This area is not now accessible by a low city transportation fare, but is likely to be so served in time.

55. *South Gate Recreation Grounds.*

At South Gate 600 to 700 acres of river bottom land is proposed to be acquired as a park reservation. In this area very large athletic fields can be developed to serve the southeast section. This area is 9 miles out, and it is not on a car line at present but is served by the South Gate Municipal Bus Lines and is a fine field for ultimate development.

57. *Whittier Narrows Recreation Park.*

This park, proposed as another large river-bottom reservation, has a large acreage in which athletic fields can be developed eventually. This area is 10 miles from the center of the city, is near Montebello, Whittier, El Monte and Alhambra, and may in time be served by a single fare city transportation line, although it is not now so served.

59. *Lincoln Park and Recreation Grounds.*

East of and including the present Lincoln Park, a large area is easily accessible from all of the east side of the city by North Broadway and North Main Street by street cars for a single fare, and is crossed by the Pacific Electric line. It includes rough but usable land that could be made into athletic fields. Part of the area is now occupied by the Ascot Racetrack, of doubtful value as such, and there is an auto camp on the Alhambra Avenue side, but the land is now nearly vacant and should be acquired for the purpose, including boundaries satisfactory for the proposed east and west parkway as well.

61. *Brookside Park, Pasadena.*

Pasadena now owns large areas in the Arroyo Seco at Brookside Park that serve in part the purposes of a great athletic field. This park will doubtless be further developed on a large scale for such uses. Brookside Park is now divided for uses as follows:

Playground equipment	3 acres
Tennis	1 acre
Major sports	18 acres
Picnic areas	18 acres
Automobile parking	5 acres
Planted areas	13 acres
	58 acres
Stadium	22 acres
Automobile parking	150 acres
Golf course and undeveloped area	290 acres
Total	520 acres

62. *Elysian Park (Chavez Ravine Section).*

Elysian Park, near the heart of Los Angeles, on the northerly side, is now chiefly rugged hilltops, but in the plans to extend the park to include Chavez Ravine and the adjacent slopes space will be available, especially in the lower section of the ravine, where a great athletic field can be developed to meet the requirements of large numbers of people, surrounded by other park features.

64. *Griffith Park Playground.*

The city now has Griffith Park Playground, on a 20 acre tract, a playground and athletic field of limited extent. This area could be very materially extended to include some of the adjacent water lands. The adjacent lands on the easterly side of the river are subdivided and becoming built up in small houses, but it is possible that a fairly large area of such lands can be acquired also, at less cost for extension to the plant already established, than could an equally satisfactory space be found elsewhere. This area is easily accessible from Glendale and from Edendale and the easterly end of Hollywood.

92. *Eaton Canyon Wash.*

In Eaton Canyon Wash 500 acres of the wash and adjacent slopes are recommended for acquirement, and in that area a large athletic field to serve the east side of Pasadena and adjacent towns on the east can be developed.

ESTIMATE OF COSTS

An estimate has been made of the probable cost for acquisition of areas not yet owned and for development of athletic grounds at each area, insofar as such development is likely to be needed for some time to come. This follows:

Cost of acquisition	$4,700,000
Improvements	2,500,000
Total	$7,200,000

This calls for relatively little cost on some areas and high cost on others. For those areas where a much larger reservation is recommended in the general park plan than is needed for athletics alone, a fair portion of the total estimated cost has been included here.

CHAPTER VII

RECOMMENDATIONS FOR LARGE RESERVATIONS IN

MOUNTAINS, CANYONS, DESERTS AND ISLANDS

THE main Los Angeles Region as herein considered, lying between the mountains and the sea, obviously does not include all the areas of recreational value to the people of the region. With the great use of the automobile, the range for pleasure seekers even in large numbers has been greatly extended, and the need for special provision for recreation in the outlying regions has already been keenly felt.

The County has acquired and developed several areas for recreation in the mountains, and the City of Los Angeles has developed four recreation camps at a long distance from the city. The Government also has developed recreational areas in the Angeles National Forest, and there are other areas far within the interior of the forest, of limited extent and widely separated one from another, that could be used by a large number of visitors if made sufficiently accessible. They can be made accessible by providing reasonably safe and direct roads, and by providing the necessary conveniences, such as running water, some forms of shelter, toilet facilities and sanitation, and stores for food and camping supplies.

With the construction of dams in the San Gabriel Canyon, the present route through the Canyon will necessarily be diverted and may be superseded at least in part by a route farther east through Little Dalton Canyon and the east fork of the San Gabriel River to Vincent Gulch and Big Rock Creek and to the desert beyond with a connection also to Big Pines Recreation Camp. This would be distinctly a canyon bottom route, and while it would have many attractive features, it will lack that particular interest which is to be found in a high-level route through the high mountains. The San Gabriel Canyon road is now being extended to Crystal Lake, and some road will doubtless be carried from there over the mountains also to Big Rock Creek, but will be fairly steep. A mountain road to afford the greatest scenic value, however, should start near La Canada, pass around the head of the Arroyo Seco as now planned by the State Division of Highways, follow the ridges from there around the west end of the San Gabriel Canyon to open up the mountain plateaus along the ridge, then drop down into Rock Creek and there connect with the Big Pines Recreation Camp road. Farther west in the mountains there have been suggestions for roads over the mountains to Palmdale for commercial use, either along the Arroyo Seco and around the head of the Tujunga Canyon, or through a canyon farther west. Neither of those routes, however, will reach land that has any very great recreational value.

In the mountains and in the desert in the northern part of the County there are several features of recreational value and public interest, notably the top of Liebre Mountain in the National Forest, now partly in private ownership, together with its delightful northern slopes; the Joshua trees and the open des-

PLATE 40. San Gabriel mountains from mouth of Tujunga Canyon, showing steep, barren hillsides, offering little or no recreation space above the valley floor. (*Photo by Fiss.*)

ert along the north County line, including the bed of Rosamond Lake, which is dry much of the time, but is a typical desert feature with its frequent mirages of considerable scenic interest; and the big Joshua trees at the east end of the Antelope Valley. To get into those areas through fairly agreeable pleasure routes, it would be possible to construct a pleasureway circuit from Newhall Tunnel northward, along the western base of the mountains, east of the occupied areas of Newhall and Saugus; then to follow up the Elizabeth Lake road to Radium Springs; then to climb up to near the top of the ridges of Sawmill Mountain and into Liebre Mountain, with a branch down the northeast slope of Liebre Mountain through Oakgrove Canyon, and from there to the large group of Joshua trees near Neenach; thence cross the desert, north of the cultivated areas, to Rosamond Lake and to the grove of big Joshua trees between Antelope Valley and Wilsona Valley, and connect from there southward to the Big Pines Recreation Camp road and the roadways in and over the mountains toward Pasadena, Glendora and the other foothill cities. All the privately owned lands along such routes are of very low economic value and the public ownership of a liberal margin of land along such routes, kept in its natural condition, would be of great scenic and recreational value to the people of the Los Angeles Region. In the Owens Valley, far north of the County line, the City of Los Angeles owns many thousands of acres of land formerly cultivated but

PLATE 41. Top of Liebre Mountain, looking down onto nearby ridges, showing native growth not yet ruined by fire or cutting; should be developed as a public recreation park.

now returned to desert because the water has been taken for city use. This area even though remote has some value for recreation and may eventually attract many pleasure seekers, especially in winter.

Within the County there are also the islands lying some distance off the coast, having very considerable possible value for recreation for those who can afford the time and expense required to reach them. Santa Catalina is privately owned and is developed in part for commercial recreation. San Clemente, lying farther out, is owned by the National Government, under the Lighthouse Department, and should be valuable eventually as a County or State recreation and camping place when there is enough demand to warrant the expense of equipping and running a recreation station there and of establishing transportation routes by air or by water or both. It is now chiefly barren, and almost without water, and unin-

habited, but has a fair harbor and a large area with some very attractive features, canyons, cliffs, and volcanic cones as well as interesting shores. So too, the westerly end of Santa Catalina, with the harbor at the isthmus would make an excellent public reservation.

Other recreational areas, such as those in the San Bernardino and San Jacinto Mountains, draw heavily from Los Angeles, and might eventually be included in a plan either as an extension of the Los Angeles System or as State Parks, or as parts of other Metropolitan Systems for the counties east of Los Angeles.

The Park system as proposed provides also for 12 or 13 outlets at the County boundaries from which extensions should be developed eventually through adjacent counties, and to which especial attention of the adjacent counties may well be invited.

In the mountain areas the largest cost to

provide for recreation will undoubtedly be that for road construction, and the value of the investment in these roads will depend largely on the methods and manner of road construction and the control of adjacent lands. The use of the roads involves four kinds of activities: first, driving along and enjoying views and events of the road; second, pausing in the car to enjoy points of special scenic interest; third, stopping to picnic or to enjoy other forms of isolated outdoor recreation near the car; and fourth, parking the car usually at some parking center and leaving it to go elsewhere on foot. Each of these four interests can be, and should be, provided for in the mountain roads, without at the same time detracting from the enjoyment of the road in other ways. Cars parked or pausing on the outer edge of the road necessarily reduce the enjoyment of the road from passing cars. So, too, cars in the outer lane of travel seriously cut off the enjoyment for people traveling next the hillside and even the widening of the roadway to provide for several lines of travel cuts off the plunging mountain views from persons using the inner lanes. Therefore, where roads are made for enjoyment at so high a cost per mile as is inevitable in the mountains, some additional cost can well be justified to obviate this feature, by extra grading and planting if need be, through providing even small hillside or woodland "nooks" or detours, near to but screened from and not in the way of the main traffic. Such nooks can be on higher or lower levels, and as stub ends or as loops, so long as they afford space enough for a few cars and a chance to turn around.

Where many cars will be parked in a scenic region it is well worth spending a considerable amount of money and of ingenuity to render the mass of cars less conspicuous, either behind belts of planting or by parking in "groves," the cars being at least partly hidden under and among the trees.

Where the volume of traffic in both directions is a considerable one, in mountain regions and where cross-overs are not needed at frequent intervals, there is a great advantage in having two one-way roads of limited width and each on its independent location. The advantage of safety in travel as well as the added opportunity for enjoying the scenery, free from interruption by vehicles passing in the opposite direction, is of very great importance. The danger of meeting on the turns of mountain roads, the glare of headlights at night, and the constant passing of vehicles is a factor of considerable irritation that can be eliminated by one-way roads. Two roads may cost more than one wider one, and two may provide less effectively for travel when the peak load is chiefly going in one direction, but two roads will give infinitely more enjoyment to the travelers whose chief reason for traveling is to find enjoyment. Where preliminary construction calls for making a two-way road, twenty or twenty-five feet wide now, but where a greater capacity will be needed later, it is often possible to plan the location so that the additional width can later be provided in an independent second road, so as to give ultimately the advantages of two one-way roads.

Enjoyment of scenery from an automobile, moving as fast as practicable, is much more possible with broad open scenery from high level roads where the nearby features are unimportant than in narrow canyons and intimate small scale landscape where the scenes are passed so rapidly that no really good views are possible. In general, the canyons should be protected from the rush of through travel, and main roads should be placed where possible on the view-commanding slopes and ridges, where they will also best serve for fire protection.

Summary of Proposed Outlying Reservations and Parkways

(The lettered classes are referred to in the last column of the next table.)

Class		Miles	Acres
A.	Large Reservations in forests	14	19,745
B.	Large Reservations in desert	10	7,500
C.	Island Reservations		60,000
D.	Connecting park roads in forests	97	
E.	Connecting park roads not in forests	81	4,800
F.	Camps in mountains		285
Total		202	92,330

List of Existing and Proposed Park Reservations and Parkways in Outlying Regions

(Numbers on the left margin refer to numbers on Plate No. 42. Letters at the right refer to the class of use for which each is recommended.)

	Width in Feet	Length in Miles	Area in Acres	Class
201—Newhall Parkway	200-500	20	1000	E
202—Elizabeth Lake Canyon and Liebre Mt. Road (mostly through forest land)	200-500	20		D
203—Liebre Mountain Reservation (10,000 acres of National Forest lands)	15,000	7	12,000	A
204—Neenach Parkway	500	8	500	E
205—Neenach Joshua trees reservation	5,000	5	2,500	B
206—Antelope Valley Parkway	500	35	2,200	E
207—Lovejoy Joshua trees reservation	10,000	5	5,000	B
208—Rock Creek Parkway	500	18	1,100	E
209—Big Pines Park Road	500	5		D
210—Big Pines Recreation Camp (existing county reservaton)		5	4,200	A
211—Rock Creek to Arroyo Seco Ridge Road and Reservations	500-5,000	42		D
212—Mt. Islip Roads		3		D

	Width in Feet	Length in Miles	Area in Acres	Class
213—Crystal Lake Reservation (existing county reservation)		2	1,290	A
214—Devil's Canyon Road		7		D
215—Big Pines Vincent Gulch and Little Dalton Road		20		D
216—Camp Seeley, City of Los Angeles			25	F
217—Camp Radford, City of Los Angeles			82	F
218—Camp High Sierra, City of Los Angeles			160	F
219—Camp Oak Flats, City of Los Angeles			18	F
220—San Clemente Island (Owned by U. S.)			50,000	C
221—Angeles National Forest, Miscellaneous Areas that should be acquired (The Angeles National Forest contains 670,682 acres within the county of which 41,622 acres are alienated, leaving 629,060 acres U. S. land)			2,255	A
222—Portion of Santa Catalina Island			10,000	C

Detailed Recommendations
201. Newhall Parkway.

From San Fernando Valley toward the northwest there is now a main traveled highway through the Newhall Tunnel, and another parallel to it and a little farther westward is being developed, and through the pass runs also the Southern Pacific Railroad. A parkway route should be developed farther eastward through Grapevine Canyon to cross the foothills a little above the pass and to follow along the easterly side of the railroad along the present highway for a mile or so, then to follow undeveloped lands east of the railroad, to cross over the railroad and highways at Soledad Canyon and to follow around the easterly side of the Santa Clara River Valley, up the easterly side of the Castaic Valley, parallel to

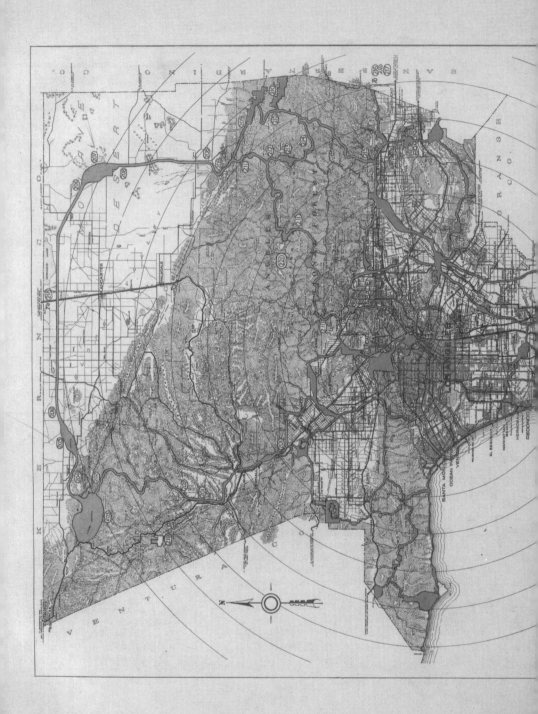

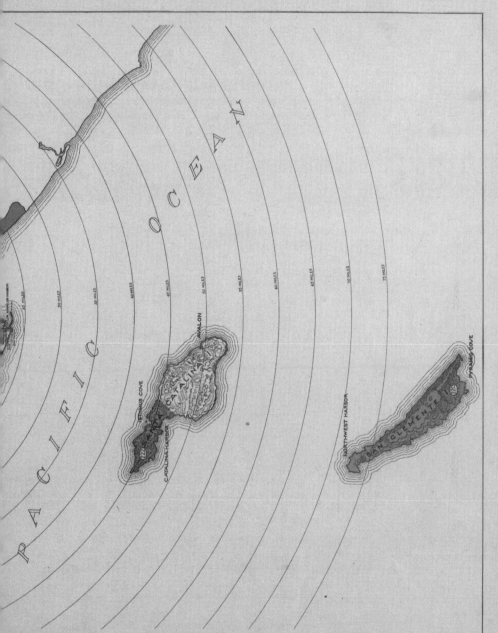

PLATE 42. General plan for large reservations in mountains, canyons, deserts and islands (shown in red), in extension of the plan for parks and parkways in the main Los Angeles Region (shown in green).

but separated from the Ridge Route. Through Elizabeth Lake Canyon it should turn north-eastward to the forest boundary.

This route would involve some heavy construction, but passes through interesting country that, if protected from fire and from devastation, can be kept attractive. Much of the land is of limited commercial value and a wide right of way should be acquired.

202. Elizabeth Lake Canyon and Liebre Mountain Road.

Above the forest line the park road should follow the valley for some distance above Warm Springs. The entire valley should be held as a reservation and the few private holdings should be publicly acquired. Above Warm Springs the canyon becomes narrow and very crooked and about two and one-half miles from the springs the road should turn westward in a branch canyon to rise to the saddle at its head; then should follow the side of Sawmill Mountain, rising northwestward to the notch between this and Liebre Mountain. This section will involve very heavy construction and need not be considered until the demand for it becomes sufficient to warrant the work or until Liebre Mountain is made a popular recreation camp, but the right of way should be planned and it is possible that a fire road might well be built along the line in an effort to prevent further great fire losses, and that the forest area may recover sufficiently in time from the last great fires to make the route more inviting than it is now.

203. Liebre Mountain Reservation.

In the northwest corner of the Angeles National Forest there is a fine rolling mountain top just a mile above sea level, extending for several miles eastward from the Ridge Route at Sandbergs, and having a native forest cover not yet ruined by fire, where a large recreation park somewhat similar in function to the Big Pines Recreation Camp, but radically different in landscape character, might be developed. A small portion of the hill is privately owned, and should be acquired at once by the public. At the base of the north slope of the mountain, there are attractive small valleys containing some fine oaks and pines and beautiful pastoral scenes that should be made a part of the reservation by acquiring the privately owned lands. Through the reservation a road from the Ridge Route eastward along the top, then branching both ways to descend to Sawmill Mountain Notch would serve to afford access and to open up the interior, and from there westward down the north slope it would afford access to the pastoral lands at the base of the mountain.

204. Neenach Parkway.

From Sawmill Notch a park road should follow westward down the north face of Liebre Mountain to meet the old road where it crosses the saddle, then turn northeastward along the old road out Oakgrove Canyon, and follow the Los Angeles Aqueduct eastward into the Antelope Valley, where the large groups of Joshua trees now stand, a distance of eight miles through interesting country and some trees, though the region has recently been terribly devastated by fire.

205. Neenach Joshua Trees Reservation.

Near Neenach there is a group of Joshua trees on a sandy plain sloping gently toward the north, several thousand acres in extent. The land now has little value. This is an interesting bit of the desert, within fairly easy reach of Los Angeles, and it can well be preserved unchanged in its natural condition.

206. Antelope Valley Parkway.

From the Neenach Joshua trees eastward across the Antelope Valley for a distance of 35 miles a parkway is proposed, to follow along the north edge of the farming district around Lancaster close to the County boundary, and to include a strip of desert land wide enough to form a foreground of desert conditions and to control some of the views over the valley and surrounding hills. This strip should be 400 to 500 feet wide, and wider where interesting buttes and other features occur, and should extend in places to the edge of Rosamond Lake, usually dry, where fine mirages are to be found. East of Rosamond Lake it should turn southeast toward the big Joshua trees in the Lovejoy Buttes and the bed of Rock Creek.

207. *Lovejoy Joshua Trees Reservation.*

At the eastern end of Antelope Valley and just north of the Rock Creek entrance into the mountains, there is a large expanse of waste desert land, some of which should be included in a reservation to preserve its natural character. The reservation should include the very large Joshua trees, some of the river bed, and some of the buttes that have little value for any economic use but are very picturesque and interesting as landscape features.

208. *Rock Creek Parkway.*

From the Lovejoy Joshua trees to the mountains the route should follow the easterly side of Rock Creek Wash up to a point where it can cross the creek to join the present road into the mountains.

209. *Big Pines Park Road.*

From the mouth of Rock Creek Canyon to Big Pines Recreation Camp a new road has recently been constructed on good lines and grades to serve both as a general highway and as a parkway to the recreation camp. In time this road will have to be widened and it is possible that in places two one-way roads can be made to serve better than a single broad road. As this is primarily a pleasure route special care should be taken to protect the scenery along the way, and any private property that

now exists, should either be acquired, or else restricted against building for some distance back from the road.

210. *Big Pines Recreation Camp.*

To meet the urgent need for big open recreation grounds in the mountains near the city, the County of Los Angeles has wisely acquired a large reservation at Big Pines, containing a variety of most interesting and attractive scenery. This area has been made available to the public by building good roads and by providing shelters, fireplaces, stores and other necessary accommodations. In order to meet the needs of a large number of visitors, some for a day, some for longer, a number of local recreational facilities have been developed and doubtless more will follow.

The success of the camp with its large attendance is leading to serious problems of wear and tear and of congestion. The big pines and firs, among the chief charms of the region, can stand only a limited amount of trampling and cutting and regrading about their roots, and intensive use of the grounds may so affect these trees that they will become weakened and will fall ready prey to the ravages of pests and diseases. Therefore, it may be necessary very soon to limit the use to a part of the grounds under the trees in a way to give others a chance to grow.

Other problems of handling many automobiles and of adding buildings will have to be met. Ingenuity and skill may permit more intensive use without destroying the charm of the place; but in any case there are limits on the amount of use that can safely be permitted. Such conditions are acutely felt now at the Yosemite and among the "big trees" where large crowds gather to enjoy the natural conditions, and by so gathering tend to destroy those very conditions they have come to enjoy.

211. *Rock Creek to Arroyo Seco, Ridge Road and Reservations.*

From the existing roads in Rock Creek to

the Arroyo Seco, a distance of over 20 miles, there is now no way to travel through the mountains. Various plans have been considered for roads for through travel, for fire protection, and for access to recreation areas in the mountains. Surveys have been considered for short routes from Pasadena and from Azusa or San Dimas to the desert, and in 1919 a report was made by Mr. J. B. Lippincott to the Automobile Club of Southern California recommending a consolidation of efforts to develop one master road over the ridges between Rock Creek and Arroyo Seco.

Already the State is planning to construct a road up the side of Arroyo Seco to the saddle back of Mount Wilson at Red Box, and the Forest Service has built a narrow road from Mount Wilson through Red Box to Barley Flats and along the ridge from there east and north to Little Pine Flats and beyond. Along that route, one road or two one-way roads, dodging heavy construction and high scars where possible, but passing through the most interesting points and areas, will serve as a parkway, a traffic road, and a means of protecting the forest reservation.

Along this route there are only a few sites, of limited area, suitable for general recreation. Those areas can be made accessible only at very large cost, but have a high recreational value. Plans have been considered by the Forest Service for leasing cabin sites at Barley Flats and for turning over to Pasadena a large area at Little Pine Flats. Those areas will represent actually millions of dollars of value by the time safe and satisfactory roads are completed to them, and they may have very high value for general recreation at that time. Therefore, it is believed that those and other areas along the proposed roadway should be reserved for the general public and be developed under such plans as may produce the most general benefit rather than be devoted to private cabin sites. Possibly small sites in those areas should be leased to cities or clubs for special development in such a way as to start activities and encourage their use.

All private holdings along this route should be publicly acquired now in advance of road building before high values in them may have been created at public expense.

212. Crystal Lake Reservation.

The County has recently acquired a reservation of 1,290 acres around Crystal Lake to include the fine canyon basin and pine groves. A road is being built into the basin and development is proposed for this area. A considerable plant for recreational purposes will be needed here and it is possible that under a carefully designed plan a complete plant can be developed in a way to preserve the natural charm of the basin and still to make adequate provision for the needs of the people. Such a plan should be made with much care, to avoid possible wasteful and destructive changes that otherwise may prove necessary later, and to preserve as much as possible of the natural charm.

214. Devil's Canyon Road.

From Crystal Lake a road is being built down the canyon to Coldbrook Camp and beyond. Below Coldbrook this road may be cut off by a San Gabriel Reservoir and a new road will be needed to the east fork of the San Gabriel. Such a road probably can best cross from near Coldbrook to the head of Devil's Canyon; then drop down across the cliffs of the ridge to Iron Canyon, and down Iron Canyon to the floor of East San Gabriel Gorge, though such a route will involve heavy construction through extremely rugged country.

215. Big Pines—Vincent Gulch and Little Dalton Canyon Road.

Portions of a road are now being built that will make a fairly direct route between Big Pines Camp and San Dimas, running over Blue Ridge from the camp, then dropping to

he Pass at the head of Vincent Gulch, then
.own the gulch and the gorge of the San Ga-
▶riel to the head of the proposed San Gabriel
Reservoir. From there the road should turn
westward to rise around the basin of Horse
Canyon and to cross the front range; then to
wind down the head of Little Dalton Canyon
and to connect with roads already built up the
anyon.

216. *Camp Seeley.*

25 acres in San Bernardino National Forest.

217. *Camp Radford.*

82 acres in San Bernardino National Forest.

218. *Camp High Sierra.*

160 acres in Inyo National Forest.

219. *Camp Oak Flats.*

18 acres in Angeles National Forest.

These four camps operated by the City of
Los Angeles are designed to serve vacation-
ists and campers primarily, and are located far
from the city, where attractive conditions exist.

220. *San Clemente Island.*

The Island of San Clemente is 50 miles
south of Point Fermin. It belongs to the National Government and has been reserved for
lighthouse purposes. The island, 20 miles long
and 3 to 5 miles wide, contains about 50,000
acres. It is now leased for sheep grazing and
the steeper, attractive north slopes are being
badly eroded, due to trampling and grazing.
The entire island should eventually be used
for a public pleasure resort. There is no water
on the island, but a reservoir can be built in
one of the larger canyons to hold enough water
for domestic uses. Bathing beaches and a fine
small harbor at the southeast end offer chance

for bathing and boating. The larger area could
be treated as a game and bird preserve.

221. *Angeles National Forest and Miscellaneous Areas Therein That Should be Acquired.*

The Angeles National Forest contains in
all 690,540 acres, of which 670,682 acres lie
in the County. This area includes 41,622 acres
that have been alienated, leaving 629,060 acres
of public lands. About two-fifths of this area
is in the forest above Saugus and three-fifths
in the nearer section. Most of the areas alienated are held as water preserves, but there are
a number of small areas in private hands that
should be publicly acquired to protect the reservation for general recreation. In all, about
2,255 acres of such holdings have been listed
by the United States Forest Service as likely
to lead to undesirable development or usage
if not so acquired, and these should be acquired
at once by the Los Angeles Region, since the
Forest Service is not now in a position to acquire them, and since it is mainly for the service of the people of the Region that they are
needed.

222. *Santa Catalina Island.*

The westerly end of Santa Catalina Island
is now unused and is of limited commercial
value. The isthmus and its small harbor, with
the nearby slopes on the east and with the
westerly end of the island, might well be acquired as a public reservation to be developed
when demand is sufficient to warrant the necessary expense.

ESTIMATE OF COSTS

An estimate has been made of the probable
cost of acquiring and of improving all of the
above listed units, based on the present sales
values of property near each unit, and on the
amount of work deemed justifiable to make
each unit available to the public. These estimates are as follows:

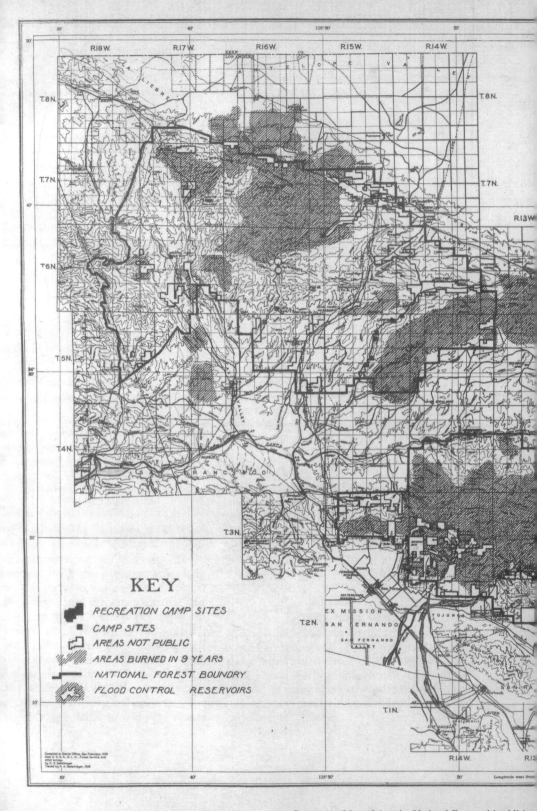

KEY

⬛	RECREATION CAMP SITES
▪	CAMP SITES
⬚	AREAS NOT PUBLIC
▨	AREAS BURNED IN 9 YEARS
▬	NATIONAL FOREST BOUNDRY
▧	FLOOD CONTROL RESERVOIRS

Compiled at District Office, San Francisco, 1926
from U. S. G. S. & L. O., Forest Service, and
other surveys
by H. A. Sebelmeyer
Traced by H. A. Sebelmeyer, 1926

PLATE 43. Map of Angeles National Forest with addition
burned over in the last ten years.

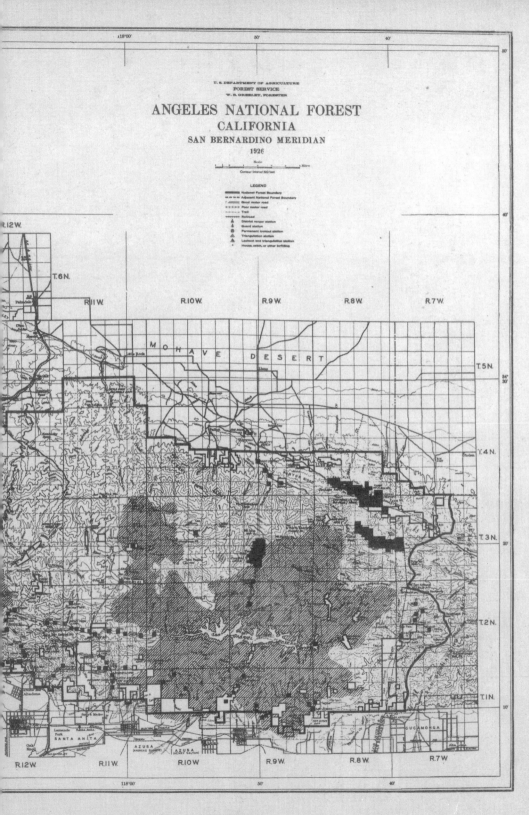

sites, areas in private ownership, reservoirs, and large areas

	Length Miles	Area in Acres	Cost of Acquisition	Cost of Improvement	Total Cost
A. Large Reservations in Forests	14.0	19,745	$140,000	$ 800,000	$ 940,000
B. Large Reservations in Desert	10.0	7,500	110,000	200,000	310,000
C. Island Reservations		60,000	100,000*	500,000	500,000
D. Connecting park roads in Forests	97.0		50,000	9,000,000	9,050,000
E. Connecting park roads not in Forests	81.0	4,800	300,000	2,300,000	2,700,000
F. Public Camps in Mountains		285			
	202	92,330	$700,000	$12,800,000	$13,500,000

*The cost of acquiring the islands must depend on negotiations, possible concessions or gifts and other factors; therefore, only a nominal figure is used here.

On the basis of the above figures a relatively small amount of money is needed for the acquisition of lands, while a large amount is needed for road building and making the areas available for use, especially in the mountains. The improvements may be made gradually over a long period of years. Doubtless a considerable share will be paid by the State Division of Highways and the National Forest Service, and many of the roads will be built by the County, whether a systematic park program is adopted or not. But many of the land acquirements are now urgent.

CHAPTER VIII

RECOMMENDATIONS FOR PLEASUREWAY PARKS OR PARKWAYS AND RELATED LARGE PARKS

THE most extensive and possibly the most urgently needed class of park and recreation facilities recommended for the Los Angeles Region is that of parkways and related large parks. The general considerations controlling this group of subjects, the meaning of the term "pleasureway parks" or parkways, as used in this report, and the extraordinary importance of such parks to a metropolis of the automobile age and particularly for Los Angeles, are set forth in Chapter I, pages 12-14. Their relation to flood control and water conservation problems is discussed in Chapter I, page 14. The general character of such parks and the contrast between them and more or less decorated highways to which the terms "boulevard" and "parkway" are often applied, are indicated by the illustrations (Plates 4, 5, 53 and 56).

Westchester County, in the New York Region, offers the most up-to-date example in this sort of development, which is everywhere becoming urgent in response to the demands of a new age. It had in 1927 a length of approximately 140 miles of parkways in a total county area of less than 450 square miles, with 5.6 per cent its total area in parks, mainly of this type. Westchester County occupies a position corresponding to the outer parts of the Los Angeles Region, having an average density of population in 1927 of a little less than two per acre, but directly in the tide of outer suburban residential development of the bet-

ter sort. What this would mean in the Los Angeles Region is suggested in a diagram (Plate 44).

Elsewhere in the New York Region and in many other metropolitan regions—such as Boston, Cleveland, Chicago, Minneapolis, Kansas City, Seattle, Portland, Oregon, and Portland, Maine—there are excellent examples of real parkways; and in most metropolitan regions there are intermediate types shading off gradually from real parks, through admirable but generally narrower and more citified parkways, both informal and formal, to so-called parkways and boulevards which are but slightly glorified streets.

In creating any extensive system of parks in a region like that of Los Angeles where urban and suburban growth has been active, critical places are almost inevitably encountered through which it is of the utmost importance to secure a reasonably pleasant and convenient connection but where the cost or physical difficulties of securing a parkway really worthy of the name would be prohibitive. There it is the part of wisdom to introduce a different sort of link in the chain, good of its sort but different. An occasional narrow neck of no appreciable length with ample widenings on either end of the neck need not impair the park-like quality at all. Much irregularity of boundaries is in fact desirable as facilitating the introduction of many special features of park value which could nowhere be secured if the width were less fluctuating. A general trimming down of width for considerable distances, however, would result in an unprofitable compromise, costing as much but less effective than if part of the length were an adequate park, with good scenery and opportunities for many park functions besides mere driving through, and the rest were a narrower parkway of a frankly different type. Some cross sections at various parts of the proposed system have been made to illustrate what should be done (Plate No. 48).

There is no standard for the amount of area that should be devoted to large parks in any one region, to say nothing of real parkways, which are a peculiarly modern need that has only recently begun to be met. But the lack of large parks in most sections of the Los Angeles Region and the absolute lack of real parkways, is evident (See Plate No. 17). In the 1,500 square miles of the Region, there are now 33 parks of over 25 acres each, and only 12 of these are of more than 100 acres. The 12 have an aggregate area of 7,539 acres, or about one-half of one per cent of the total area of the region, and even then approximately half the acreage consists of steep and rugged mountain lands in Griffith, Elysian and Brand Parks.

In the large central urban area, approximately 20 miles in diameter, where most of the people live, there is now but one possible parkway extending east and west through Elysian and Griffith Parks, and but one route north through the Arroyo Seco that possibly can be extended southward from Elysian Park to the Baldwin Hills. In this urban area, there are a large number of radial streets leading out in various directions, many of which have been designated as "boulevards" and on some of which an effort is made to maintain trees and to keep the routes attractive, but the general demand for very wide pavements for large volumes of traffic has been so great that most of these interior routes have been paved for almost their entire width, and very little space is left for planting.

Therefore, most of the travel originating within the urban district must probably continue in the future as it has in the past, to find its way through existing highways out to the regions in which parks and parkways can reasonably be established, and travel from the outside must either find its way around the city through the proposed parkway system, or cross through the center by the ordinary highways even though this area, 20 miles in diameter contains the people most in need of access to park facilities, and is nearly as large as the region in which the entire Boston system of City and Metropolitan Parks has been developed (See Plate No. 45).

The plans as proposed contemplate the acquisition of a relatively large amount of land but the areas have been selected, so far as possible, to use much land which, though less valuable for commercial, industrial, or residential use, has great value for park and recreation purposes.

The total area of this proposed regional system of parkways and large parks, including 16,000 acres of existing publicly owned parks water lands, and similar areas is approximately 70,000 acres, and the aggregate length of the proposed routes is 440 miles. Seventy thousand acres is a large amount of park land, but looking to the future of this extraordinary region, it seems entirely reasonable. It is only about 7 1/3 per cent of the total area of the region. This percentage would be almost imperceptibly increased by including the limited area of the beaches, which cannot be precisely expressed in acres because of their indefinite outer boundary, while the gradual increase with the spread of population, of local playgrounds and other strictly local recreation areas, not included in this regional system might be expected ultimately to increase the percentage a few points further. The islands deserts, forests and mountains with relatively large acreages for recreation, lie wholly outside the Region.

As an *objective*, and for a metropolis that i

growing up under 20th century conditions, with the special urge to outdoor recreation which the people of the Los Angeles Region must feel, compare this with the fact that Chicago *already has* within Cook County over 6 per cent of the total area in parks; that Greater New York already has 5.5 per cent in parks; and that three adjoining counties of the New York Metropolitan District already have from 4.9 to 5.6 per cent in parks (from 5.8 to 13.4 per cent in parks and municipal watershed lands combined); and that they are all diligently striving for more.

In the following pages there are descriptions, unit by unit, under numbers which refer to the accompanying map (Plate 46), of a proposed complete system of parkways and associated large parks for the entire region, such as appears reasonable in connection with the other types of units discussed in other chapters. The proposed system is grouped chiefly along three main east and west routes and six north and south routes as follows:

Three Easterly and Westerly Chains

The Mountain Chain:

Extending along the base of the mountains from the Newhall Tunnel to the eastern County line and connecting with all roads into the mountains, it is in large part placed high enough on the slopes to be above most of the urban development, so as to command superb views over the plains and cities, and should be always *wide enough* to keep forever open in park areas the foregrounds of these views as seen from the main roadway. The parks in this chain in places directly adjoin the Angeles National Forest lands and constitute an extension or rectification of the present southerly forest boundaries. Elsewhere they leave considerable private lands above them. But any private lands, either above or below, should front upon separate border roads or other supplementary roads and *not* crowd in upon the main roadway. The units along this chain are Nos. 18 to 21, 75 to 80, and 86 to 97.

The Coast Chain:

Along or near the coast from Ventura County to and into Orange County, designed to meet requirements for through pleasure travel and for pleasant following of the shores, the value of this chain will depend very largely upon the amount of public control of lands lying between the roadways and the sea. From El Segundo to the east end of Long Beach this route is inland, passing through Nigger Slough and over Signal Hill to connect the best points of interest along the route. The units along this chain are Nos. 1 to 3, 33, 38, 41, 43 and 46 to 52.

The Hilltop Chain:

From Triunfo to Pomona along the Santa Monica Mountains, Griffith, Elysian and Lincoln Parks, the Montebello Hills and Puente Hills, a scenic middle route connecting a large number of points of interest and tapping a large number of urban streets. This route commands some of the finest views into the mountains and over the plains and cities. It includes units Nos. 6 to 9, 25 and 26, and 57 to 60, and 62 to 74.

Six Northerly and Southerly Chains

The San Gabriel Chain:

From the mountains to the sea along the San Gabriel River, a route having the advantage of following the drainage channel. This includes units Nos. 53 and 81, 82 and 83.

The Rio Hondo and Eaton Wash Chain:

From the mountains to Long Beach near the sea, parallel to and just west of the San Gabriel Chain, this route taps the cities on its borders and benefits by following the large drainage channels with their points of interest. This chain includes units Nos. 54 to 57, 84, 85 and 92.

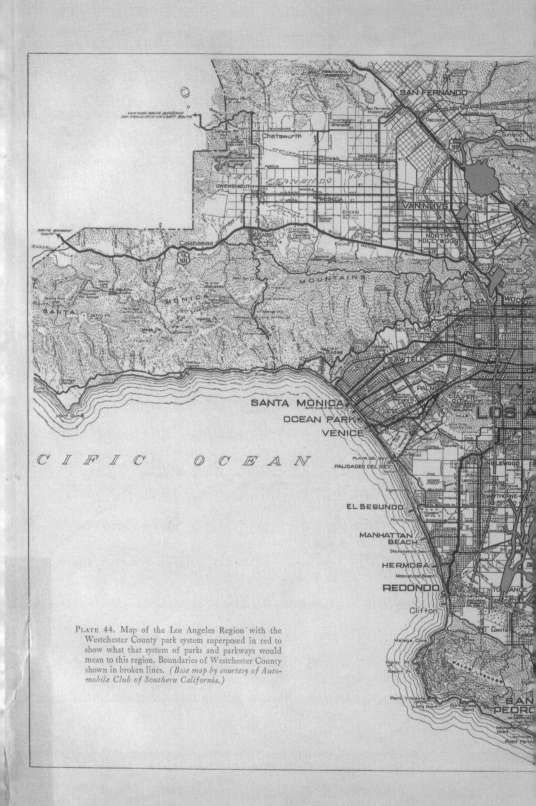

PLATE 44. Map of the Los Angeles Region with the Westchester County park system superposed in red to show what that system of parks and parkways would mean to this region. Boundaries of Westchester County shown in broken lines. (*Base map by courtesy of Automobile Club of Southern California.*)

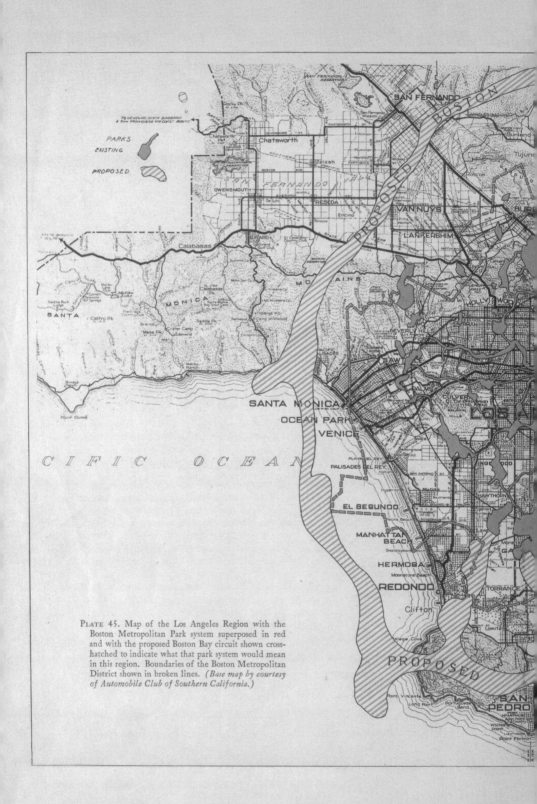

PLATE 45. Map of the Los Angeles Region with the
Boston Metropolitan Park system superposed in red
and with the proposed Boston Bay circuit shown cross-
hatched to indicate what that park system would mean
in this region. Boundaries of the Boston Metropolitan
District shown in broken lines. (*Base map by courtesy
of Automobile Club of Southern California.*)

PLATE 46. General plan for a complete system of parkways and large parks for the Los Angeles Region. (*Base
map by courtesy of Automobile Club of Southern California.*)

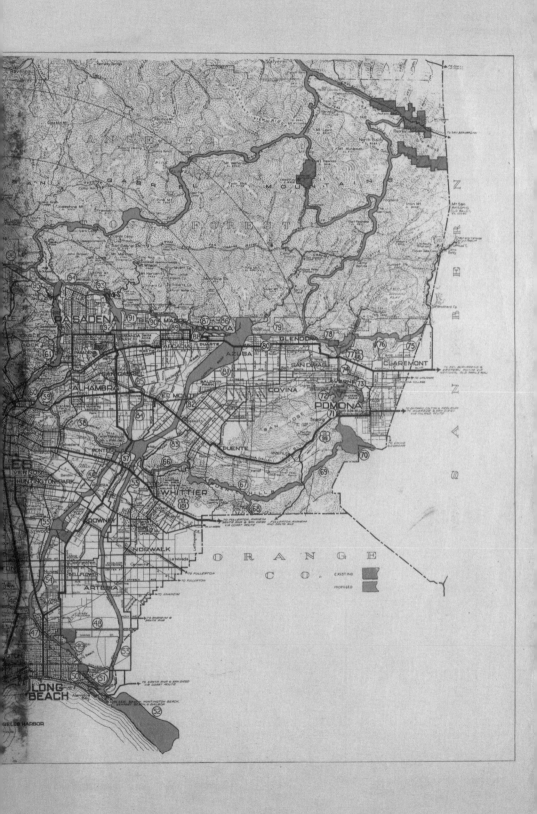

Arroyo Seco and Palos Verdes
Loop Chain:

From the mountains to the sea through the heart of the city. This chain follows the present large public holdings in the Arroyo Seco and Elysian Park with a proposed extension through Exposition Park to the slopes of Baldwin Hills, and from there south to the sea at Palos Verdes, with a loop around the Palos Verdes shores and back to Nigger Slough, tapping the heart of the city and affording a pleasant outlet in both directions for a very large population. This chain includes Nos. 35 to 40, 44 and 45, 61 and 62.

Tujunga Valley and Ballona
Creek Chain:

From the mountains to the sea over the Santa Monica hills. This chain follows the wash and valley of the Tujunga to a favorable place to cross over the hills, dropping down along the Franklin Canyon Reservoirs to cross the west side of Beverly Hills along the various Golf Courses to the Baldwin Hills, then to follow Ballona Creek to the Ballona Slough at Del Rey. It includes units Nos. 21 to 24, and 26 to 33.

Newhall, Chatsworth and
Topanga Canyon Chain:

Also from the mountains to the sea. This chain passes the two large reservoirs, skirts the head of San Fernando Valley to pass over the Santa Monica hills and down Topanga Canyon. It includes a number of points of interest and forms an important route. It includes units Nos. 10 to 17.

Dume Canyon Chain:

From Ventura Boulevard at Triunfo across

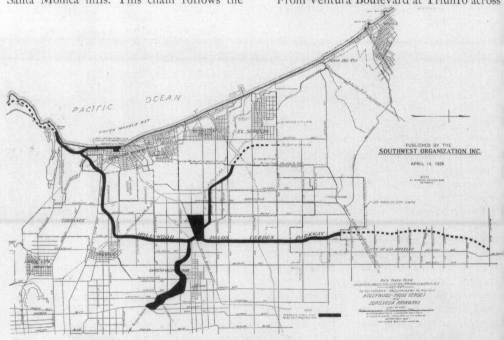

Plate 47. Parkway from Los Angeles to Palos Verdes now being planned by the County as the first real parkway in the Los Angeles Region; the plan shows also Alondra Park in the center and the proposed Sepulveda Parkway and Gardena Valley Park across the center.

202

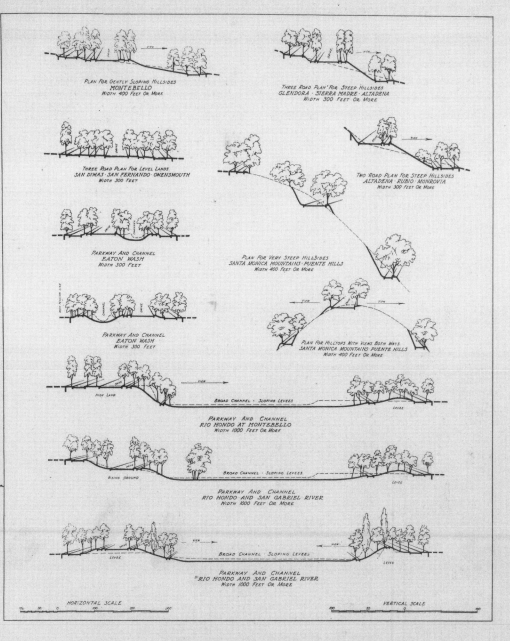

PLAN FOR GENTLY SLOPING HILLSIDES
MONTEBELLO
WIDTH 400 FEET OR MORE

THREE ROAD PLAN FOR STEEP HILLSIDES
GLENDORA · SIERRA MADRE · ALTADENA
WIDTH 300 FEET OR MORE

THREE ROAD PLAN FOR LEVEL LANDS
SAN DIMAS · SAN FERNANDO · ONENSMOUTH
WIDTH 300 FEET

TWO ROAD PLAN FOR STEEP HILLSIDES
ALTADENA · RUBIO · MONROVIA
WIDTH 300 FEET OR MORE

PARKWAY AND CHANNEL
EATON WASH
WIDTH 300 FEET

PLAN FOR VERY STEEP HILLSIDES
SANTA MONICA MOUNTAINS · PUENTE HILLS
WIDTH 400 FEET OR MORE

PARKWAY AND CHANNEL
EATON WASH
WIDTH 300 FEET

PLAN FOR HILLTOPS WITH VIEWS BOTH WAYS
SANTA MONICA MOUNTAINS · PUENTE HILLS
WIDTH 400 FEET OR MORE

PARKWAY AND CHANNEL
RIO HONDO AT MONTEBELLO
WIDTH 1000 FEET OR MORE

PARKWAY AND CHANNEL
RIO HONDO AND SAN GABRIEL RIVER
WIDTH 1000 FEET OR MORE

PARKWAY AND CHANNEL
RIO HONDO AND SAN GABRIEL RIVER
WIDTH 1000 FEET OR MORE

HORIZONTAL SCALE

VERTICAL SCALE

PLATE 48. Typical sections for parkways, showing how various slopes may be treated in a way to produce interesting variety and to protect good views and interesting scenery.

the westerly end of the Santa Monica Mountains to the proposed large terminal park and beach reservation in Dume Canyon. This chain includes Nos. 4 and 5.

SUMMARY OF RECOMMENDATIONS

The areas considered have been numbered for convenience as approximately 100 units and these have been grouped and classified as follows:

Class		Length Miles	Area Acres
A.	Shore Front Roads and Park Areas	36.5	6,690
B.	Large Upland Reservations	87.5	30,575
C.	Large Drainage Basin Reservations	34.3	11,600
D.	Narrower Drainage Basin Reservations	53.9	6,270
E.	Connecting Parkways	214.0	11,560
F.	Enlargements specially valuable for athletic fields, golf, etc.	13.8	4,515
	TOTALS	440.0	71,310

LIST OF PROPOSED PARKWAYS AND RELATED LARGE PARKS

Giving the approximate width, length and area of each, together with the class of purpose for which it is recommended, and numbered as on the General Plan (Plate No. 46).

	Approx. Width in Feet	Length in Miles	Area in Acres	Class
1. Venice and Santa Monica Shore Parkway (land now public)	200-400	7.0	40	A
2. Lower Malibu Coast Parkway (partly in existing highway)	200-400	15.0	350	A
3. Upper Malibu Coast Parkway (partly in existing highway)	200-400	4.0	100	A
4. Dume Canyon Park (including 464 acres U. S. water lands in Ramirez Canyon)		6.0	4500	B
5. Dume Canyon Parkway and Cliffs	400-7000	6.0	2000	E
6. Russell Valley Park		2.0	1400	B
7. Triunfo Canyon Parkway and Cliffs	400-2500	9.0	2200	C
8. Saddle Peak Parkway and Reservation	300-3500	12.0	1000	E
9. Topanga-Mulholland Parkway	300-600	5.0	250	E
10. Lower Topanga Canyon and Cliffs (now highway)	500-1500	5.0	500	E
11. Old Topanga and Dry Canyon Parkway and Cliffs (now highway)	300-2500	6.0	300	E
12. Calabasas Parkway	300	2.3	80	E
13. Escorpion Park		1.1	300	B
14. Escorpion Parkway	300	1.7	60	E
15. Chatsworth Reservoir Park (1170 acres now public)		2.6	2700	B
16. Chatsworth Parkway	300	9.3	500	E
17. San Fernando Reservoir Park (1154 acres now public)		7.7	2750	B
18. San Fernando Parkway	300	4.9	180	E
19. Pacoima Wash Reservation (partly for drainage and percolation)		2.1	400	C
20. Pacoima Parkway	300	3.0	250	E
21. Tujunga Valley Park (partly for drainage and percolation)		4.5	1400	C
22. Tujunga Wash (partly for drainage and percolation)	1200-3500	4.9	1300	C
23. San Fernando Mission Parkway (partly for drainage)	150-400	4.7	190	E
24. Lower Tujunga Parkway (partly existing parks)	300-1200	6.0	530	E
25. Mulholland Parkway (now a highway)	300-600	17.0	500	E
26. Mulholland-Tujunga Parkway	200-600	3.0	150	E
27. Franklin Reservoir Reservations (322 acres in reservoir)		5.0	500	E
28. Beverly Hills Parkway	200-300	4.0	60	E
29. Culver Park Reservation		1.0	150	B
30. Culver Connection	225	0.5	10	E

	Approx. Width in Feet	Length in Miles	Area in Acres	Class
31. Culver Recreation Field		0.2	160	F
32. Ballona Creek Parkway (part for drainage)	600–1000	5.9	430	D
33. Del Rey Park and Bird Refuge (part for drainage) (549 acres in Gun Clubs)		2.0	1000	A
34. Baldwin Hills Parkway	225–600	3.2	90	E
35. Rancho Cienega Recreation Field		0.5	125	F
36. In-town Parkway (including Exposition Park 114 acres)	200–300	8.0	350	E
37. Inglewood Parkway (Plans for acquisition now being completed for southerly portion)	225–300	8.2	225	E
38. Alondra Park (now public)		0.5	315	B
39. Alondra-Palos Verdes Parkway (Plans for acquisition now being completed)	225	8.3	250	E
40. Palos Verdes Coast Road (now in part dedicated)	170–300	9.0	200	A
41. Alondra-Del Rey Parkway	200	9.1	250	E
42. Gardena Valley Park and Parkway Reservation (Plans for acquisition now being completed)		3.9	500	B
43. Nigger Slough Reservation (part for drainage)		3.0	2000	B
44. San Pedro Parkway	225	10.0	300	E
45. San Pedro Hills Reservation		2.1	800	B
46. Dominguez Ranch Parkway	225	2.6	70	E
47. Los Cerritos Parkway		3.0	150	E
48. Bixby Ranch Parkway and Reservation (including 680 acres water and airport lands of Long Beach)	225	5.3	780	E

	Approx. Width in Feet	Length in Miles	Area in Acres	Class
49. Signal Hill Park and Parkway		6.0	400	B
50. Long Beach Recreation Park (now public 400 acres)		3.0	420	B
51. San Gabriel River Mouth (Partly for drainage)	1000	2.3	300	D
52. Bolsa Chica Park Reservation, Bird Refuge and Beach (Outside County limits) (2200 acres in Bolsa Chica Gun Club)		5.5	5000	A
53. Lower San Gabriel River Parkway (partly for drainage)	1000	17.2	2300	D
54. Lower Los Angeles River Parkway (partly for drainage)	1000	6.8	830	D
55. South Gate Recreation Area		1.7	670	F
56. Lower Rio Hondo Parkway (partly for drainage)	1000	6.4	800	D
57. Whittier Narrows Recreation Park and Drainage Basin		6.0	1250	F
58. Montebello Parkway	225–400	12.5	270	E
59. Lincoln Park and Recreation grounds (46.0 acres in existing Park)		0.7	230	F
60. Lincoln-Arroyo Seco Parkway	225	1.8	50	E
61. Arroyo Seco Park and Parkway, including—Sycamore Grove, 15 acres; Victory Park No. 1, 160 acres; Victory Park No. 2, 187 acres; Lower Arroyo, 70 acres; Arroyo Seco, 90 acres; Brookside, 521 acres; Oakgrove and water lands, 334 acres	1377	11.0	1420	B

	Approx. Width in Feet	Length in Miles	Area in Acres	Class
62. Elysian Park (600 acres now public)		3.0	1020	B
63. Los Angeles River Parkway	250–500	2.8	50	E
64. Griffith Park and Adjacent areas (including Griffith Park, 3752 acres; water lands, 443 acres; water lands, 43 acres; water lands, 24 acres; water lands, 42 acres; Playground, 20 acres; total 4324 acres		4.0	4330	B
65. Upper Los Angeles River Parkway (also includes drainage channel)	225–1500	4.0	500	E
66. Turnbull Ridge Parkway	225–400	5.3	210	E
67. West Puente Hills Parkway and Reservation		12.9	1700	B
68. La Habra Connection	300	1.5	50	E
69. East Puente Hills Parkway and Reservation		4.9	620	B
70. Pomona Basin Reservation		3.0	2400	B
71. Pomona Parkway	225	1.3	35	E
72. Puddingstone Reservoir Park (500 acres now in flood control basin)		2.8	1700	B
73. Ganesha Parkway		4.2	90	E
74. La Verne Parkway	225	1.9	50	E
75. San Antonio Cone Reservation (partly for drainage and percolation)		1.7	200	C
76. Live Oak Park and Parkway		3.8	500	B
77. San Dimas Cone Reservation (partly drainage and percolation)		2.1	600	C
78. Glendora-San Dimas Park and Parkway (96 acres now in parks)		3.4	165	E
79. Glendora-Azusa Parkway		4.2	150	E
80. Azusa Golf Grounds Site		0.5	120	F
81. San Gabriel Wash Reservation (partly for drainage and percolation)		7.2	5000	C
82. Upper San Gabriel River Parkway (partly for drainage)	1000–1200	5.5	750	D
83. San Gabriel River Golf Grounds		0.5	360	F
84. Upper Rio Hondo Parkway (partly for drainage)	1000	3.2	500	D
85. Eaton Wash Parkway (partly for drainage)	300–400	6.6	360	D
86. Monrovia-Mt. Olivet Parkway		1.7	190	E
87. Monrovia Parkway		2.1	80	E
88. Monrovia Golf Grounds Site		0.5	250	F
89. Santa Anita Canyon Park and Parkway		1.5	220	B
90. Sierra Madre Parkway (including 70 acres of public water lands)	300	3.8	140	E
91. Sierra Madre Golf Grounds Site		0.2	250	F
92. Eaton Canyon Wash Reservation (partly for drainage and percolation)		2.8	500	C
93. Mt. Rubio Parkway	300	1.7	70	E
94. Altadena Parkway	225	1.9	50	E
95. Arroyo Seco Canyon Parkway to Angeles Mountain Road	300	3.0	100	E
96. La Canada Parkway	300	1.7	85	E
97. Verdugo Creek-Tujunga Parkway	300	5.0	300	E
98. Whiting's Woods and Brand Park Reservation (park now 616 acres)		4.0	1100	F
99. Glendale Parkway	225	2.0	100	E

DETAILED RECOMMENDATIONS

These areas, numbered geographically and not in their order of relative urgency or importance, are described briefly below according to the numbers assigned them.

1. *Venice and Santa Monica Shore Parkway.*

Much of the shore at Venice and a part of that at Santa Monica is now owned by the public to a line just above extreme high-tide line in a way to provide considerable space for bathing and beach recreation, but not wide enough to provide for long-shore pleasure travel. The land under water is publicly owned, and can be developed when the need becomes sufficiently urgent. If groins or underwater longitudinal breakwaters are built, the upland can be widened seaward onto the shallow areas far enough to provide some space at least for pleasure travel parallel to the shore along the fronts of private property. A possible scheme is shown on Plate No. 31. Such a plan would have the objectionable feature, however, of introducing a busy thoroughfare between users of the beach and users of adjacent buildings. Another possible plan that would involve heavy cost but that may in time be justified as already suggested under beaches (Chapters I and V) would be to extend a mole out to sea at the Del Rey marshes and to carry it along two to four thousand feet outside the bathing beaches parallel to the shore, where the water is now 25 to 40 feet deep, to meet the shore again above the private holdings of Santa Monica. Such a plan if developed upon a generous scale, would enclose a large pleasure harbor, would provide relatively still water for bathing, would carry through travel around outside the throngs of beach users and would provide a considerable parking space for autos as well, out of the way of the beach crowds. Bridges in the mole could be made to permit free flow of tides and afford access to small pleasure boats. An outer harbor

has been suggested above the pleasure bay that would care for sailboats and other craft too large to pass under the bridges. As a feature in the general long-shore travel, such a mole would also have great value.

2. *Lower Malibu Coast Parkway.*

From Santa Monica westward to Dume Canyon, the State has acquired a right of way near the shore and has opened a thoroughfare that is destined to be a busy one, especially on holidays and Sundays. This thoroughfare, designed to carry a large volume of traffic, now has an 80 foot right of way for most of its length. It is designed for a single roadway, in a relatively narrow belt of lowland. It extends to publicly owned tidelands on the seaward side in only a few places; there are almost no side roads above it into which parking of cars or congestion of traffic can be diverted, and there is little chance for such roads or areas to be developed because of the cliffs above the road for much of its length.

Most of the pleasure travel that will follow this route will be attracted by the cool sea breezes, the hope of enjoying sea views and the desire to travel along the coast or to stop at the beaches. More than this 80 feet of width will soon be needed, and should be provided. Where the highway is near the shore, few if any buildings should be permitted to interfere with the enjoyment of this route. Where the highway is farther back, private property can be left to develop; but the right of way should be wide enough to permit widening the roads very materially in the future, or possibly creating two or three separate roads for division of traffic either by classes or in one-way roads.

Already the creation of the roadway has led to much activity in use of the adjacent lands and to large increase in land values, and soon this development will create a serious obstacle to any possibility for widening. A right of way 200 feet or more in width would protect the public traffic and pleasure needs for all time; and this, in connection with the acquisition of

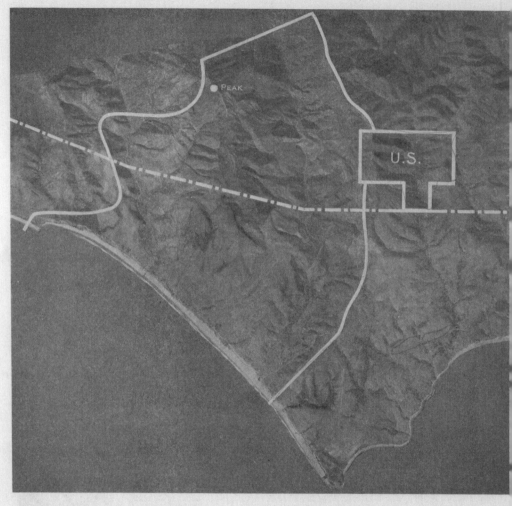

PLATE 49. Airplane view of Dume Canyon and Dume Point, showing in dash the Rancho line and in solid line the areas including the beach, the mesa near the shore, the hill slopes and the peak suited for development of a fine oceanside park, and showing United States land in Ramirez Canyon that should be included. (*Photo by Fairchild.*)

such frontage as may be needed for beach uses, should be accomplished now before further increase in developments is permitted. The County now owns a number of remnants of roadway along parts of this route that might well be exchanged for additional width in the main shore road.

3. *Upper Malibu Coast Parkway.*

Above Dume Canyon, still within the County limits but more remote from the Metropolitan District of Los Angeles, the highway follows the coast for a part of the way, then runs farther inland on the coastal mesa. In this region also a widening of the right of way should be made to 200 feet or more, or the route should be doubled for the same reasons as for Section 2, and in this section State aid may be available both for that part lying within the County and for the part following the shore in Ventura County.

4. *Dume Canyon Park.*

Northwest of Point Dume at Zuma Beach there is a fine shore, about three miles of sandy beach, with the highway just above the storm tide-line, and above this beach the coastal mesa widens out enough to afford space for a fine water-front park having the advantages of the cool ocean-front climate. It is at a reasonable distance from the city for a large terminal reservation; it contains beautiful trees, canyons, and gentle slopes, where park and recreation features in great variety can be developed; and back of this mesa the hills rise to prominent points offering reasonable opportunity for hill climbing and more vigorous exercises, with fine scenery.

The area as a whole is surrounded by natural boundaries that should be recognized, and on the east the United States now has a reservation under lighthouse control in Ramirez Canyon that should also be acquired, and, subject to Government requirements, be made a part of the reservation.

To acquire the beach and mesa land will doubtless prove costly, but the hills and mountain lands comprising possibly 2/3 of the total area are of limited value. The entire project, properly developed, would be of enormous value to great numbers of pleasure-seeking, auto-driving people who will come from the cities and all the inland regions, as well as to visitors from afar. Once acquired, the land may well be held for the present largely as a reservation open to the public. Buildings can be added, conveniences developed and various types of usage encouraged by improvements, as the demand may warrant.

5. *Dume Canyon Parkway and Cliffs.*

From the proposed park above described there should be a cross road leading inland. This should climb the hills above Dume Canyon and should be kept attractive by the preservation of the canyon slopes below and the hill slopes above. In the small basin at the upper end of Dume Canyon, subdivision has started. The valley is so attractive that it would be desirable to preserve this basin also, but that may not prove feasible. The lower end should be 7,000 feet or more in width to include all of Dume Canyon, but at the head of the canyon this can be reduced to 300 or 400 feet, and from there to Triunfo Canyon the road should drop down Sierra Canyon in a reservation that need not be over 300 to 400 feet wide in places, but up to 1,000 feet in others. The land should be acquired now before further improvements are started. The boundaries should preferably follow either ridge lines or be high enough to protect views from proposed roads, in which case they can well be placed on lines where boundary roads may eventually be developed.

Dume Canyon is narrow and very rugged, with high cliffs especially on the east. There are huge boulders in the bottom of the canyon, with sycamores in the lower reaches and fine oaks in the upper end. La Sierra Canyon is more like a broad basin, less picturesque and not so interesting, but is well clothed with shrub growth and has ample room in which to construct a satisfactory parkway, although there is already some inexpensive development along the route.

6. *Russell Valley Park.*

In the northerly corner of the west end of the County, the head of Russell Valley with rolling plains and open areas and with fine oaks offers a place where an inland rural park reservation of large proportions may well be set aside, a space where golf, horseback riding, ball fields, picnics and camping can be encouraged with ample open surroundings. The southeasterly boundary should follow the hills 500 or 600 feet higher south of Triunfo Canyon to include in all about 1,400 acres between the County line, Ventura Boulevard, the old Rancho El Conejo boundary and the slopes above Triunfo Canyon.

7. *Triunfo Canyon Parkway and Cliffs.*

From Russell Park and Sierra Canyon eastward down Triunfo Canyon to Malibu Creek Canyon there is chance for a parkway of remarkable scenic interest and beauty. The boundaries should include the bottom of the valley and so far as possible the cliffs and side slopes as high as can be seen from a satisfactory road line. A width of 400 feet to 2,500 feet should be reserved west of Sierra Canyon, while 250 to 300 feet may suffice in places east from there to Malibu Lake. Around the lake both shores should be protected, with space for a park roadway along the northerly side, and possibly a second local road above that. From the lake eastward to Las Virgenes Canyon Road the reservation should include the narrow valley and some of the Goat Butte lands on the south. The buttes have almost no value for development but are extremely bold and picturesque and should be protected against despoliation.

From there to Cold Creek is a charming bit of pastoral scenery and agricultural development bordering the existing roads. Land that has limited cabin value, but great park value, should have the boundaries far enough back to preserve the scenery and some of the adjacent canyons as well.

The basin at the head of Malibu Canyon offers a fine place for picnics and camping, and there also a widening of the reservation should be made. From there a reservation down Malibu Canyon might well be made eventually, and that too would make an interesting reservation, more picturesque than Topanga Canyon, but this has not been included. No road should ever be built in the bottom of that canyon and a parkway up on the slopes would be very difficult and very costly to construct.

Where the parkway will pass through relatively open areas it may be of limited width, but the boundaries should be so chosen that border roads can be developed. In the gorges the entire bottom and slopes should be acquired. In some of the side valleys it is possible that groups of coast redwoods can be established and many existing trees can be preserved, with ample space for recreation and camping and possibly for golf and other sports as well.

8. *Saddle Peak Parkway and Reservation.*

The top of Saddle Peak is the highest point in the front row of hills; it is a fine outlook point and is being considered as a possible site for an observatory. Already a road has been built up to the peak from the east, and even though very difficult to construct, this road should be extended westward toward Triunfo Canyon in a strip of sufficient width to protect the scenery and to provide a few places at least for automobiles to stop. A road has been surveyed by the County from Cold Creek at the head of Malibu Canyon to Coal Creek on the coast highway to provide a local outlet. This road can be followed from Cold Creek up the hill to the point where it begins to descend and can be continued from there to the Peak on a suitable line.

Following the road recently constructed from the Peak to the Tuna Canyon Road the parkway should turn north at the point where that road begins to descend steeply, and from there at about elevation 1,250 a new route on easier grades and above the local subdivisions should drop down to Topanga Canyon to enter just above Topanga Post Office.

9. *Topanga-Mulholland Parkway.*

From Topanga Canyon and the proposed Saddle Peak route eastward there is now no direct route towards the city, and Mulholland

PLATE 50. Rugged and picturesque cliffs along Lower Topanga Canyon, where land has little value for houses and should be preserved for scenery. (*Photo by Stagg.*)

Highway itself does not command any fine views toward the ocean. Therefore, from a point about 2,500 feet above Topanga Post Office in Old Topanga Canyon a new route is proposed to bridge over the Topanga Canyon Road and to climb gradually to the ridges and then follow the crest northeastward to Mulholland Highway. Throughout a considerable portion of its length where the side slopes are not too rugged and steep, this reservation should be wide enough to allow for development eventually of border roads as well as the central way, and in all the higher portions, at least, the borders should be far enough from the roadway to protect views and to preserve an uninterrupted open foreground.

The route is for the most part through rugged mountain country, but near the westerly end it passes the Trippet Ranch on rolling hills. The mountains are covered with shrubby growth and south of the Trippet Ranch there are fine live oaks.

10. Lower Topanga Canyon and Cliffs.

Extending back from the Coast Highway through an extremely rugged canyon and gorge the lower Topanga Canyon Road is now one of the notable scenic features of the region. Much of the route is still unspoiled, although economic pressure on landowners to realize on the adjacent lands, and desire on the part of others to stop amidst such surroundings is leading to a kind of development that bids fair to destroy much of the character that now forms the chief attraction to the canyon. Much of the land along the lower canyon is unsuited to residential uses, is needed for possible roadway improvements, paths and local stopping places, and has some value for roadside recreation in addition to its large value purely for scenic purposes.

The slopes above the road on both sides should be acquired up to the practical limits of views, and should be kept undefiled. The bottom of the canyon also should be acquired to be kept for general recreation, relatively free from buildings throughout most of the distance, including all of the lowland at and near the mouth of the canyon, where a number of small cottages now occupy land that would otherwise have great value for the gathering of very large numbers of pleasure seekers around camp fires and stoves and in pleasant groves, with a few general buildings capable of caring for very large numbers of people.

11. Old Topanga and Dry Canyon Parkway and Cliffs.

Above Topanga Post Office a new road is now being completed to Calabasas through old Topanga Canyon and Dry Canyon. This road passes through some very attractive small basins having good trees and local open spaces. Cabins are being spread over these areas, and the public is being confined more and more to the limits of the roadway. These areas have very great recreational value for picnics and general enjoyment and the entire canyon bottom with some of the side slopes should be publicly owned. Near the divide there are some very interesting rocks and crags, having

little commercial value, that should be included in the proposed reservation.

Along the route where the roadway necessarily occupies one side of the canyon the land above the road need be little more than 100 feet wide from the center of the road, but on the other side the bottom of the canyon and the slopes for some distance above form a part of the scenery and on that side the reservation should be from 200 feet or 300 feet wide to 1,200 feet or more in places.

12. Calabasas Parkway.

From Ventura Boulevard northward, in extension of the Topanga Parkway, a route is proposed through open land and a few walnut and fruit orchards. This should be a 300-foot three-road parkway, with live oaks, peppers and simple dignified planting.

13. Escorpion Park.

At the extreme western end of the San Fernando Valley the old Rancho Escorpion with grazing land and a few scattered trees on rolling hills offers a chance for an enlargement in the parkway much like an English country park, with possible space for golf and other forms of open land recreation, near to but in addition to the proposed reservation at Chatsworth Reservoir.

14. Escorpion Parkway.

Like the Calabasas route this section also can well be made a simple three-road way, 300 feet or so in width, partly through citrus groves.

15. Chatsworth Reservoir Park.

At the Chatsworth Reservoir there is now a reservation of 1,170 acres of water lands, and around this area there are a number of hills and slopes that should be added to the reservation with the definite purpose of using the areas for recreational purposes, insofar as that will not interfere with reservoir requirements.

PLATE 51. Upper San Fernando Valley with rocks of Chatsworth in the distance, along the base of which the proposed Chatsworth parkway should extend. (*Photo by Fiss.*)

The existence of a large reservation will make possible development of park-like character, and the presence of water will add charm to the park scenery even though the body of water itself cannot be used for recreation.

The boundaries should be selected on reasonable lines for boundary streets, and it is suggested that on the northwest the boundary should extend into Ventura County. The northerly boundary should extend to Oakwood Cemetery.

The area proposed should be treated as a large reservation, to be kept undefiled and to be planted in places, and, as demand increases, to be adapted to use for various appropriate kinds of recreation.

16. Chatsworth Parkway.

Following north and east around the head of the San Fernando Valley from the Chatsworth Reservoir to the San Fernando Reservoir a route is proposed, to be about 300 feet wide and 9 miles long, to be treated most of the way with three roads and planting, with en-

largements for recreation and views at the mouth of Limekiln Canyon, at Mission Canyon, and on the mesa just west of San Fernando Reservoir Park. At the easterly end near the San Fernando Reservoir, the route enters Bull Canyon, there to cross the canyon and follow the easterly side northward through pasture land, leaving houses and citrus groves undisturbed in the westerly portion, and making the existing road along the westerly edge of the barranca the park boundary.

17. San Fernando Reservoir Park.

San Fernando Reservoir is in a reservation of 1,154 acres, and like the Chatsworth Reservoir this area affords a nucleus for a large reservation. The westerly boundary should include the hills to the small valley north from Bull Creek, with a possible road from there to the San Fernando Road. The northerly boundary should follow the latter; the easterly boundary should follow a satisfactory line for a border road, and the southerly line should follow the bottom of the hills, where a road

PLATE 52. San Fernando Reservoir and surrounding hills that should be included in a reservation to be made attractive.

can be built near the edge of existing cultivation and should provide for an outlet toward the San Fernando Mission. The Reservation should be acquired and planted in part and held for gradual development as recommended for Chatsworth Reservoir.

18. San Fernando Parkway.

From the reservoir north and east around the back of San Fernando and along the border of the Olive View Sanatorium to Pacoima Wash a parkway five miles long and 300 feet wide, with space for three roads and planting, is proposed. This route, chiefly through relatively flat land, can be in part formally treated with rows of large growing trees.

19. Pacoima Wash Reservation.

Extending from the forest boundary on the north to Mulholland Street on the south, the Pacoima Wash should be reserved to serve as a drainage channel and percolation basin, and as an interesting park feature as well. The boundary on the west of the southerly portion should follow the top of the steep bank of the wash far enough back to allow for a border road in addition to a park drive. Farther north it should be kept far enough west to allow for a border road only.

On the east the boundary may well follow ranch lines and the city boundary. With the existence of the new dam above this wash, the danger of violent floods is greatly reduced and the area, while occasionally used for percolation, can be used at other times for recreation and can be planted to trees, in part at least, to make an attractive open space.

20. Pacoima Parkway.

From the Pacoima Wash eastward to the Tujunga Valley a route is proposed around the base of the mountain and down the little Tujunga Wash. The northerly boundary should extend to the Edison Power Line above Mulholland Street to avoid leaving a strip of waste land. From Mulholland Street east a 300-foot strip is proposed, suitable for a three-road way, to Kagel Canyon. The parkway will connect with the road to the Dexter Canyon Park now being developed by the County. At Little Tujunga Wash the parkway should be widened to include much of the wash and possibly to extend into the forest, although this canyon has relatively little park value. The wash could serve in part at least for flood control and percolation.

21. Tujunga Valley Park.

Tujunga Valley, three-quarters of a mile wide where the highway crosses, and nearly five miles long from the Edison Power Line at the westerly end to the forest boundaries on the east, is a flat mostly of gravel and boulders with scattering bushes and a few trees. It is now subject to occasional violent floods, but will be less so when the proposed dams in Tujunga Canyon shall have been constructed.

In addition to use for flood control and percolation, this area can be made useful for certain kinds of recreation and should be developed as a simple open landscape reservation. The boundaries along the north should follow along or near the highway in the central portion, leaving considerable valuable acreage be-

PLATE 53. Shores of lake in Prospect Park, Brooklyn, suggesting the kind of development that could be made around the large reservoirs.

tween to the westward and rising on the steep hillsides to the eastward to include much or all the land between the valley and the forest boundary. The south boundary should include all the wash land and enough of the slope to allow for construction of a suitable border road on that side.

The westerly end of the wash is held by a natural dike, so it may prove desirable and feasible to remove the gravel from a portion of the areas to create a lake as a valuable park feature.

An arm of the park should be extended southward from near the easterly end to connect with the existing park in Sunland, and to include some or all of the small buttes to the west of it, north of Michigan Avenue.

22. *Tujunga Wash.*

Extending for 5 miles southward from the Tujunga Valley, the Tujunga Wash and Cone has spread very wide and made several channels, but this is now being confined to a single channel of sufficient width to allow for drainage and percolation, and, for that purpose, it has been estimated that nearly a thousand acres will be needed. In addition to the area needed for flood control, the edges of the wash should be acquired wide enough for ample driveways. It is possible that if the area is wide enough so that water can be spread very wide and shallow, the park roadways can then be carried along within the basin, subject occasionally to actual flooding rather than to be placed upon border dikes close to adjacent private holdings. Under such a plan border roads should follow both sides of the basin in addition to the park drive.

Any plan for a satisfactory improvement of the wash as a park feature is necessarily com-

Plate 54. Large area in Tujunga Wash that is subject to occasional flooding and is likely to be made hideous by costly "developments" if not acquired as an interesting and useful public open space. (*Photo by Fiss.*)

plicated by the existence of enormous gravel plants that operate and should continue to operate in the valley, and also by the need for definite flood control channels that are likely to be very unattractive unless designed on a broad general scheme for a double service of both park and protective purposes. Already some levees have been constructed and others doubtless must be put in to confine flood waters, but if these are kept far enough apart to allow for shallow water, the possibility of developing the area for added park values will be far greater than with narrow, deep channels.

Along this route the question of crossing railroads and busy highways will doubtless lead in time to the consideration of grade separations and probably will mean that the park drive must go over as the other routes are already developed down close to flood levels, leaving little chance for going under them.

23. San Fernando Mission Parkway.

From the Pacoima Wash near the San Fernando Mission to the Tujunga Wash, plans are being developed for a drainage channel to protect Van Nuys. This channel parallels but does not follow the two great power lines and the proposed Whitnall Highway. A parkway should follow that channel from San Fernando Reservoir past the Mission to connect with the Tujunga Wash, nearly 5 miles away.

At the southerly end Payton Avenue can be made the easterly boundary. The drainage channel, to be 200 feet, should have an additional 250 feet for park roads or even more if the channel can be widened and flattened to give it a more park-like character and border roads. Northerly from Pacoima Wash the park road can follow the westerly side of the power

PLATE 55. San Fernando Mission, a point of interest
on proposed line of parkway.

line and parallel to the Whitnall Highway,
where an additional width of 150 feet should
suffice.

At the Mission the boundaries should be
widened out to provide for proper street intersections and for proper relation to the Mission itself.

In the development of the plan space should
be available for borders of eucalyptus trees
with alders and other deciduous planting along
the channel, such as poplars, sycamores and
more brilliant autumn trees, including sour
gums and sweet gums. Possibly palms and
other semi-tropical plants should be used also.

24. Lower Tujunga Parkway.

Passing Van Nuys the drainage channel follows the nearest wash to the eastward, but will
occupy a relatively narrow and deep channel,
while in the wash next farther east there are
now several parks and there are other stretches
of the old wash that could be acquired. Therefore the best location for the next six miles
southward follows that wash and the parks already established.

A width of 300 feet or 400 feet up to 1,200
feet or 1,400 feet should be acquired to allow
ample space for local recreation and park requirements in addition to pleasure travel. Near
the Los Angeles River, south of Second Street

and east of Tujunga Avenue, the parkway
should turn south to the Los Angeles River
and to Ventura Boulevard.

25. Mulholland Parkway.

From Calabasas and the Topanga Canyon
roads eastward to Franklin Canyon, Mulholland Highway should be made a part of the
main park system. From there eastward to
Griffith Park the highway becomes more of
an urban highway and probably should be
considered as such, especially as a parkway is
needed from the Franklin Reservoir to the
Los Angeles River and to the Tujunga Wash
on the north and another to connect with Beverly Hills and the cities beyond on the south.

The question has been raised as to vacating
portions of the 200 foot right of way deeded
for the Mulholland Highway, since the extra
width is not being used, and is not part of any
existing plan for use. If the highway is to be
made a part of the park system, however, a
definite plan should be made for ample parkway development with proper protection of
fine views, space for planting and improvements, allowance for widening and improving
the roadways, and for double roadways in
places and with proper provision for border
roads where feasible and for other connections to adjacent lands. Such plans may permit
abandoning or exchanging certain areas, but
in general should provide rather for acquiring
more land for public use and enjoyment, and
land enough so that satisfactory roads for access can be developed to serve the adjacent remaining private lands.

From Calabasas to the mountains, the highway should be made 300 feet wide with provision for border roads and central road and
ample space for planting. To be of really great
park value the lines of roads should be somewhat modified; in places the roadways can be
doubled to follow both sides of small summits
and there the summits should be acquired also.
So much has been done now that it would be

unfortunate not to carry the work farther to a satisfactory completion. Where the proposed route from Topanga Post Office joins the highway a relatively large summit exists that will be surrounded if the junction is made in both directions, and this might also be added to the reservation.

26. Mulholland-Tujunga Parkway.

From Mulholland Highway at Franklin Reservoir down to the Los Angeles River and the proposed Tujunga Parkway a fairly direct route for comparatively easy construction would drop down through the corner of the Hollywood Country Club lands to the straight portion of Laurel Canyon Road, then rise slightly toward the east to pass around the south and east sides of the subdivided area to meet the Tujunga Parkway just west of Universal City. This route should be 200 feet to 600 feet in width, wide enough to permit proper development of a central roadway with one or two border roads and with space for trees and planting, and with control over the local and distant views.

27. Franklin Reservoir Reservations.

There are now two water land reservations in Franklin Canyon containing 322 acres and there is a road up through the canyon toward Mulholland Highway. The reservoirs form objects of interest. The land reserved provides definite open space that can be made attractive, and offers a possible route for a parkway for part of the distance through the canyon. From the top of the canyon down to a point below the lower reservoir, the park drive should follow the canyon below the reservoirs, but back of most of the development of Beverly Hills the road should turn westward across the foothills and down Peavine Canyon to the mouth of Benedict Canyon.

28. Beverly Hills Parkway.

Four miles from Benedict Canyon to the Hillcrest Country Club, crossing the lower end of Benedict Canyon, the route should follow the westerly edge of the canyon floor southward along the easterly edge of the Los Angeles Country Club to cross Wilshire and Santa Monica Boulevards at the Beverly Hills west city line, continuing along the easterly line of the Westwood Public Golf Course to cross Pico Boulevard and cut through the northeast corner of Hillcrest Country Club and eastward along the old ranch line to the vacant hills beyond. The three country clubs following most of the route are now interesting and probably will remain so for some time to come. As a connecting link through costly lands the reservation may be made relatively narrow. Along the golf courses there will be no need for a border road on that side and a two-road way may prove sufficient with an understanding that should the golf clubs be subdivided, a service road and park strip is to be added by them at that time. In crossing Beverly Boulevard, the route follows that road for 1,000 feet and a special plan for crossing and for parallel roads will be needed and eventually grade separations there and at Wilshire, Santa Monica and Pico Boulevards respectively may also be required. The taking of land now should be sufficient to permit such changes within the park lands when required.

29. Culver Park Reservation.

East of Hillcrest Country Club on the vacant hills of the Arnaz tract, 150 acres of land along the proposed route is now available and is recommended for a local and general park. This area may be reduced somewhat if the area farther east is acquired as recommended for a large recreation center. Boundaries suggested are, on the north the old ranch line and existing streets, on the east existing streets, on the south and west arbitrary lines to enclose an area of about 150 acres.

30. Culver Connection.

From the Arnaz tract to La Cienega Boulevard, a little over a mile, there is now compara-

PLATE 56. Back Bay tidal marshes in Boston converted into an attractive waterside park, such as may be possible for the Del Rey marshes.

tively vacant land between Cadillac and David Avenues that should be acquired, and those street lines should be extended eastward to serve as border roads for a parkway.

31. Culver Recreation Field.

East of La Cienega Boulevard and north of the Pacific Electric Railway there is a triangular tract of 165 acres or so, that is still vacant, that would serve as a fine location for a large regional athletic field and recreation center. It is low and subject to occasional flooding and is not ideal for building uses, but could be used for play. It is within a mile and a half of the city car lines, and is on the Pacific Electric.

32. Ballona Creek Parkway.

From Culver City to the sea the channel of Ballona Creek runs on a very flat gradient. This creek will receive a very large volume of water in occasional storms, from paved streets and roofs of the urban regions above it. The volume of water it may be called on to carry is likely to be much larger at times than is now possible in existing channels and bridges. The new bridge at Culver City has an opening 80 feet wide by 20 feet high. The older bridges are smaller and the channel as defined has less capacity. If the city is allowed to grow around the channel and then widening proves necessary, the economic loss to the community will be very great. It is possible that a channel 10 or 12 feet deep and three or four hundred feet wide may be needed eventually, especially in the lower reaches of the creek. Such a channel if merely walled in is likely to become a very ugly feature in the district, standing empty and dry most of the year, a receptacle for papers and rubbish. The channel can better be developed as part of a parkway. The bottom can have pools and basins in places and a relatively narrow channel for a small run-off with the remaining floor on a slightly higher level to be covered with low growth and occasional trees. In a broad, low channel it would be possible, as suggested for the Tujunga Wash, to have a park driveway within the channel, above all ordinary floods, but subject to occasional flooding, with border streets on still higher levels to afford access to adjacent properties. The big problem today is to acquire a wide right of way 600 feet 1,000 feet wide while much of the land is still open, and to determine on ultimate lines and grades for border roads where private property will certainly be safe from flooding.

33. Del Rey Park and Bird Refuge.

At the mouth of Ballona Creek at Del Rey, near Venice, there is a large area of marsh land and low upland subject to occasional flooding and close to sea level. This area might be made usable in part for housing by filling, especially if other portions are dredged to form lakes or canals and the material is thus obtained nearby. Such work necessarily is costly and the result would have no particular advantages over equal areas on the nearby uplands. The marshes are now frequented by swarms of shore birds, especially in rough weather, and 549 acres of the area is owned by two gun clubs. The entire area has already been considered for a boating harbor, lagoons and a seaside park. Any plan for a pleasure harbor at Venice and ... ...ing additional throngs to the seashore will need a large inland area for auto parking, family picnics, shallow water for small boats, and other forms of recreation, and under a general plan for complete development this marsh area can be made of great recreational value aside from but in connection with the beaches, and some space can still be reserved as a bird refuge.

The entire area should be acquired for such purposes. The boundaries should include nearly all the lands between the two railway lines and, on the west, the ridge and the lagoon near the sea, with one or two broad connections across the occupied sandy strip next to the seashore, and with space enough to allow for a large outlet from Ballona Creek to the still waters of the proposed pleasure harbor.

34. Baldwin Hills Parkway.

From Ballona Creek at Culver City eastward along the north face of the Baldwin Hills a route is planned on a line high enough to command views over the city and to the San Gabriel and San Bernardino Mountains. This strip should be wide enough for a good border road above the park drive to serve the uplands and for another border roadway far enough below the drive to keep buildings from encroaching on the views, and to allow space for planting as well. The width should vary from 225 feet to 600 feet at the steeper places. From the northeast corner of the hills a route to the heart of the city is suggested to cross Mesa Drive and the open lands beyond. Around the east side of the hills the parkway should continue southward to take all land between two existing border streets, and the line should run parallel to and one to two blocks west of Mesa Drive to connect with the Inglewood Parkway. This portion of the route will run through a built-up section and a number of houses will have to be removed. The houses are of good quality, rather above the average, but will be less costly than any plan to widen Mesa Drive to a suitable width, even if that were feasible.

35. Rancho Cienega Recreation Field.

East of Mesa Drive and south of the Pacific Electric Railway there is now a large area of vacant low-lying flat land that would make an ideal site for a regional athletic field. This area of 125 acres should extend from the line of Exposition Boulevard south to the location for the In-town Parkway (No. 36) and from near Mesa Drive eastward across the open lands.

36. In-town Parkway.

From the Baldwin Hills and the proposed routes to Ballona Creek and to Palos Verdes several plans have been considered for a connection toward the center of the city or along the westerly side to Hollywood and Griffith Park or to Silver Lake and Elysian Park. Such plans have been found to involve very great costs through the destruction of expensive buildings without reaching the heart of the city. Just west of the business district of the city in a region of many small houses and shops of less costly character there is a possible location for a connection from the Baldwin Hills to Exposition Park, the campus of the University of Southern California and Elysian Park. This route should be projected at once before big buildings on Sixth Street, Wilshire Boulevard, Seventh Street and elsewhere introduce still further obstacles. For such a route it is possible that some aid may be obtainable from the major highway funds. The route that appears most feasible from a preliminary study runs from Baldwin Hills diagonally across Mesa Drive and the open land to follow the southerly side of Thirty-eighth Place to Thirty-ninth street at Exposition Park; then north across the corners of private property and the park to follow the west side of Hoover and lower Severance Street, and the east side of upper Severance Street through St. James Park and along the east side of Norwood Street, Oak Street, Albany Street and Whittier Street to Seventh Street; then to follow the west side of lower Witmer Street, Hartford Avenue and upper Witmer Street to Beverly Boulevard; then to curve eastward across the small blocks and steep grades to follow the west side of Toluca Street and East Edgeware Road and the east side of Marion Avenue to Sunset Boulevard; then to turn westerly along the south side of Everett Street to the proposed extension of Elysian Park.

This route will enter the proposed extension of the park at an interesting point, where it can bridge over the road in Chavez Ravine to connect with park driveways beyond.

Grade separations at Seventh Street, Wilshire, Sixth Street, Beverly Boulevard, Glendale Boulevard, and Sunset Boulevard will doubtless be required in time and any plan for complete improvements should include sufficient space for such possibilities.

37. Inglewood Parkway.

From Slauson Avenue south to Alondra Park, the route has been designed to follow a block west of and parallel to Mesa Drive south to the city limits, and to remove a number of houses now in the way. The width is planned to be one block part of the way and half a block farther south. At the Santa Fe Railway, plans should provide for ultimately passing under the railroad, but a grade crossing will doubtless be necessary at present.

South of the railroad the Inglewood Cemetery occupies a large area just west of the route and possibly the park lands should bend westward to skirt the cemetery for some distance, then bend eastward again to connect with the parkway 225 feet wide, now being designed from the city line southward to Alondra Park and beyond, passing the Potrero Country Club and following the line of Cypress Street much of the way.

38. Alondra Park.

Southwest of the city in a section where there was no large park of any sort, the County recently acquired 315 acres of gently rolling agricultural land on which to develop a park of both local and regional character. A plan has been made for complete development of the area, to include local playgrounds in the two southern corners, a general athletic field in the central portion, ball fields in the northeast corner and a golf course in the westerly portion, with walks and drives through the area and ample spaces for planting to produce a general park-like character. (See Plate 58.)

39. Alondra-Palos Verdes Parkway.

Much land has been acquired, some construction has been started and plans have been

PLATE 57. Sketch for a broad, dignified and attractive parkway 225 feet in width with three road-ways planned to extend from Los Angeles city to the sea at Palos Verdes.

largely completed for the acquisition and improvement of this section of the proposed Hollywood-Palos Verdes Parkway by the County (known as A. & I. No. 15). Designed as a three-road parkway 225 feet or more in width, this bids fair to be the first real parkway in the Los Angeles Region; one to become an important link in a pleasure route from the city to the seashore. In the plans provision has been made for ultimate separation of grades at several crossings.

40. Palos Verdes Coast Road.

Following along or near the top of the cliffs of the rugged coast line of the hills of Palos Verdes, from the beaches of Redondo to the proposed park reservation near San Pedro, a pleasure road is already built and in use, and in part has been dedicated of ample width to ensure to the public for all time a route through pleasant surroundings with fine views over the ocean. For the first four miles south of Redondo the parkway has been established 180 feet or more in width between building lines, and for nearly half this distance the land between the highway and the ocean is established as a quasi-public park never to be built upon. The right of way has been restricted against commercial traffic under restrictions that are designed to continue in perpetuity.

Through the unsubdivided areas farther south the present Coast Road has been designed to be 170 feet in width, with reservation of the coastal areas for a part of the way, and

PLATE 58. Design for Alondra Park, 315 acres, recently acquired by the County.

with double roadways wherever possible to afford fine outlooks for travelers in both directions.

41. Alondra-Del Rey Parkway.

From the Del Rey Marshes and the proposed terminal park there south and eastward, a parkway connection is needed. Two routes for this offer advantages: one following the shore to the beach cities, then following the hilltops back of the built-up areas to cross to Alondra Park or some point farther south; the other route to follow the line of proposed Sepulveda cut-off that has already been surveyed and planned as a proposed County improvement, making a direct connection from Del Rey Marshes to Alondra Park through areas now mostly undeveloped, but Mines Field, oil wells and other activities now developing may prove serious obstacles to this line. The shore route offers the advantage that the city now has about 200 acres in the Hyperion Sewer Farm, much of which may be available for the creation of a large shore front park just west of El Segundo, all in close connection with a shore front parkway.

42. Gardena Valley Park and Parkway Reservation.

Plans have already been considered under a County Project (A. & I. No. 15) to acquire the bottom of Gardena Valley and the side slopes, including border road locations, and a general plan has been made for ultimate development as a pleasant rural park with lakes, boathouses, ball fields, picnic groves and many attractive features. The entire area should be acquired at once, the boundary roads should be developed, and planted; some planting should be done in the interior and the balance can be held as a reservation for more intensive improvement from time to time as demand may warrant. This valley is subject to heavy flooding at rare intervals and the lower end is so near sea level that it will drain very slowly. The area can be used for park purposes even if flooded occasionally, but is not suitable for other uses. This park reservation should be materially extended through the lower valley as described in the next section.

43. Nigger Slough Reservation.

In connection with and in extension of the proposed Gardena Valley Reservation, the broad flat flood plane of Nigger Slough now unfit for residential or commercial uses should be made a park.

Nigger Slough is one of several large areas in the County where the elevation of the land is so near sea level that ordinary methods of gravity drainage by open channels and by storm sewers, whether undertaken at the general expense by the Flood Control District or at local expense by local drainage districts, cannot possibly protect the land from constantly repeated serious inundations, unless the surface of the land is raised in a wholesale manner by filling. (See Appendix No. III.)

This area could be developed as a large lowland park, having interesting interior park character with ample space for various forms of recreation, with possible extension of lakes and pools and water sports suggested for Gardena Valley also.

44. San Pedro Parkway.

From Nigger Slough to the hills back of San Pedro a parkway 225 feet or more in width as a connection from the Nigger Slough to the Palos Verdes Coast Road is proposed. This route should cross the lowlands back of Wilmington and Harbor City, skirting the slopes north of San Pedro to the hills overlooking the shore. The route can possibly be designed in a way to benefit by the park reservations already set aside in the Miraleste section of Palos Verdes. The south end of the reservation should be wide enough to connect with both the uphill and the down-hill hairpin turns of the existing Palos Verdes Coast Road.

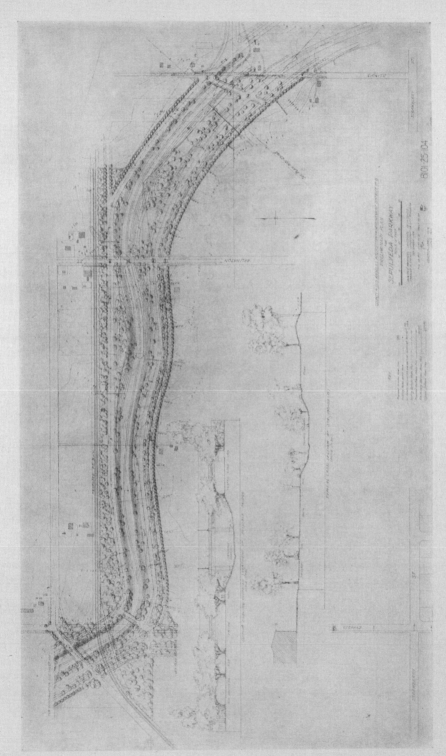

PLATE 59. Design for a parkway through Gardena Valley and Nigger Slough with two border roads, a park drive and a channel for drainage.

45. *San Pedro Hills Reservation.*

San Pedro Hill, just back of San Pedro and close to the sea, rises to a height of 1,480 feet above sea level. It commands views in all directions over the sea and over the coastal plains and the surrounding cities back into the mountains 100 miles or more away. The face of the hill offers space for park development where the cool climate of the sea can be enjoyed. The base of the hills includes the rock coast and cliffs above the sea and connects with the Coast Road toward the west and the Royal Palms Golf Course and possible roads into San Pedro toward the east.

The small amount of fairly level area on the slopes above the sea could be developed for picnic areas and parking of a large number of cars, as that will be a necessary feature of any park in this region. Such a park may offer unusual opportunities for such public interests as a marine biological station and museum, or a botanic garden with experimental stations.

46. *Dominguez Ranch Parkway.*

From Nigger Slough eastward to the Los Angeles River a connecting route is needed as a link in the one main east and west parkway between Los Angeles and the ocean. This section offers no particular interest and should be as direct as possible. It will necessarily pass through industrial areas and cross busy highways. It should be 225 feet or more in width to be ample for planting and for three roadways.

47. *Los Cerritos Parkway.*

From the Pacific Electric bridge over the Los Angeles River at Los Cerritos southeastward to the Union Pacific Railroad at Signal Hill a route is planned, to be 225 feet or more in width. For much of the way the location will be on a side hill and a greater width will be needed for border roadways at the top and bottom of the slopes. There are many oil wells along this route which can be left to operate within the reservation under special agreements until abandoned.

48. *Bixby Ranch Parkway and Reservation.*

The City of Long Beach now owns nearly 700 acres of airport and water lands north of Signal Hill, most of which should be included in a reservation in connection with a parkway eastward and as a large athletic field or should be correlated in a way to be mutually beneficial for park uses and other uses. East of the water lands, the route crosses flat land and can be 225 feet or more in width, crossing the San Gabriel River to the Orange County line at a point from which it can be extended eventually farther eastward. Through the water lands, two connections toward the southwest are possible, one to Signal Hill on the south, the other near the Union Pacific Railroad to the proposed Signal Hill Parkway.

49. *Signal Hill Park and Parkway.*

Overlooking the City of Long Beach and the plains behind it, Signal Hill stands out alone as a commanding hill. It is now covered with oil wells and shops and oil sumps, but those features are temporary as compared to the life of the city. The time is not far off when activities will slacken and some of the land will be released from oil uses, and gradually the entire area will be opened for other uses.

Under a plan for gradual development, much of the land could doubtless be acquired now, subject to sub-surface rights and partial use of the surface where needed. Possibly much of the surface of the land could be obtained practically without cost in exchange for certain privileges and relinquishments under proper negotiations.

The first need on the hill will be for a through east and west roadway as a link in the park system, and it is possible that this could be developed among the derricks and shops while they are still in active use. At the easterly end, there is a reservoir that should be included within the limits of the plans.

The park drive should follow one or both sides of the hill high enough in places to afford fine views over the country, the city and the harbor. The hill itself eventually can be made a striking feature in the landscape with forest trees in place of the present oil derricks, with possibly a bowl for concerts, and other park features.

50. *Long Beach Recreation Park.*

The City of Long Beach has a park of 400 acres in the line of the proposed main parkway, extending from Anaheim Road to the San Gabriel River near the County line. The park contains within its boundaries several private holdings that should be eliminated. The width of the easterly end is scarcely sufficient to afford a satisfactory location for a through roadway toward the coast unless the water area be reduced or additional land be acquired. The park doubtless should continue chiefly as a local park and some form of agreement should be made between the city and such authority as may be established to deal with the larger problems of regional pleasure travel.

51. *San Gabriel River Mouth.*

Below Anaheim Street, the San Gabriel River has been relocated to flow between dikes in a relatively narrow channel 300 feet to 330 feet wide. A park strip should be added along each side, several hundred feet in width and so designed that the entire river mouth can be treated as a broad, open parkway.

The southwesterly boundary should extend to the east line of Recreation Park and the south boundary should extend to Alamitos Bay, and a connection toward the southeast should extend to the County line and the Bolsa Chica Marshes.

52. *Bolsa Chica Park Reservation, Bird Refuge and Beach.*

Just outside the southeast County line the

large marsh area of Bolsa Chica and Los Alamitos and the beach from Anaheim Landing to Huntington Beach offers a fine location for a big water-front reservation similar to that proposed for the Del Rey Marshes, but more extensive, and to include more actual ocean front. This area, lying in Orange County, but on the main diagonal coast road from Long Beach and the Los Angeles Region southward, offers great possibilities for the development of a large and important recreational area, pleasure bays, picnic grounds, and wild reservations all within easy access of a very large proportion of the people of the metropolitan region.

The beach (as discussed in Chapter V on beaches) is being cut up into small lots and has a number of small houses upon it, but its greatest value would be attained if it were kept open for large numbers of the general public. The marshes have little value, except at the back where oil has been found, and the boundaries should either exclude the oil wells or include them subject to the life of their operations.

Five and one-half miles long by a mile and a half wide, the area that could reasonably be set aside for public use and enjoyment includes about 5,000 acres.

A part of this area, about 2,200 acres, is owned by the Bolsa Chica Gun Club, and that part might reasonably be acquired subject to certain rights and reservations for a definite period of time to permit them to continue to occupy it until the public requires the area.

This reservation should be of much value not only to Los Angeles and Orange County, but also to Riverside and San Bernardino Counties, as it is one of their nearest shores, and one that can be reached without passing through busy urban areas.

53. *Lower San Gabriel River Parkway.*

From the San Gabriel River mouth below Anaheim Road, northward to the Whittier Narrows, a distance of over 17 miles, plans are now being considered for acquiring a channel for flood control for the San Gabriel River.

PLATE 60. San Gabriel River near the Narrows, showing area needed for drainage that has park value, especially if the border vegetation can be preserved. (*Photo by Fiss.*)

The river bed is several hundred feet wide but under control may be narrowed and deepened, thus destroying the not unpleasant tree-bordered wash that now exists. For a parkway it would be far more attractive to preserve much of the character of the present bed, to develop border roads and dikes farther apart in a less formal manner and to make some uses of the land in the bed of the stream during most of the year when little or no water is running.

Just what plan can be developed to bring to the community the most interest and enjoyment from the river treatment will depend on many factors, but of these the first and most important will mean the acquisition of a strip not less than 1,000 feet wide outside which private property may be encouraged to develop, and to hold the central area for carefully de-vised plans for use and control, and not to change the present character until a definite plan for a satisfactory result has been adopted.

Any plan for development will be somewhat complicated by the existence of electric power lines and railroad lines along the banks in places, and the boundaries should be adjusted to relate properly to these also.

Already a few subdivisions have extended into the line of desired reservation, but not extensively. In places the boundaries should include existing streets subject to right of use.

The most serious question in any plan for improvement will necessarily be that of providing satisfactory and effective revetments or other forms of river control without seriously injuring the landscape value of the river bed. The prospect of a dam in the mountains to control the river offers a possibility of materially

PLATE 61. Riverway in Boston, once a pestilential drainage channel but redeemed under a joint plan for drainage and park uses.

reducing the size of revetments required.

The river banks offer opportunities for special types of tree growth and special effects of foliage with cottonwoods, sycamores, willows and poplars, wild grapes and even sweet gums and sour gums. The already interesting foliage masses can be kept and made a striking feature of the district instead of giving way to an ugly vacant channel.

At the northerly end on the east bank is the old Pio Pico Adobe House, owned by the State, that should be included within the parkway reservation.

54. *Lower Los Angeles River Parkway.*

From Long Beach northward to the Rio Hondo at South Gate the Lower Los Angeles River offers much the same problem as the Lower San Gabriel. Below Los Cerritos the river has already been confined between revetments 300 feet apart and commercial use of the edges has been encouraged and made possible so that parkway construction of an interesting character would be difficult and costly if attempted, but above there where a right of way 400 feet or 500 feet wide is needed for flood control a width of 1,000 feet or so should be acquired, and above Center Street where the channel is broad and meandering a width of 1,500 feet or so in places seems desirable.

55. *South Gate Recreational Area at the County Farm.*

Between the County Farm and the Rio Hondo and in the point of land between that and the Los Angeles River for a distance of nearly two miles to the Stewart and Gray Road, and for a width of 4,500 feet or so, there is an area that should be acquired for a public

PLATE 62. Gorge in Montebello Hills not yet invaded by development, where a parkway can be located. (*Photo by Fiss.*)

reservation in connection with park and drainage problems and to serve as a large athletic field as well. This area should be acquired in advance of intensive development and held as a reservation to be made more and more useful to the public as the need for it increases. It is possible that the area might be acquired by the County and used as an extension of the County Farm in part at least, but held as a public trust to become available for recreation when demand for its use becomes sufficiently urgent.

As the Region grows and values increase the time may come that a part or all of the County Farm of 480 acres may be diverted to other uses, or may be available as an extension of the proposed recreation area and it is quite possible that a portion of the farm may be made accessible to the general public in connection with a general plan for the development of the park and recreational features, and that on the other hand a part of the reservation may be used for grazing by the County live stock in a way to improve the pastoral type of scenery and to add interest to the reservation itself.

56. *Lower Rio Hondo Parkway.*

Above the County Farm to Montebello and the Whittier Narrows for a distance of 6 miles, the same flood channel problem exists. There again a width of 1,000 feet or more would afford ample space for a satisfactory development. North of Telegraph Road the west shore rises in steep bluffs and offers some interesting problems in locating park drives and border roads. Some small private houses in Montebello should be removed. On the west bank south of Telegraph Road is one of the original adobe ranch houses of the great Spanish grant to Don Antonio Maria Lugo. This house, which was later the home of Henry T. Gage, one of California's notable governors, with its adjacent grounds, should be included in the reservation.

57. *Whittier Narrows Recreation Park and Drainage Basin.*

Between the hills at Whittier and at Montebello, the San Gabriel and the Rio Hondo Rivers run parallel and little over a mile apart. There the underground river waters come to the surface forced up by the natural dike that crosses the narrows. In this area, two proposed routes from the south, two from the north and one each from the east and the west converge, so into this area a large amount of pleasure travel will be brought from all directions. Therefore, the entire area should be made a public reservation and recreation field. The boundaries should include both rivers and extend to Lincoln Avenue on the west and to Durfee Road on the north, and should include under agreement the 49 acre water reserve of Pasadena in the valley and extend south to the existing cross street.

In the northwest portion, there are oil wells that should be included in the area but may be allowed to continue to operate under a suitable agreement.

In this area it may be possible to develop lagoons for bathing and boating and to afford various other forms of recreation.

58. *Montebello Parkway.*

From Whittier Narrows west to Lincoln Park a parkway just above the base of Montebello hills is proposed. This route will run through open land most of the way, although plans are being made now for the subdivision of one large tract that should be crossed.

Oil fields will be crossed near the easterly end where special concessions may prove necessary. Just south of Third Street, west of Montebello, a cut 60 or 80 feet in depth will be

PLATE 63. Plan for parkway through gorge in Montebello Hills as prepared by Regional Planning Commission.

necessary through a narrow ridge. West from there to Coyote Pass and Garvey Avenue a side hill parkway is proposed where three roads should be planned, the middle park drive high enough above the lower border road to protect forever a view out over the city, and another border drive above on a satisfactory location. In this section a width of 250 feet to 300 feet at least will be needed. West of Coyote Pass the route should turn northward in the deep canyon already considered by the Regional Planning Commission for a parkway, then turn west at the Pacific Electric tracks, cross the tracks through the pass and then cross Alhambra Avenue to the back of Ascot Speedway. This route will involve considerable heavy construction and some costly land takings, but it follows the most feasible line to enter Los Angeles city from the east, and it offers some interesting scenic features along the route. Plans should provide sufficient space for possible grade separations where likely to be needed in the future.

59. Lincoln Park and Recreation Grounds.

Los Angeles City now has 46 acres in Lincoln Park developed as a neighborhood park. Just east of this park is a large area as yet undeveloped or slightly used, including the Ascot Track. The entire area, containing possibly 180 acres, should be acquired as one of several proposed regional athletic fields, to be developed for intensive use by a large number of athletic teams and players in various games.

North of Lincoln Park is the Selig Zoo that should be added to the park as a city feature if it can be obtained on advantageous terms. The city now has no satisfactory zoo within easy access and a well-organized public zoo would afford pleasure to many people.

60. Lincoln-Arroyo Seco Parkway.

From Lincoln Park to the Arroyo Seco and toward the city a connection is needed, and for that a satisfactory route is not easily found. The best location seems to be to cross Mission Road from Lincoln Park on a viaduct and to skirt the base of the hills northward to the Arroyo. Possibly the small hill opposite Lincoln Park should be included in the taking to provide material for fill and location for an overhead crossing over Mission Road and over North Broadway also. The route if kept east of Pasadena Avenue can drop down into the Arroyo to join with other park roads toward the city. Part of the way the width may be less than 225 feet; in other portions it should be wider to meet existing street and lot lines.

61. Arroyo Seco Park and Parkway.

From the Los Angeles River at Elysian Park to the mountains, already much of the land for a park and parkway system up the Arroyo Seco has been acquired, including Sycamore Grove, two Victory Parks, Lower Arroyo Park, Arroyo Seco Park, Brookside Park, Oak Grove Park, and the water lands, 1,377 acres in all. About 43 acres more will be needed to eliminate various small holdings and to complete the route, or more if boundaries are adjusted to allow space for really ample park driveways where narrow streets now exist.

From Riverside Drive at Elysian Park the park road should either cross on the Dayton Avenue bridge or dip down and follow the river bed, or both, then follow the edges of Arroyo Seco low enough to pass under bridges, with connections up to the streets in places.

Through the parks from Victory Park to the mountains some remnants of private property should be acquired and park drives and border streets of ample width are needed to afford pleasant continuous travel from the city to the mountains. At Devil's Gate Dam there is need for a good connection around the dam on one or both sides and possibly for some additional lands to protect park views and park features.

Under the Colorado Street bridge there is still some vacant land in private ownership that should be publicly owned.

62. Elysian Park.

The City of Los Angeles now owns 600 acres in Elysian Park hilltops, but does not own the enclosed valleys toward the south. About 420 acres more should be acquired to increase the value of this close-in public property and plans are now being considered by the city to acquire a large additional area. This additional area is partly vacant and should be acquired before large sums are spent to develop it for other uses. A street has been suggested through Chavez Ravine, but it will be much better if that entire ravine can be devoted to recreation and made a part of the park. From the proposed In-town parkway at the southwest corner a drive should extend along the westerly ridge through the pass at the head of Chavez Ravine to connect with the proposed Los Angeles River Parkway in both directions along the northerly face of the hills.

With the proposed extension of the area, various types of park scenery can be developed within the park itself, and recreation can be encouraged in a way not possible in the hilltops alone. Insofar as possible, the steep slopes surrounding the ravine should be included in the park extension to control the park scenery and to keep private development from detracting from the park value.

The bottom of Chavez Ravine near the easterly end is easily accessible from the city and would make an ideal place for athletic fields of large size to serve large crowds, and on the slopes a golf course may be possible.

63. *Los Angeles River Parkway*.

Riverside Drive from Elysian Park to Griffith Park has been considered as a possible route for a parkway. It is now being developed as a busy street and is destined to become simply another traffic artery. The south bank of the Los Angeles River on the other hand is a region of low valuations and poor developments, and from the Dayton Avenue bridge to Griffith Park the bank of the river and the river bed should be acquired with enough upland to afford ample space for park-like treatment. This route should connect with the Arroyo Seco under the Dayton Avenue bridge, and with the Elysian Park entrance where it now enters Riverside Drive northwest of the park.

64. *Griffith Park*.

Griffith Park is the largest public area in the Los Angeles Region, outside the National Forest reserves, available for park and recreation

purposes. The park contains nearly 4,000 acres, largely in steep mountain lands of relatively limited recreational value. About one-quarter of its area, however, is level enough to be used for active recreation. Of this intensively usable land nearly one-fourth has recently been cut off from the main park by Victory Boulevard, a busy highway along the river bottom through the park.

In addition to Griffith Park lands there are now also several other areas of adjacent water lands in public ownership, having high value for park and recreational uses, that should be and doubtless can be made a part of the park reservation. Nearly 600 acres of such lands might be made available and thus serve to almost double the intensively usable area of this great park reservation.

The park and water lands also are unfortunately cut in two by the highway above referred to, so that there is little possibility for creating a single large area having a fine quality of interior park scenery and unity unless that road can be diverted around the park, but in the northwesterly section where much of the water land lies there is still space that can possibly be dedicated to a high type of park use if properly guarded. Victory Boulevard can be and should be relocated east of the river along the power line and the intervening small parcels should be publicly acquired.

In Griffith Park itself there are possibilities for the development of park features and park scenery of far greater value than have as yet been brought out. In time, space should be found elsewhere on land of less value for the propagating houses and shops and work yards so that the interior of the great park area can be made more park-like and beautiful and those fine open spaces can be kept free from obstructions as open scenery for public enjoyment. The valley sections of the park itself can be made finer and finer as time goes on by the gradual development of suitable enclosing and surrounding foliage masses, and by development of interior groups and masses of vegetation with finely proportioned, varied and interesting open spaces where most appropriate.

There is an enormous value to the people at large in a simple, quiet, beautiful open space screened in and kept free from all evidences of commercial activities and from the less attractive conditions of the outside world. This value can be created and developed only in such an area as Griffith Park or other large reservations, and it is worth creating even to the exclusion of some of the many kinds of activities that insist on finding a place in the best part of every large park.

65. Upper Los Angeles River Parkway.

Four miles from Griffith Park westward to the Tujunga Wash, the upper Los Angeles River with adjacent water lands and necessary drainage channels offers a good location for a parkway westward. Already the river is being constricted to an ugly deep channel and the channel is being crowded on both sides. A strip wide enough to provide reasonable space for border streets, and a pleasant roadway should be from four or five hundred feet wide to twelve or fifteen hundred feet in places. Near Griffith Park all of the pleasant valley on the south side of the river should be included in the boundaries. Farther west the present private road may well serve for the south boundary as a park drive and border street. Through Universal City and west to the sharp bend in Ventura Boulevard the local street should form the south boundary.

The banks along the river range from five to thirty feet in height and are higher along the south than the north shore most of the way. The park drive doubtless should follow the southerly shore.

66. Turnbull Ridge Parkway.

From the Whittier Narrows eastward up the Puente hillsides to Turnbull Canyon Road, several possible routes for a parkway two hundred and twenty-five to four hundred feet or more in width have been considered, but the most practical and most attractive route climbs the southerly face of the hills from the Workman Mill Road along the route recently surveyed for a roadway by the County. A width of two hundred and fifty feet along Workman Mill Road is needed to continue that road as a fairly wide traffic road on the easterly edge of the parkway. This route would make a veritable skyline drive overlooking the valley and plains to the south.

67. West Puente Hills Parkway.

From the Turnbull Ridge Parkway an extension nearly thirteen miles long and from three hundred to four thousand feet in width is proposed to include the hilltops down to reasonable locations for side roads. This route following along or near the line recently surveyed by the County for a ridge road from Turnbull Canyon to Brea Canyon Road, passes through some interesting canyon tops and upland valleys with attractive native growth and with the finest views toward the mountains. A few oil wells will be encountered and land acquisition can be made subject to existing operating privileges. This is one of the routes where the owners of large areas might well be persuaded to set aside land for a really *fine* public parkway and reservation as a splendid monument to the donors. The plan should be so designed that the remaining property along the sides can be developed to the best advantage and will benefit by being near a really fine public-way.

68. La Habra Connection.

From the proposed parkway above mentioned, a branch toward La Habra as far as the County line should be acquired to meet the possible location that may seem best in Orange County for future extensions.

69. *East Puente Hills Parkway and Reservation.*

East of Brea Canyon Road across the Diamond Bar Ranch to the big basin southwest of Pomona, a route is proposed following the ridge line as surveyed by the County for a short distance, then turning northward across the head of the broad upland valley of the Diamond Bar Ranch to enter the big basin from the west.

A number of fine upland features along the route should be preserved and boundaries have been suggested to include these.

At the head of Rodeo Canyon, two miles east of Brea Canyon Road, where the route turns north, a rugged and picturesque gorge is encountered that will involve heavy construction.

This parkway should be ample in width as proposed for the West Puente Hills Section, and this is another section that might possibly be acquired by gift on the same basis as that suggested for West Puente Hills (No. 67 above).

70. *Pomona Basin Reservation.*

Southwest of the City of Pomona at the east end of the Puente Hills lies a large basin surrounded by rolling hills. The basin with the slopes to the rim of the hills includes about 2,400 acres. The entire area with one farm group and with fine oaks and sycamores in the canyons would make a complete self-contained unit for an extensive rural park of the finest type, with ample space for all sorts of recreation activities, such as golf, ball games, picnic groves, auto camps and hiking trails. The area should be acquired and reserved for later development. It is apparently now in only one or two large ownerships and should be acquired before it may be broken up.

71. *Pomona Parkway.*

From the Pomona basin northward to the Puddingstone Reservoir to cross the upper end of the Spadra Valley at its narrowest point a connection is planned to drop gradually from the rim of the above mentioned basin along the face of the slopes among existing native walnut trees and in fine command of views of the mountains. Crossing the valley, where two highways and the railroad are in close proximity, plans for the parkway should provide for ultimately bridging over all of them, even though grade crossings may be necessary at present. North of the railroad, walnut groves on flat lands are to be crossed and a three-road parkway 225 feet or 250 feet wide should be made. From there the route should climb northeasterly toward the Puddingstone Reservoir.

72. *Puddingstone Reservoir Park.*

The Puddingstone dam now subjects 500 acres or so of land to flooding and may create at times a fairly large lake, fluctuating with rainy conditions and, therefore, of limited recreational value. The reservoir lies in a basin at the east end of the San Jose Hills. A reservation surrounding the basin and extending to reasonable lines for boundary streets is suggested. Most of the land is unimproved, except some areas lying so low that they will be flooded by the reservoir.

73. *Ganesha Parkway.*

East of the Puddingstone Reservoir, the County owns 73 acres of fair grounds, and south of that the City of Pomona owns 61 acres in Ganesha Park. From the proposed reservation at Puddingstone Reservoir a connection to these two areas may well be made, although not an essential link in the proposed park system.

74. *La Verne Parkway.*

From Puddingstone Reservoir northward to the mountains across the upper end of Walnut Creek and of San Dimas Valley a route is proposed as a short link between the hills and the mountains. This connection, involving no particular local problems, can best be acquired along the east side of Artesia Avenue, leaving that street for the westerly road of a three-road parkway.

75. *San Antonio Cone Reservation.*

As the easterly unit of the proposed route along the base of the mountains, the San Antonio Cone extending from the County east line to the flood control basin at Palmer Canyon offers a peculiar type of landscape scenery. At the mouth of the San Antonio Canyon a perfect cone has formed as a half circle several miles across, extending into Claremont and far into San Bernardino County. High up on this cone against the base of the mountains, the parkway is planned to cross the cone, and on the cone a broad strip of land having relatively low commercial value should be included in the plan, wide enough to preserve a bit of the natural character of this type of country and wide enough to keep a fairly open view in both directions over the length of the route. This area may doubtless have some value for absorption of water as well. The northerly boundary may well include the existing road along the base of the mountains and an extension of its line westerly. The width should be not less than 1,200 feet to 1,500 feet for much of the distance, to be in scale with the country.

Oaks, sycamores, yuccas, holly and other native growth should be developed to frame the scenery along this route.

76. *Live Oak Park and Parkway.*

From the Palmer Canyon Flood Basin westward to San Dimas Wash the route should pass above the foothills around the branches of Thompson Creek and across Live Oak Creek and Marshall Creek through most interesting rolling uplands of wild and rugged waste lands. The reservation should be broad enough to control local scenery and to include many interesting local features; the boundaries where practical should follow lines where border roads can be made to encourage favorable development of the adjacent areas. Both sides of Marshall Creek should be included in the taking, and west of these Wheeler Street can form the southerly boundary of the proposed reservation; a width of 800 feet to 1,000 feet is desirable.

Along this section ample space should be available for picnic grounds and many forms of recreation for auto parties. This will form one of the most picturesque and attractive sections of the foothills chain of parkways.

77. *San Dimas Cone Reservation.*

From the San Dimas Canyon two miles westward to Artesia Avenue a reservation is proposed on the San Dimas Cone. This cone is less conspicuous as a geological feature than the San Antonio Cone and it has been deeply eroded. The plan proposes to acquire the wash and some of the land to the north of it up to the forest boundary, and to include the 16-acre County park at Artesia Avenue and the 80-acre park on the hills above. The main park driveway may follow one or both of two routes, one along the San Dimas Road to the small park, then turning northwest; the other to cross on the foothills higher up and to connect also with the route from La Verne (No. 74).

78. *Glendora-San Dimas Parkway.*

From Artesia Avenue the route should run west to the Dalton Washes across the foothills high above most of the present developments. This is another picturesque and attractive link in the proposed system, through grazing and wild lands, having much natural charm along the way that should be preserved, and commanding fine outlooks and views over the valley.

79. *Glendora-Azusa Parkway.*

From the Dalton Washes across the foot-hills above Glendora and Azusa to the San Gabriel Wash, a straight line location has been surveyed by the County for a main highway. This line should be followed, taking a width of 300 feet or so from Sierra Madre Avenue southward to provide for a three-road attractive formal parkway. This route crosses land well developed in citrus orchards, and it is possible that the land can be acquired for three roads to be developed when needed and the citrus groves can be continued in use for many years.

80. *Azusa Golf Grounds Site.*

Northeast of Azusa the hilly spur projecting from the mountain mass and lying south of Sierra Madre Avenue, offers an unusually interesting site for golf grounds and picnic grounds, and for local park uses as well. The land is now undeveloped and should not be costly.

81. *San Gabriel Wash Reservation.*

From the south boundary of the forest at the mouth of San Gabriel Canyon southwestward to the Whittier Narrows, the San Gabriel River has spread out across a basin three or four miles in width, forming an enormous wash in which the river is now partly confined to a limited channel. In the wash are large gravel pits and gravel washing machines, and in places houses and cultivation have spread into the wash, but there is still a large area of waste land subject to possible flooding at long intervals and unsuitable for agricultural or residential development. In this area a spreading basin of several thousand acres is needed for flood waters, and around this area definite boundaries for a good type of development should be established. Within the boundaries of the wash, plans should be made for the most satisfactory development of basins, dikes, gravel pits, highway crossings, recreation areas and general park scenery of a type suited to the situation and attractive as a foreground over which to enjoy views of the mountains from border streets and park drives. A plan has been studied to include within the wash from the Forest on the north to Los Angeles Street west of Baldwin Park a strip 4,000 feet to 9,000 feet wide and seven miles long, containing 5,000 acres, within which area the land should be definitely withdrawn from real estate development to form a public reservation to be used under a well-devised and appropriate plan for the various purposes it can best be made to serve. In places gravel pits are being sunk to a tremendous depth so close to existing highways and railways that trouble will certainly arise, and conditions are likely to become still worse in time unless properly controlled.

While it is evident that a plan for broad and extensive development is needed to lead toward a satisfactory permanent result in this great area, such as can be produced only under general public control, it is difficult to say just what that plan should be until far more time and study has been given the problem than is possible in a preliminary survey. That such a plan is needed is evident and it is believed that a large reservation such as is here proposed should be made at once subject to joint planning by flood control authorities, park authorities, and suitable agreements regulating the gravel removal that can be and should be permitted or encouraged to continue to operate within the area.

In the area the County already owns gravel pits, various road plans are already being developed and flood control dikes have been built, but so far there is yet no definite plan designed to lead to a complete and satisfactory solution of the problems of the entire area under the many more or less conflicting interests. At the upper end the mountain-side parkway should cross, and border streets and park drives along both sides of the wash should eventually serve as important north and south routes.

82. Upper San Gabriel River Parkway.

From the wash above described southward for five and a half miles to the Whittier Narrows the river wash becomes more constricted. A few hundred feet of width will be required for flood waters and a few hundred feet more should be added for park drives and border streets, making a total of 1,000 feet to 1,200 feet that should be acquired, within which the flood channel can be left rather irrregular in outline and less sluice-like than would be necessary within a narrower space.

83. San Gabriel River Golf Grounds.

Between the Workman Mill Road and the river north of the Puente Hills, two miles above the Whittier Narrows, there is an area of 360 acres that would make an excellent golf site on rolling mesa land that could well be made a part of the reservation to be reached by pleasant parkways from various directions. The lowland is farmed and the upland is dry farm or pasture land with some fine trees and with room for generous planting when developed.

84. Upper Rio Hondo Parkway.

From the Whittier Narrows northward to Eaton Wash, a distance of three miles, a channel 400 feet to 500 feet in width is needed for flood control with three channels entering from the north. Along that wash a strip 1,000 feet or so in width should be acquired for parkway development similar to that proposed for other like channels.

Near the southerly end the west boundary should be kept up on the high bluffs overlooking the valley, where a number of oil wells exist that may be allowed to continue under proper regulation as proposed for other sections also.

85. Eaton Wash Parkway.

Six and one-half miles from the Rio Hondo to Villa Avenue, Pasadena, a right of way 50 feet to 110 feet wide will be needed for flood control. Along the northerly portion of this wash the Edison Company has a power line and along the high banks and existing streets the developments suggest a very irregular boundary for a parkway 300 feet to 400 feet wide, just wide enough to include those features of interest and of necessity, and to afford room for a park driveway, and on each side for border streets.

A careful study of the route has shown that a plan can be devised to make a satisfactory parkway along the wash of varied and interesting character, but needing much detailed study to determine the exact boundaries that can best serve for the needed right of way.

86. Monrovia-Mount Olivet Parkway.

From the upper end of San Gabriel Wash for nearly two miles westward following along or near the line surveyed by the County, the route should rise gradually to the top of the mesa back of Mt. Olivet Station. In the upland section, a broad area of the rougher lands should be included to protect the scenery along the parkway and to protect fine views out over the valley from this elevated location.

Fine oaks and pines are included within proposed boundaries and afford excellent places for picnics and park enjoyment.

87. Monrovia Parkway.

From the canyon above Mt. Olivet westward for the next two miles to the line of Myrtle Avenue in Monrovia the route should follow a line higher up than the line surveyed by the County. The right of way should be 250 feet or 300 feet wide and the lines should be irregular to follow good grades and avoid existing improvements where feasible. For much of the way the route passes through one large estate, and passes along the upper edge of some fine citrus groves. Heavy grading will be necessary in crossing Monrovia Canyon.

88. *Monrovia Golf Grounds Site.*

Northeast of Monrovia on one large estate there are rolling hills, partly used for grain fields and partly in citrus groves, that would make an ideal site for a country park and golf site, from 120 acres to 250 acres or more in extent. In locating the parkway through this region it may prove more practical and better economy to take much or all of the estate than to pay dearly for a part of it and in that case this additional area most certainly should be included.

89. *Santa Anita Canyon Park and Parkway.*

Behind the mountain spur between the Myrtle Street line and Santa Anita Canyon for a distance of a mile and a half through upland valleys, practically following the line surveyed by the County, the parkway should widen out to include most of the beautiful basin at the easterly end, and all of the smaller valley descending westward to Santa Anita Canyon. Some heavy grading will be necessary in entering the canyon, but that seems unavoidable.

Live oaks, sycamores and eucalyptus trees make this route especially attractive. Some small orchards of doubtful value will be included in the boundaries.

90. *Sierra Madre Parkway.*

From Santa Anita Canyon westward to Eaton Wash, nearly four miles, the proposed route follows the line surveyed by the County part of the way, but rises above it in Sierra Madre and falls below it farther westward. In order to get a fair width the parkway should include some land above Grandview Avenue. Through Sierra Madre a number of houses will necessarily be involved and a number of streets should be included, but as a link in a long line the additional cost for this section

will be justified and the length of the improved area to be crossed is not great as compared to the length of the total scheme.

Several vineyards will be involved and some heavy grading is necessary to cross the many canyons that penetrate the mountains above. Just west of the center of Sierra Madre the 70 acres of publicly owned water land in Bailey Canyon that has been considered for a possible botanic garden joins the parkway on the north and that area should certainly be kept as a public holding with its fine canyon mouth and bit of open land.

91. *Sierra Madre Golf Grounds Site.*

South of the parkway, partly west of but chiefly east of Sierra Madre Villa Avenue, 120 to 250 acres of rolling foothills land now mostly in vineyards or vacant may well be included in the reservation to control the view out over the valley from the parkway and to afford space for a bit of country park and possibly golf grounds.

92. *Eaton Canyon Wash Reservation.*

From Villa Avenue, Pasadena, and Eaton Wash to the mouth of Eaton Canyon proper, a distance of nearly three miles, the wash widens out from 2,000 feet to 3,000 feet in width, forming a broad basin that should be entirely included in a reservation. A drive should follow the westerly rim of the basin, the foothills parkway should swing into the basin from the east on the face of the bluffs to reach the bottom near the head of the basin where the reservation will be relatively narrow, and from there it should follow the northerly face just above the floor along the line surveyed by the County to the upper end of the wash, and cross the Mt. Wilson Toll Road.

The upper end of the wash above New York Avenue is beautifully wooded with oaks and sycamores, and offers a fine place for picnics, regional recreation, and local park interests as well. Extremely fine views over the valley are found from the high mesa along the proposed upper roadway. About 120 acres of the upper end is now owned by the City of Pasadena as water land.

93. Mt. Rubio Parkway.

From Eaton Wash westward about two miles along the line surveyed by the County to Rubio Canyon at Lake Avenue, the route follows a high location through a corner of the National Forest and chiefly back of developed areas. The National Forest section contains some fine eucalyptus trees and there are oaks and sycamores in Rubio Wash. This section should be wide enough to provide for two or three roadways and to control the views below, possibly 250 feet to 300 feet.

94. Altadena Parkway.

From Lake Avenue to the Arroyo Seco at Millard Canyon, approximately two miles, the route should follow the surveyed line, except at Millard Canyon, where a higher line is proposed to avoid a dip in the profile. Loma Alta Drive can be used as the lower road of a three-road plan, 225 feet to 300 feet in width. There is little development of costly character above Loma Alta Drive.

At Millard Canyon some costly grading will be required to drop down into and across the canyon. There is now a plan for a State Highway bridge across the mouth of Arroyo Seco, but that will probably be needed primarily for local traffic from many nearby streets.

At the mouth of Arroyo Seco the parkways will meet one of the most agreeable and attractive of the existing canyons lying within the forest boundaries, but now largely privately owned by water companies and others. For the protection of the water, the City of Pasadena would be better served if all private holdings were eliminated and the canyon were closed as a water reservation. The canyon has, however, a very large recreational value, and it is believed that most of the private holdings should be acquired for this purpose. The build-ings should nearly all be removed and the public should be admitted only under such restrictions as will ensure proper protection of the water. Under any plan the entire floor of the canyon and the adjacent slopes should be acquired as public or semi-public lands.

95. Arroyo Seco to Angeles Mountain Road Parkway.

From the mouth of Arroyo Seco Canyon westward, climbing the face of the steep, rugged hills on a five or six per cent grade, the route is planned to rise to the mesa near the Edison Substation overlooking the canyon to the north and the valleys toward the south, and to connect with the proposed Angeles Mountain Road now being planned by the State. (See Chapter VII, No. 211.)

96. Angeles Mountain Road to La Canada and Whiting's Woods Parkway.

From the Angeles Mountain Road near the Edison Substation westward along the proposed new State Highway line to Haskell Street and from there westward to cross Michigan Avenue near Rosemont Avenue, and to cross blocks diagonally southwest to Whiting's Woods, a parkway four miles long is planned, most of the way through area partly subdivided and sparsely occupied. This should be 225 feet to 300 feet wide with additional area at a few places where fine views should be protected.

97. Verdugo Creek-Tujunga Parkway.

From Whiting's Woods westward the route should follow Verdugo Creek, taking in the drainage channel, which should be 25 feet to 80 feet wide, with enough of the side slopes to include trees and shrubby growth and to preserve the natural charm of the valley, and with width enough also for a broad pleasure drive and for additional border roads. Near the upper end of Verdugo Creek the small open basin should be included to make an attractive local park. At the head of the valley the route should cross diagonally over to the mountains to wind down around the north side of the City of Tujunga to the saddle where the canyon road now crosses over into Tujunga Canyon. From there the roadway should wind down the north face of the small butte westward to the canyon floor to connect with proposed roads in the Tujunga Wash and with roads into the forest area.·

98. Whiting's Woods and Brand Park Reservation.

On the south side of Verdugo Hills there is now a public area of 616 acres in Brand Park that is undeveloped and little used. North of this park on the northerly slopes is an attractive wooded canyon and basin at Whiting's Woods that has been suggested for park purposes. The lower portion of the woods offers a fine place for picnics and a small woodland park. The basin back of it affords space for a pleasureway on winding lines and easy grades up to the summit in Brand Park 3,000 feet above the sea with a connection through the saddle a few hundred feet lower, from which the park drive can again wind down the southerly slope in Brand Park to the canyon in its southwesterly boundary to meet the proposed Glendale Parkway to Griffith Park. This proposed road over the hill having the advantage of large park reservations along the route and fine views from the summit will form the only practicable cross connection for a parkway in a distance of ten or fifteen miles between the Tujunga Wash and the Arroyo Seco. Much heavy construction will be involved in making a satisfactory road.

99. Glendale Parkway.

From Brand Park to Griffith Park across Glendale a parkway connection is proposed to loop westward, then southeastward back of Glendale, then to cross Grand View Avenue

PLATE 64. Whiting's Woods, a shady spot in the north face of Verdugo Hills that should be included in a public reservation. (*Photo by Fiss.*)

and to turn south parallel to the avenue to the northeast corner of Griffith Park. Some improvements will have to be crossed through Glendale to reach Griffith Park, but the most feasible route should be acquired or made a part of definite plans.

ESTIMATE OF COSTS

A detailed estimate of probable cost for acquisition and for improvement has been made for each unit of the system on the basis of present selling values for acreage and lots in each neighborhood, on the assumption of purchases and of improvements adapted to the conditions near each section.

Table of Estimated Probable Purchase Costs and Improvement Costs for Each Type of Park and Parkway

Type of Project Proposed	Length in Miles	Area in Acres	Cost of Acquisition	Cost of Improvements	Total Cost
A. Shore Front Roads and Park Areas (not including costs estimated under Beaches)	36.5	6,690	$ 7,400,000	$18,400,000	$ 25,800,000
B. Large Upland Reservations	87.5	30,575	22,670,000	6,260,000	28,930,000
C. Large Drainage Basin Reservations	34.3	11,600	9,250,000	2,410,000	11,660,000
D. Narrower Drainage Basin Reservations	53.9	6,270	12,800,000	3,150,000	15,950,000
E. Connecting Parkways	214.0	11,560	39,830,000	13,610,000	53,440,000
F. Special sites for large athletic fields, or golf courses or other uses (not including costs included under Regional Athletic Fields)	13.8	4,515	7,220,000	850,000	8,070,000
Totals	440.0	71,310	$99,170,000	$44,680,000	$143,850,000

Conclusion

The above list of park and parkway projects covers the complete system proposed for the Los Angeles Region south of the National Forest and the mountains. It does include many but not all the existing parks, some of which are fairly large and important. It does not include beaches, strictly local parks and playgrounds, or the more remote reservations in the mountains, deserts and islands, which are discussed in other chapters.

A large number of units involving a large total acreage has been discussed, extending over a great variety of kinds of land and involving many problems. *No attempt has been made to indicate the order of urgency or preference for them*, as such a selection must depend upon local factors that are constantly changing, and that should be determined as the work proceeds and as conditions affecting the various plans call for action.

Two distinct problems are involved in the plans, first the acquisition of lands and second the improvement of the projects to meet existing demands. The need for acquisition of lands is urgent now for nearly all projects before further obstacles make acquisition more difficult. The need for improvement in a general preliminary way is fairly urgent now for most of the plans, but apparently is not realized by the public in general probably because the great possibilities for better things that might be done here and the immense opportunities for better things that are being lost through lack of plans and action have not yet been made sufficiently evident.

APPENDICES

APPENDIX NO. I

List of Schools in the Los Angeles Region Having More Than Five Acres Each of Available Playground Space

(District and Unit Numbers refer to Plate 25 on Page 52.)

District No.	Unit No.		Area of Site in Acres	Area of Recreation Space in Acres
A-2	2	Owensmouth High	25.2	6.89
A-5	4	Van Nuys High	23.2	10.32
A-6	23	Lankershim High	18.2	14.0
A-8	9	Broadway High, Glendale	24.0	22.34
A-8	18	New High (to be built), Glendale	19.95	10.00
A-8	19	Eleanor Toll Junior High, Glendale	9.23	8.
B-1	31	Santa Monica High	13.78	6.89
B-1	42	Venice High (Jr. & Sr.)	24.95	14.9
B-2	6	Fairfax High, L. A.	24.3	9.5
B-2	21	John Burroughs Junior High	10.4	5.28
B-2	23	Los Angeles High	18.5	9.3
B-2	30	Beverly Hills High	18.1	12.1
B-3	43	J. A. Foshay Junior High, L. A.	7.4	5.3
C-1	1	El Segundo Elementary	7.21	5.
C-1	2	El Segundo High	18.92	15.
C-2	9	Inglewood Union High, Lawndale	10.	5.
C-2	18	Wiseburn Elementary, Hawthorne	10.	7.
C-3	9	Jefferson High, L. A.	18.4	6.86
C-3	34	George Washington High, L. A.	16.75	11.55
C-3	47	John C. Fremont High, Los Angeles	26.1	10.9
C-3	51	Hyde Park Elementary	9.8	5.12
C-5	4	Enterprise Elementary, Compton	9.	6.3
C-5	6	Compton High	13.7	6.85
C-5	7	Abraham Lincoln, Compton	8.4	5.88
C-6	2	Narbonne High, Lomita	11.1	9.38
C-6	8	Phineas Banning High, Wilmington	9.5	8.33
C-7	5	Valmonte Elementary Site, Palos Verdes	11.23	7.86
C-7	19	Montemalaga Elementary Site, Palos Verdes	9.67	6.77
C-7	22	Zurita Elementary Site, Palos Verdes	10.15	7.11
C-7	35	Coronel Park High Site, Palos Verdes	45.83	23.
C-7	43	Lunada Bay Elementary Site, Palos Verdes	10.58	7.41
C-7	47	Margate Elementary, Palos Verdes	27.73	19.4
D-1	4	Huntington Park High	20.	10.
D-1	19	High School Site, Huntington Park	18.	9.
D-1	30	Lindbergh Elementary, Compton	8.6	6.02
D-1	33	Poinsettia Elementary, Compton	7.5	5.25
D-3	2	East Whittier Elementary	8.48	5.94
D-3	13	Whittier High	13.4	6.7
D-3	20	Excelsior Union High, Norwalk	18.66	9.4
D-5	3	Lowell Elementary, Long Beach	12.02	8.4

District No.	Unit No.		Area of Site in Acres	Area of Recreation Space in Acres	District No.	Unit No.		Area of Site in Acres	Area of Recreation Space in Acres
D-5	5	Wilson High, Long Beach	13.56	6.78	F-3	1	San Marino Elementary	12.	6.
D-5	27	Long Beach Polytechnic High	19.16	9.58	F-3	5	Garfield Elementary, Pasadena	11.5	8.05
E-2	617	Hollenbeck Junior High and Boyle Heights School, L.A.	9.86	6.1	F-3	12	High School, Alhambra	17.82	8.9
					F-3	21	Alhambra High	8.66	6.1
E-3	30	James A. Garfield Junior High, L. A.	15.	11.5	F-4	11	High School, Monrovia	23.6	11.8
E-3	3	Washington Elementary, Los Angeles	7.5	5.25	F-4	17	Huntington Elementary, Monrovia	7.3	5.1
E-3	4	Montebello High	12.0	6.	F-4	18	Monrovia High	8.5	5.95
F-1	2	Eagle Rock High	12.5	6.25	F-4	24	Woodrow Wilson Junior High, Pasadena	14.98	13.73
F-2	9	Pasadena High School	38.0	12.66	F-5	2	El Monte High	17.	9.
F-2	11	McKinley Junior High, Pasadena	8.05	6.05	F-5	3	Columbia Elementary, El Monte	12.1	8.47
F-2	15	John Muir Technology, Pasadena	15.	11.	F-6	4	Citrus Union High, Glendora	15.68	7.89
F-2	17	Thos. Jefferson School, Pasadena	10.57	7.	F-6	19	Puente High	10.71	5.85
F-2	18	John Marshall Junior High, Pasadena	14.37	10.8	F-8	3	Bonita High, San Dimas	22.41	11.25
F-2	21	Henry W. Longfellow School, Pasadena	7.75	5.	F-8	4	La Verne Elementary	8.6	6.
					F-8	6	Claremont High	18.22	9.1
F-2	22	Washington Junior High, Pasadena	12.64	10.5	F-8	13	Pomona High	7.9	5.53
					Y-4	2	Torrance High	18.75	10.58
F-2	41	South Pasadena City High	15.	7.5	Y-4	3	Torrance Elementary	7.55	5.3
							Total		636.82*

*Since the above was written the Redondo Union High has acquired a 22-acre athletic field.

APPENDIX NO. II

List of Existing Public and Quasi-Public Open Spaces, Each of One Acre or More, in the Los Angeles Region (Not Including School Grounds)

(District and Unit Numbers refer to Plate 25 on Page 52.)

SUMMARY BY CLASSES

Public Recreation Areas:	No. of Areas	No. of Acres
A. Parks and playgrounds 1 to 5 acres each	95	247
B. Parks and playgrounds 5 to 25 acres each	69	839
C. Parks and playgrounds 25 to 100 acres each	19	934
D. Parks and playgrounds 100 to 1,000 acres each	12	3,896
E. Parks and playgrounds over 1,000 acres	1	3,752
Total	196	9,668
Quasi-Public Recreation Areas:		
F. Golf Clubs and Country Clubs (outside of park areas)	42	6,179
Quasi-Public Areas Having Possibly Some Recreational Value:		
G. Water Lands	53	6,523
H. Cemeteries	17	1,347
I. Public Institutions and other quasi-public lands (County, City, State and private)	36	6,267
J. Airports (not including small landing fields)	31	2,991

DETAILED LIST OF UNITS *

District No.	Unit No.		Class	Areas in Acres
A-1	4	Chatsworth Reservoir Lands	G	1,309
A-1	5	Oakwood Cemetery, Chatsworth	H	200
A-2	8	Encino Park, Ventura Blvd.	A	4
A-2	9	El Caballero Country Club	F	120
A-2	10	St. Andrews Golf Club	F	120
A-4	6	Brand Park at San Fernando Mission	B	6
A-4	8	County Rock Quarry at Pacoima on San Fernando Road	I	191
A-4	11	San Fernando Reservoir Lands	G	1,154
A-4	12	Olive View Sanatorium, San Fernando	I	656
A-4	14	San Fernando Mission	I	4
A-4	15	San Fernando Mission Gardens	I	38
A-4	16	Maclay Reservoir Site, San Fernando	G	6
A-4	17	Gravel Pit on San Fernando Road	I	40
A-4	18	Dexter Park, near Little Tujunga Canyon	K	40
A-5	9	Sherman Way, San Fernando Valley	I	24
A-5	10	Whitley Park Country Club, North Hollywood	F	210
A-5	11	Hollywood Country Club, North Hollywood	F	104
A-5	13	Eagle Airport, North Hollywood	J	33
A-5	14	Hollywood Heights Polo and Hunting Club	F	78
A-6	9	Pioneer Park, Burbank	C	35
A-6	22	North Hollywood Park and Playground	C	90
A-6	26	Burbank Park, Burbank	A	2
A-6	28	Lakeside Golf Club, North Hollywood	F	100
A-6	30	Glendale Airport, Glendale	J	20
A-6	31	Burbank Civic Center	B	20
A-6	32	Lockheed Airport, Burbank	J	16
A-6	33	Panorama Airport, Burbank	J	38
A-6	34	Valhalla Cemetery, Burbank	H	135
A-6	35	Hollywood Aero Corporation Field, North Hollywood	J	40
A-6	37	Fernangeles Park, North Hollywood	B	10

*Since this table was compiled, Metropolitan Airport, near Van Nuys, Boeing Airport, in Burbank, Western Air Express Field, in Alhambra, and possibly some others, have been opened, while some airports have been discontinued. Areas included in this table under one acre in extent are shown as one acre; other fractions have also been omitted.

District No.	Unit No.		Class	Areas in Acres
A-6	38	Stonehurst Park, near San Fernando	B	15
A-6	39	Lopez Water Lands in Burbank	G	53
A-6	40	Lopez Water Lands in Burbank	G	43
A-6	41	Lopez Water Lands in Burbank	G	10
A-6	42	Pomeroy-Hooker Water Land in Burbank	G	445
A-6	43	Los Angeles Water Land in Burbank	G	22
A-6	45	Victory-Van Owen Park, North Hollywood	D	172
A-7	2	Monte Vista Park, Sunland	B	6
A-7	11	Flintridge Country Club	F	70
A-7	13	Oakmont Country Club, Glendale	F	80
A-8	13	Nibley Park, Glendale	A	2
A-8	16	Brockmont Park, Glendale	A	1
A-8	31	Hawley Playground (leased), Los Angeles	B	5
A-8	32	Griffith Park Playground	B	20
A-8	34	Verdugo Park Site, Glendale	B	10
A-8	35	Griffith Park Airport, Los Angeles	J	157
A-8	37	Raymond Reservoir Site, Glendale	G	6
A-8	39	Grandview Cemetery, Glendale	H	30
A-8	45	Glendale Reservoir Park	A	2
A-8	49	Campbell Street Reservoir Site, Glendale	G	14
A-8	52	Glendale Reservoir Site	G	9
A-8	57	Hunters Highland Tract—L.A. Water (San Fernando Road)	G	9
A-8	58	L. A. Water Land on Los Angeles River	G	23
A-8	59	L. A. Water Land on Glendale Boulevard	G	44
B-1	2	Riviera Golf Club at Santa Monica	F	300
B-1	3	Brentwood Country Club at Santa Monica	F	140
B-1	7	U.C.L.A. Campus	I	430
B-1	10	Los Angeles Country Club at Beverly Hills	F	334
B-1	11	Westwood Golf Club at Beverly Hills	F	180
B-1	12	Hillcrest Country Club at Beverly Hills	F	141
B-1	13	Rancho Country Club at Beverly Hills	F	187
B-1	17	Sawtelle Playground	B	7
B-1	18	Clover Field Airport, Santa Monica	J	55
B-1	19	Santa Monica Golf Course	D	109

District No.	Unit No.		Clas
B-1	24	Palisades Avenue Park, Santa Monica	A
B-1	26	Palisades Park, Santa Monica	C
B-1	27	Lincoln Park, Santa Monica	B
B-1	34	Santa Monica Playground	A
B-1	40	Machado Park, Venice	A
B-1	47	Westward Ho Country Club at Venice	F
B-1	49	Lindbergh Park, Culver City	A
B-1	50	Victory Park, Culver City	A
B-1	53	California Country Club at Culver City	F
B-1	57	South Side Park, Santa Monica	A
B-1	58	Holmby Park, near Beverly Hills	B
B-1	61	Lindbergh Park, Santa Monica	A
B-1	62	Santa Monica Park	A
B-1	63	Woodlawn Cemetery, Santa Monica	H
B-1	64	Venice Beach	B
B-1	66	Soldiers' Home, Sawtelle	I
B-1	68	Santa Monica Reservoir Site	G
B-1	71	Centinela Sewer Lands, Mesmer City	I
B-1	73	Del Rey Gun Club, Venice	F
B-1	74	Recreation Gun Club, Venice	F
B-2	1	Beverly Hills Park	A
B-2	3	Beverly Hills Park	A
B-2	9	Poinsettia Playground, Hollywood	B
B-2	14	De Longpre Park, Hollywood	A
B-2	19	Wilshire Country Club	F
B-2	22	Los Angeles High School Memorial Park, Wilshire District	A
B-2	25	Hancock Park, Wilshire District	B
B-2	27	La Cienega Playground, Beverly Hills	B
B-2	29	Roxbury Playground, Beverly Hills	B
B-2	38	Queen Anne Playground, Wilshire District	A
B-2	41	Vermont Avenue Parkway, Hollywood	B
B-2	42	Vineyard Playground, Wilshire District	A
B-2	46	Hollywood Cemetery	H
B-2	47	California Aerial Transport Field, near Beverly Hills	J
B-3	5	Yale Playground, Los Angeles	A
B-3	11	Echo Park Playground, Los Angeles	A
B-3	64	Barnsdall Park, Los Angeles	B
B-3	65	Silver Lake Reservoir Land, Los Angeles	G

District No.	Unit No.		Class	Areas in Acres
B-3	68	Echo Park, Los Angeles	C	27
B-3	69	Everett Park, Los Angeles	A	1
B-3	70	Old U.C.L.A. Campus, Los Angeles	I	25
B-3	72	La Fayette Park, Los Angeles	B	11
B-3	73	Westlake Park, Los Angeles	C	32
B-3	74	Terrace Park	A	1
B-3	75	University of Southern California Campus	I	10
B-3	76	Occidental Boulevard Park, Los Angeles	A	1
B-3	77	St. James Park, Los Angeles	A	1
B-3	78	Rosedale Cemetery, Los Angeles	H	50
B-3	79	Belleview Reservoir Land, Los Angeles	G	9
B-3	80	Rowena Reservoir Land, Los Angeles	G	10
B-3	81	Darby Street Reservoir Land, Los Angeles	G	9
C-1	3	El Segundo Park	A	3
C-1	4	Los Angeles University Lands, Del Rey Hills	I	1.00
C-1	5	Loyola University, Del Rey Hills	I	100
C-1	6	Del Rey Beach Park	B	10
C-1	7	Hyperion Sewer Land, near El Segundo	I	200
C-1	9	Mines Field Airport, near Inglewood	J	640
C-2	1	Fox Hills Country Club, near Culver City	F	280
C-2	3	Inglewood Park	C	50
C-2	8	Potrero Country Club, Inglewood	F	100
C-2	15	Western Avenue Golf Course, near Inglewood	F	160
C-2	22	Alondra Park, near Lawndale	D	315
C-2	25	Grevillea Avenue Park, Inglewood	A	5
C-2	29	Inglewood Cemetery	H	300
C-2	30	Los Angeles Airways Field, near Inglewood	J	40
C-2	31	Master Aircraft Corporation Field, near Inglewood	J	115
C-2	32	Aero Corporation of California Field, near Inglewood	J	18
C-2	33	Kelly Airport, Hawthorne	J	80
C-2	34	Belleview Golf Course, near Inglewood	F	98
C-2	35	Dycers Airport, near Gardena	J	160
C-3	4	Central Playground, Los Angeles	A	1

District No.	Unit No.		Class	Areas in Acres
C-3	10	Ross Snyder Playground, Los Angeles	B	10
C-3	12	Slauson Community Playground, Los Angeles	A	1
C-3	15	Slauson Playground, Los Angeles	A	5
C-3	43	Manchester Playground, Los Angeles	B	16
C-3	59	Harvard Playground, Los Angeles	B	15
C-3	61	Chesterfield Square Park, Los Angeles	A	2
C-3	67	South Park, Los Angeles	B	19
C-3	75	Vermont Square Park, Los Angeles	A	2
C-3	80	Exposition Park, Los Angeles	D	114
C-3	87	Pacific Air Transport Field, at Baldwin Hills	J	17
C-3	88	Lincoln Air Line Field, at Baldwin Hills	J	17
C-3	89	American Aircraft Field, at Baldwin Hills	J	38
C-3	90	Rogers Airport, at Baldwin Hills	J	14
C-3	94	Sunset Golf Course, Baldwin Hills	F	306
C-4	1	Manhattan Beach Park	A	3
C-4	2	Manhattan Beach Park	B	6
C-4	14	Redondo Beach City Park	B	8
C-4	18	Vincent Park, Redondo Beach	A	2
C-4	19	Hermosa Beach Park	A	1
C-4	20	Redondo Beach Country Club	F	176
C-4	21	County Beach at Manhattan Beach	A	4
C-4	22	City Beach at Manhattan Beach	A	1
C-4	26	Hermosa and Redondo Public Beaches	B	16
C-4	24	Palos Verdes Airport, near Palos Verdes	J	30
C-5	12	Southwest Airport, near Gardena	J	14
C-5	13	Short Airport, near Gardena	J	23
C-5	14	Compton Airport	J	90
C-5	16	Roosevelt Cemetery, Gardena	H	40
C-6	9	Banning Park & Playground, Wilmington	B	22
C-6	12	Wilmington Water Land	G	9
C-7	1 to 4	Val Monte Park, Palos Verdes	C	35
C-7	7	Val Monte Parkway, Palos Verdes	A	2
C-7	9	Malaga Strip, Palos Verdes	B	11
C-7	10	Malaga Park, Palos Verdes	D	249

District No.	Unit No.		Class	Areas in Acres
C-7	14	Malaga Hills Park, Palos Verdes	C	62
C-7	16	Martins Park, Palos Verdes	A	2
C-7	21	Zurita Canyon Park, Palos Verdes	B	17
C-7	23	Margate Canyon Park, Palos Verdes	C	35
C-7	24	Douglas Hillsides, Palos Verdes	C	60
C-7	26	Del Sol Hillsides, Palos Verdes	B	6
C-7	27	La Costa Hillsides, Palos Verdes	A	5
C-7	28	Malaga Bluffs, Palos Verdes	B	9
C-7	29	Bluff Cove Shores, Palos Verdes	C	69
C-7	30	Margate Parkway, Palos Verdes	A	2
C-7	31	Estudillo Hillsides, Palos Verdes	A	5
C-7	32	Landetta Hillsides, Palos Verdes	B	10
C-7	33	Coronel Canyon, Palos Verdes	B	9
C-7	34	Mirola Hill, Palos Verdes	A	5
C-7	37	Zumaya Trail, Palos Verdes	B	6
C-7	38	Zumaya Canyon Park, Palos Verdes	A	5
C-7	40	Lunada Canyon Park, Palos Verdes	C	35
C-7	42	Paseo Lunado, Palos Verdes	A	3
C-7	44	Resort Point Bluff, Palos Verdes	B	17
C-7	45	Lunada Bay Shore, Palos Verdes	B	25
C-7	46	Rocky Point Bluff, Palos Verdes	B	12
C-8	5	Averill Park, San Pedro	B	11
C-8	8	Anderson Playground, San Pedro	A	1
C-8	10	Alma Park, San Pedro	A	2
C-8	14	Point Fermin Park, San Pedro	B	23
C-8	15	Leland Park, San Pedro	B	12
C-8	18	Harbor Playgrounds, San Pedro	B	9
C-8	19	San Pedro Cemetery, San Pedro	H	3
C-8	20	Fort McArthur, San Pedro	I	50
C-8	23	Royal Palms Golf and Country Club, San Pedro	F	220
D-1	8	City Park, Huntington Park	B	8
D-2	5	Rio Hondo Country Club, near Downey	F	220
D-2	7	Security Airport, Montebello	J	36
D-2	8	Pasadena Water Lands, Montebello	G	49
D-3	6	Alta Park, Whittier	A	3
D-3	7	Central Park, Whittier	A	2
D-3	9	Loftus Park, Whittier	A	1
D-3	25	Broadway Park, Whittier	A	1
D-3	27	Whittier Water Land, Whittier	G	5
D-3	28	Pio Pico Mansion, Whittier	I	6
D-3	32	Mt. Olive Cemetery, Whittier	H	10
D-3	34	State Hospital, at Norwalk	I	300
D-3	36	State School for Boys, Whittier	I	150
D-4	10	Houghton Park, Long Beach	C	29
D-4	12	Virginia Country Club, Long Beach	F	130
D-4	13	Long Beach Water Land & Airport	G	680
D-4	15	Long Beach Water Land	G	10
D-4	16	Long Beach Water Land	G	95
D-4	18	County Farm, near Downey	I	482
D-5	4	Recreation Park, Long Beach	D	400
D-5	10	Bluff Park, Long Beach	B	7
D-5	11	Bixby Park, Long Beach	B	10
D-5	22	Lincoln Park, Long Beach	A	5
D-5	31	Los Cerritos Park, Long Beach	A	2
D-5	34	Knoll Park, Long Beach	A	2
D-5	36	Santa Cruz Park, Long Beach	A	.1
D-5	37	Lookout Park, Long Beach	A	2
D-5	38	Ocean Avenue Parks, Long Beach	B	6
D-5	46	Alamitos Beach Park, Long Beach	A	5
D-5	48	Long Beach Reservoir Land	G	25
D-5	49	Long Beach Water Land	G	20
D-5	50	Long Beach, Beach	A	5
D-5	53	Long Beach Public Beach and Auditorium	B	20
E-1	12	Downey Playground, Los Angeles	A	5
E-1	13	Recreation Center Playground, Los Angeles	A	1
E-2	3	Whittier Playground, Los Angeles	A	3
E-2	9	Evergreen Playground, Los Angeles	B	6
E-2	13	Pecan Playground, Los Angeles	A	1
E-2	17	Prospect Park, Los Angeles	A	3
E-2	18	State Street Playground, Los Angeles	A	1
E-2	54	Hazard Park and Playground, Los Angeles	C	36
E-2	56	Hollenbeck Park, Los Angeles	B	21
E-2	57	Hostetter Playground, Los Angeles	A	2
E-2	58	Lincoln Park, Los Angeles	C	46
E-2	59	Evergreen Cemetery, Los Angeles	H	100
E-2	60	New Calvary Cemetery, Belvedere District	H	140
E-2	61	B'nai B'rith Cemetery, Belvedere District	H	13
E-2	62	California Airways Field, Belvedere District	J	66
E-2	63	County Hospital, Los Angeles	I	74
E-2	66	I.O.O.F. Cemetery, Belvedere District	H	30
E-3	1	Montebello Golf Club	F	120
E-3	5	Montebello Park	B	15

District No.	Unit No.		Class	Areas in Acres
E-3	11	Montebello Playground	A	1
E-3	14	Belvedere Park, Belvedere District	A	3
E-3	15	Monarch Airport, near Montebello	J	135
E-3	16	Vail Field Airport, near Montebello,	J	411
F-1	3	Yosemite Playground, Eagle Rock	B	10
F-1	4	Occidental College Campus, Eagle Rock	I	39
F-1	7	Sycamore Grove Park, Los Angeles	B	15
F-1	8	(Arroyo Seco) Victory Park No. 1 and No. 2, Los Angeles	D	347
F-1	16	Garvanza Park, Los Angeles	A	3
F-1	18	Arroyo Seco Playground, Los Angeles	A	5
F-2	47	Oak Grove Park & Water Land, Altadena	D	334
F-2	50	Garfield Park, South Pasadena	A	5
F-2	51	Raymond Golf Course, South Pasadena	F	55
F-2	52	American Legion Park, Pasadena	A	2
F-2	53	Singer Park, Pasadena	A	4
F-2	54	Central Park, Pasadena	B	10
F-2	55	Memorial Park, Pasadena	A	5
F-2	56	La Pintoresca Park, Pasadena	A	3
F-2	57	Washington Park, Pasadena	A	3
F-2	59	Pasadena Country Club, Altadena	F	115
F-2	60	California Institute of Technology, Pasadena	I	22
F-2	61	Tournament Park, Pasadena	B	23
F-2	62	San Marino Park, San Marino	C	26
F-2	63	Arroyo Seco Park, South Pasadena	C	90
F-2	64	Mission Park, South Pasadena	A	1
F-2	65	Brookside Park, Pasadena	D	521
F-2	66	Carmelita Park, Pasadena	B	13
F-2	68	Lower Arroyo Park, Pasadena	C	70
F-2	69	Huntington Estate, San Marino	I	200
F-2	70	Los Angeles County Nurseries, Altadena	I	9
F-2	73	Yard Reservoir Site, Pasadena	G	13
F-2	82–85	Pasadena Civic Center	B	12
F-2	97	Casitas Wells, Altadena	G	5
F-2	98	Mt. View Cemetery, Altadena	H	18
F-2	99	Pasadena Reservoir Site	G	19
F-3	2	San Gabriel Country Club, San Gabriel	F	100
F-3	7	Alhambra Park	B	14
F-3	10	Midwick Country Club, Alhambra	F	235
F-3	27	Savannah Park, Rosemead	A	1
F-3	28	Airport, San Gabriel	J	145
F-3	30	San Gabriel Mission	I	5
F-3	31	Pasadena Sewer Farm, San Gabriel	I	507
F-4	2	Besse Playground, Lamanda Park	A	2
F-4	4	Sierra Madre Park	A	4
F-4	7	Ross Field Airport, Etc. (U. S.), Arcadia	I	396
F-4	10	Arcadia Park	A	5
F-4	15	Monrovia Library Park	A	5
F-4	20	Monrovia Park	B	20
F-4	26	Santa Anita Riding & Hunting Club, Arcadia	F	11
F-4	27	Precipice Canyon Water Land, Altadena	G	20
F-4	28	Eaton Canyon Water Land, Altadena	G	110
F-4	31	Sierra Madre Water Land	G	69
F-4	33	Sierra Madre Water Land	G	35
F-4	34	Michillinda Park, Pasadena	A	2
F-4	35	Monrovia Water Land, Arcadia	G	15
F-4	36	Arcadia Water Lands	G	9
F-4	37	County Quarry, Azusa	I	33
F-4	38	Temple Park, Arcadia	A	2
F-4	39	Sierra Madre Water Lands	G	112
F-4	45	Monrovia Reservoir Site, Arcadia	G	10
F-4	46	Monrovia Reservoir Site, Arcadia	G	5
F-6	13	Covina Park	B	9
F-6	27	County Quarry, Azusa	I	27
F-6	28	Morgan Park, Baldwin Park	B	7
F-8	7	Pomona College, Claremont	I	38
F-8	9	County Fair Grounds, Pomona	I	73
F-8	11	Lincoln Park, Pomona	A	2
F-8	19	Washington Park, Pomona	A	5
F-8	22	Garfield Park, Pomona	A	2
F-8	23	Central Park, Pomona	A	2
F-8	31	Rodgers Field Airport, near Puente	J	23
F-8	32	Pomona Airport	J	20
F-8	37	San Dimas Park	I	96
M-1	3	Bel-Air Country Club, near Santa Monica	F	116
M-1	4	Occidental College Site, near Santa Monica	I	500
M-1	5	California Botanic Gardens, near Santa Monica	I	800
M-1	7	Hollywood Bowl	I	65

District No.	Unit No.		Class	Areas in Acres
M-1	8	Encino Country Club, Ventura Boulevard	F	210
M-1	9	Girard Country Club, Girard	F	90
M-1	10	Upper Franklin Reservoir Land, Beverly Hills	G	165
M-1	11	Lower Franklin Reservoir Land, Beverly Hills	G	157
M-1	12	Stone Canyon Water Lands, Bel-Air	G	12
M-1	13	Encino Reservoir Site, Encino	G	208
M-1	14	Stone Canyon Reservoir Site, near Santa Monica	G	285
M-1	15	Girard Reservoir Site, Girard	G	6
M-1	16	U. S. Lighthouse Water Lands, Malibu Ranch	G	464
M-5	1	Stough Park, Burbank	D	120
M-5	2	Sunset Canyon Golf Club, Burbank	F	150
M-5	3	Brand Park, Glendale	D	616
M-5	4	Burbank Reservoir	G	7
M-6	1	Chevy Chase Golf Club, Glendale	F	50
M-6	2	Glendale Reservoir Lands	G	5
M-6	3	Chevy Chase Reservoir Lands, Glendale	G	6
M-6	5	Vacant Water Land, Glendale	G	65
M-6	6	Annandale Country Club, Pasadena	F	140
M-7	1	Verdugo Playgrounds, Los Angeles	B	11
M-7	4	Forest Lawn Cemetery, Glendale	H	212
M-7	5	Ascot Reservoir Lands, Los Angeles	G	6
M-8	76	Elysian Park, Los Angeles	D	599
M-8	77	Elysian Park Playground, Los Angeles	B	9
M-8	80	Victory Heights Water Land, Los Angeles	G	5
M-8	81	Catholic Cemetery, Los Angeles	H	11
M-8	82	Pest House, Los Angeles	I	5
M-8	83	Jewish Cemetery, Los Angeles	H	5
M-8	84	Yale Playground, Los Angeles	A	1
M-9	1	Griffith Park, Los Angeles	E	3,752
M-9	3	Hollywood Reservoir Lands	G	231
M-11	2	El Tesoro Canyon Park, Palos Verdes	B	13
M-11	3	Lorraine Boundary Park, Palos Verdes	A	3
M-11	4	Frascati Canyon Park, Palos Verdes	B	8
M-11	7	Miraleste Canyon Park, Palos Verdes	B	11
M-13	1	Hacienda Country Club, La Habra	F	150
M-14	1	Mountain Meadows Country Club, Pomona	F	220
M-14	2	Ganesha Park, Pomona	C	61
Y-1	1	Plaza, Los Angeles	A	1
Y-1	2	Apablasa Playground, Los Angeles	A	2
Y-1	9	Pershing Square, Los Angeles	B	5
Y-1	10	Wall Street Playground, Los Angeles	A	1
Y-1	26	Civic Center, Los Angeles	A	5
Y-2	2	Silverado Park, Long Beach	B	13
Y-3	3	Plaza Park, San Pedro	A	4
Y-3	4	Terminal Island Playground	B	10
Y-3	5	Allen Field Airport, Terminal Island	J	450
Y-3	6	Long Beach, Beach	B	10
Y-4	4	Prado Park, Torrance	A	2
Y-4	5	Torrance Airport	J	20

APPENDIX NO. III

Copy of Letter on Nigger Slough and Other Lands Lying Below Possible Drainage Levels, Submitted by Olmsted Brothers on May 21st, 1926, to the Board of Supervisors of Los Angeles County

GENTLEMEN: Our preliminary studies of the Nigger Slough portion of Improvement No. 15 under the Mattoon Act have raised certain problems of drainage and filling, our consideration of which has drawn attention to certain fundamental questions of principle and policy affecting also other large areas of land in Los Angeles County lying wholly outside of the present southwestern improvement district.

These questions are of such far-reaching importance to the County and the need of adopting a sound general method for dealing with them is apparently becoming so urgent that we feel bound to submit this brief outline of them to you, and to advocate their prompt and thorough consideration apart from, but concurrently with, the development of plans for Improvement No. 15.

Nigger Slough is only one of several large areas in the County where the elevation of the land is so near sea level that ordinary methods of gravity drainage by open channels and storm sewers, whether undertaken at the general expense by the Flood Control District or at local expense by local drainage districts, cannot possibly be made to protect the land from constantly repeated serious inundations, unless the surface of the land is raised in a wholesale manner by filling.

For some kinds of park uses, land may be subject to occasional flooding without serious detriment, provided it can be properly drained in the intervals between floods, and the same is true of most agricultural uses. But it is obvious that conditions ought not to be allowed to arise which will subject land used for streets and for building purposes to recurring inundations.

In the absence of definite engineering determination of the elevations to which flood waters can be limited in these low areas by methods which are practicable from an engineering and from an economic standpoint, and in the absence of proper legal control of building operations on such lands, it is as certain as anything can be that, partly through ignorance and partly through unscrupulousness, these areas will be largely developed in such a manner that

in every period of heavy rainfall not only will streets be submerged but the waters will rise over the floors of houses and other buildings, causing enormous inconvenience and economic loss, creating seriously unsanitary conditions, and tending to produce the most objectionable of slums. And the worst of it is that where this condition arises there will be no practicable remedy short of raising bodily the elevation of entire districts after great sums of money may have been spent in building streets, houses and other improvements below the irreducible flood level.

The principles involved can be readily understood from the enclosed diagrams relating to the Nigger Slough basin. With variations of detail the same principles apply to other large areas, notably in the surroundings of the city of Long Beach and in the Ballona Creek Valley.

Diagram 1 is a profile along the line of the Nigger Slough drainage canal of the Flood Control District. The solid line shows the natural surface of the ground. The shaded line indicates the approximate elevation of extreme high tide. The dotted line shows the bottom of the canal as proposed, and as constructed at a temporarily reduced width, by the Flood Control District, with a gradient rising at the rate of only one foot to the mile from tidewater.

The dot and dash line shows the elevations of flood water in the canal computed by the engineers of the District, as it would be if the canal were completed as planned and for a flood discharge of only 1,050 second-feet. *With the installation of streets, buildings, and other improvements in the tributary drainage area a very much larger flood run-off than this is absolutely certain.* We are informed that the City Drainage District Department has computed the drainage area above Main Street at 74 square miles and the run-off as 2,000 second feet, on the assumption that 10% of the drainage area will be built up as industrial, 50% as residential, and 40% will remain in its present condition. Seventy-four into 2,000 gives a run-off of only 27 second-feet per square mile, the equivalent of 1/24 of an inch of rainfall per hour. While

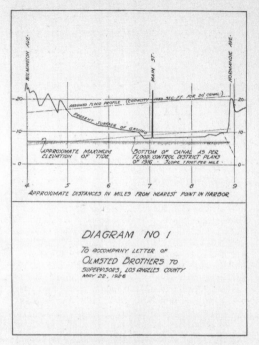

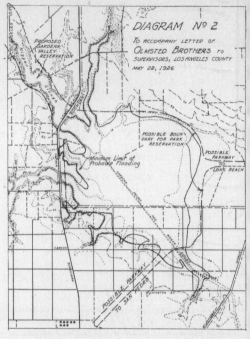

PLATE 65. Profile of Nigger Slough drainage basin, showing assumed flood profile.

PLATE 66. Plan of Nigger Slough drainage basin, showing areas likely to be flooded.

such an assumption may be entirely reasonable as a basis for any immediate construction, it seems unreasonable to assume that after urban development shall have continued for (say) two or three generations there will not occur, at rather frequent intervals, a run-off very greatly exceeding 27 second-feet per square mile. It would not be surprising if the maximum run-off in rainy years should in time grow to be five or ten times that figure, and by that time the right of way for the drainage outlet from the basin to the harbor will certainly have become walled-in by innumerable industrial plants, and will have been crossed by many street and railroad embankments, the openings through which will tend to limit the possible capacity of the channel and increase the gradient of flood water discharge.

The down-stream portion of the flood profile could be considerably lowered by dredging the bottom of the canal below high tide level, permitting tidewater to ebb and flow in the canal. This raises questions as to the probable sanitary conditions which would arise in such a long, narrow, semi-stagnant tidal canal; but even if such a deep-dredged channel proved to be feasible without creating a nuisance, it seems obvious that limitations of cost upon the depth and width of the channel, and upon the size of the

numerous street bridges across it will make it a matter of very great, if not of insuperable, cost to lower the ultimate flood profile in the neighborhood of Main Street to an elevation appreciably lower than that assumed by the Flood Control District when they figured on a channel 20 feet wide at the bottom for a run-off of less than 14 second-feet per square mile—to say nothing of the chance that floods may in time back up to even higher levels than the profile shown.

Diagram 2 shows the approximate extent of the lands East of Main Street which would be put under water by floods rising to that profile. Their area is approximately 1,500 acres.

If this and similar areas are not taken for park reservations, it seems to us that it is the clear duty of the County authorities, *first*, to determine by painstaking engineering studies the lowest elevations at which it will be practicable to hold the floods in such low areas by providing reasonable sizes of main drainage channels; *second*, to take such steps as are necessary to ensure the reservation of rights of way for such channels and for their ultimate construction at the proper time (presumably at the general expense by the Flood Control District); *third*, to determine at what minimum elevations, in relation to the prospective controlled flood levels, streets can be established and houses erected without creating conditions prejudicial to the public health, safety and general welfare; and *finally*, to establish, under proper enabling legislation, regulations prohibiting the opening of new streets not graded up to the minimum safe elevation and prohibiting the construction of buildings except at safe elevations, with proper exceptions to allow for agricultural and other improvements of a non-residential character which could be inundated without serious prejudice to the public welfare.

Agriculture and recreation are the principal uses to which such low land can properly be put without the large expense for filling them up to a level safe from disastrous flooding.

As the surrounding areas fill up with industrial and residential developments on higher ground it will be expedient and economical to acquire considerable areas of these lands for the recreation of the surrounding population, and this can be done at the price of agricultural land if, and only if, speculators are restrained from developing and marketing building lots on low lands without first filling them sufficiently to make them permanently fit for human habitation.

It is interesting to note that somewhat comparable conditions have been encountered in some of the eastern seaboard cities. In Boston and the Boston Metropolitan District there are thousands of acres where the land is, or originally was, at about the elevation of mean high tide, and therefore subject to frequent, though usually very shallow, inundation. In Boston for about the last seventy years, and for various shorter periods in the surrounding territory, no streets have been permitted to be opened at elevations lower than the standard, computed to be safe from flooding in case of coincidence of a maximum high tide with a heavy rain-storm, and no dwellings or other ordinary urban structures are permitted under the building laws except upon streets at or above the standard minimum elevations and when themselves constructed at such elevations and in such manner as to make them safe and sanitary in view of the predictable maximum water level.

Throughout the whole of the "Back Bay" residential and business district of Boston, and on other areas totaling many square miles in extent, all the streets have been filled six feet or more above the natural surface and any basements extending below street grade are required to be water tight and provided with artificial drainage depending on pumps or ejectors. In Boston and especially in the

surrounding metropolitan district, a considerable fraction of the low lands subject to inundation in their natural state have been acquired for park purposes at very reasonable prices compared with values on adjoining uplands, *because* such low lands cannot be used for building purposes without the costly filling necessary to fit them for such use.

It is to be noted further that the dangers of uncontrolled private development on lands too near sea level to be economically capable of protection from inundation are much more insidious in the Los Angeles district than in eastern seaboard cities because extreme fluctuations in rainfall here make most of these low lands during dry seasons much less unattractive for building operations than in the East, where they are generally water-soaked as often as once or twice a month even though maximum floods may occur no more often than they do here.

Park plans for the portion of Nigger Slough above Main Street have been made on the assumption that the land will be permanently subject to flooding in wet seasons up to levels approximately as high as the flood profile originally assumed by the Flood Control District, frankly recognizing that if these levels are not to be greatly exceeded the capacity of the outlet channel will in time have to be enormously increased beyond that provided for in the District's original plans; but *we cannot too strongly urge the importance of promptly facing the ultimate engineering solution of the whole problem* as affecting not merely the Nigger Slough Basin both inside and outside the Southwest Improvement District, but also the other extensive low areas of the County where subdivisions are steadily creeping in to make untold troubles for the future.

If the permanent determination of the economically practicable water levels, during dry weather and during floods, which can be permanently ensured in the Nigger Slough Basin is not made before the park improvements are actually installed in the area between Normandie Avenue and Main-Street, these park improvements will have to be constructed on a gamble, which will involve either the expenditure of a lot of money in construction that may later prove to have been unnecessary or else taking a serious risk of unsatisfactory results and later reconstructions, or both.

Respectfully submitted,
Olmsted Brothers.

APPENDIX NO. IV

Table of Comparative Powers, Duties, and Resources of Various Metropolitan Agencies of California and Elsewhere

EXISTING CALIFORNIA LEGISLATION

Features Considered	Los Angeles County Flood-Control District	County Sanitation Districts	Metropolitan Water Districts
DISTRICT			
(1) Date of Legislation	1915	1923	1927
(2) How established	Special Act	*Enabling Act	*Enabling Act
(3) Area comprised	Part of County	Cities and parts of County	Cities
(4) Formation of district by	Act	County Board of Supervisors unless 2% demand election	*Election
(5) Vote required	None	*Majority	*Majority
GOVERNING BODY:			
(6) Consists of	Board of Supervisors of Los Angeles County	Board of Directors, consisting of Executive of County and of each city	Board of Directors, representing each city
(7) Term of Service	....	....	....
(8) Appointed by	Existing	Existing	Each city
POWER AND DUTIES:			
(9) Acquisition, development and control of land	Yes	Yes	Yes
(10) Eminent domain	Yes	Yes	Yes
(11) Sale of surplus land	Yes	Yes	Yes
(12) Assessment of benefits	....	....	....
(13) Police control	....	....	....
RESOURCES:			
(14) Percentage of assessed valuation allowed in bonds	Not limited	Not limited	15%
(15) Vote required	Majority vote	⅔ vote	Majority vote
(16) Operating tax limit	10c per $100	No limit	*5c per $100
PROGRESS MADE:			
(17)	In operation since 1915. Bonds issued and authorized about $40,000,000	Nine such districts in Los Angeles County	Los Angeles and 11 other cities formed a district in 1928

*Details suitable for Los Angeles Parks are shown with a star. (*)

Park Legislation in Other States

	(Boston) Metropolitan Park District	Westchester County (New York)	New Jersey County Park Districts	Chicago South Park District	Illinois County Forest Preserve District	Missouri Public Reservation Districts
(1)	----------	----------	----------	----------	----------	----------
(2)	Special Act	Special	*Enabling Act	Special	*Enabling Act	*Enabling Act
(3)	*Several Counties	One County	One County	Local	One County	*Several Counties
(4)	Act	Act	Vote, in County of over 200,000	Act	*Petition of 500 for election	*5% petition
(5)	None	None	*Majority	None	*Majority	*Majority
(6)	*Commission of five	*Board of Six	*Commission of five	*Board of five	*Board of five	*Commission of five
(7)	5 years	3 years	5 years	----------	*4 years	5 years
(8)	*Governor	County Board of Supervisors	Presiding Judge of Supreme Court of County	First five by Governor, thereafter by Judge of Circuit Court	Chairman of County Board of Supervisors	*Governor
(9)	*Yes	Yes	Yes	Yes	Yes	Yes
(10)	*Yes	Through Supervisors	Yes	Yes	Yes	Yes
(11)	*Yes	----------	----------	Yes	----------	----------
(12)	*Yes	----------	Yes	Yes	----------	----------
(13)	*Yes	----------	Yes	----------	Yes	Yes
(14)	Special Acts	*5%	a. $2,500,000 b. $2,800,000 c. $800,000	Was 5%; now not limited	a. To acquire 35,000 acres b. 1%	a. ½ of 1% b. Additional ½ of 1%
(15)	Not required	Not required	a. Not required b. Majority c. Not required	Majority	a. Not required b. Majority	a. Not required b. ⅔ vote
(16)	Annual Legislation	Not limited	Not limited	10c per $100	Not limited	20c per $100
(17)	Large System Completed. Cost about $25,000,000	Large system being completed. Estimated cost, $60,000,000	Essex and Union Counties have systems fairly complete; others starting	Finest small parks and some large ones completed	35,000 acres of forest lands acquired; now being extended	----------

*Details suitable for Los Angeles Parks are shown with a star. (*)

APPENDIX NO. V

Shore Land Rights in California: An Opinion Submitted to the Citizens' Committee in 1928 by O'Melveney, Tuller & Myers, Attorneys at Law

SYNOPSIS

OPINION ON SHORE LAND RIGHTS IN CALIFORNIA

I. The State succeeded to Rights Similar to The Rights of the Other States in Tidelands When California Was Admitted to the Union.

It is clearly established by statute that the State owns the land "below tidewater and below ordinary high-water mark bordering upon tidewater within the State" (C. C. Sec. 670), and by the Constitution that the ownership of the State extends out into the Pacific Ocean "three English miles" (Constitution, Art. XXI). The cases clearly hold that title to such land is in the State. See:

Teschemacher v. Thompson, 18 Cal. 11, 79 Am. Dec. 151.

Ward v. Mulford, 32 Cal. 365.

Long Beach L. & W. Co. v. Richardson, 70 Cal. 206.

The United States acquired title from Mexico to all lands below navigable and tidewaters in the present State of California by the treaty of Guadalupe Hidalgo in 1848, with the exception of such submerged lands as had been previously conveyed to private owners by the Spanish or Mexican governments.

Ward v. Mulford, 32 Cal. 365.

After the admission of California to the Union, it became the owner of all lands within its borders below navigable and tidewaters by virtue of its sovereign character and not by virtue of direct grant from the general government as in the case of other public lands.

Oakland v. Oakland Water Front Co., 118 Cal. 160.

Ward v. Mulford, 32 Cal. 365.

People v. Davidson, 30 Cal. 393.

Guy v. Hermance, 5 Cal. 73.

But this sovereign character of the State is qualified by the paramount right to control navigation which is reserved to the United States under the commerce clause and other provisions of the Constitution of the United States.

Gibson v. U. S., 166 U. S. 269.

Since the title to such land is in the State, if there be any authority to lease or grant it, such authority must be exercised either by the State or some agency of the State. However, it should be noted that the courts are very reticent in construing statutes to authorize sales of tidelands. In *People v. Morrill*, 26 Cal. 336, it was decided that under the Acts of April 21, 1858, and May 13, 1861, regulating the sale of swamp and overflowed and tidelands, the shore of the ocean between ordinary high and low-water marks, and which was not susceptible of reclamation, so as to be made useful for agricultural purposes, could not be entered and converted into private ownership. Also the court in *Kimball v. Macpherson*, 46 Cal. 104, came to the same conclusion as to

the Act of March 28, 1868. See also, *Farrish v. Coon*, 40 Cal. 33.

The matter is very well stated by Shaw, J. in the opinion of the court in *People v. California Fish Company*, 166 Cal. 576, 591.

"The tidelands embraced in these statutes, under the generally accepted meaning of that term, includes the entire sea beach from the Oregon line to Mexico and shores of every bay, inlet, estuary, and navigable stream as far up as tidewater goes and until it meets the lands made swampy by the overflow and seepage of fresh water streams. It is not to be assumed that the State, which is bound by the public trust to protect and preserve this public easement and use, should have intentionally abdicated the trust as to all land not within the very limited areas of the reservations, and should have directed the sale of any and every other part of the land along the shores and beaches to exclusive private use, to the destruction of the paramount public easement, which it was its duty to protect and for the protection and regulation of which it received its title to such lands."

II. The Nature of the State's Title to Tide and Submerged Lands.

That the State of California holds the title to such lands subject to the public right of navigation, commerce and fishery. In *Weber v. State Harbor Comrs.*, Mr. Justice Field in delivering the opinion of the court said:

"Upon the admission of California into the Union upon equal footing with the original States, absolute property in and dominion over, all soils under the tidewaters within her limits passed to the State, with the consequent right to dispose of the title to any part of said soils in such manner as she might deem proper, subject only to the paramount right of navigation over the water, so far as such navigation might be required by the necessities of commerce with foreign nations or among the several States, the regulation of which was vested in the general government."

This statement appears to be a clearly correct statement of the law, unless there be vested private rights in such lands, subject to which the State holds its title. But if such rights exist and are vested they would be protected by the Fourteenth Amendment to the Federal Constitution and similar provisions of the fundamental law of the State. A person may also, because he is a member of the public, have rights in such land which must be secured to him. But assuming that no such private rights in tidelands have vested, the State and federal government possessing all-sovereign power, would seem to have complete authority to dispose of such land as seems fit.

This view seems to be supported by the court in one of the earliest cases dealing with the State's disposition of tidelands. In defining the State's authority the court used the following language:

"She holds the complete sovereignty over her navigable bays and rivers, and although her ownership is by the law of nations, and the common and civil law, attributed to her for the purpose of preserving the public easement or right of navigation, there is nothing to prevent the exercise of her power, in certain cases to destroy the easement, in order to preserve the general good, which, when done, subjects the land to private proprietorship."

Eldridge v. Cowell, 4 Cal. 80.

It is difficult to discover the basis of the following statement in *Ward v. Mulford*, 32 Cal. 365.

"The land which the State holds by virtue of her sovereignty, as is well understood, is such as is covered by the flow and ebb of the neap or ordinary tides. Such land is held by the State in trust and for the benefit of the people. The right of the State is subservient to the public rights of navigation and fishery, and theoretically, at least, the State can make no disposition of them prejudicial to the right of the public to use them for the purposes of navigation and fishery, and whatever disposition she does make of them, her grantee takes them upon the same terms upon which she holds them, and of course subject to the public rights above mentioned. But this restriction does not prevent her from disposing of them so as to advance and promote the interests of navigation. On the contrary such a disposition of them would be in keeping with the purposes of the trust in which she holds them. Nor of reclaiming them from the sea, where it can be done without prejudice to the public right of navigation, and applying them to other purposes and uses."

But this doctrine has to a certain degree at least been incorporated into our law by the California Constitution of 1879, Article XV, Section 2, which provides:

"No individual, partnership, or corporation, claiming or possessing the frontage or tidal lands of a harbor, bay, inlet, estuary, or other navigable water in this State, shall be permitted to exclude the right of way to such water whenever it is required for any public purpose, nor to destroy or obstruct the free navigation of such water; and the legislature shall enact such laws as will give the most liberal construction to this provision, so that access to the navigable waters of this State shall be always attainable for the people thereof."

It has been held that the provisions of this section operate as a limitation upon the power of the legislature in the matter of the disposition of tidelands and are to be considered as incorporated in any grant or patent of such lands, and as a result the grantee must leave the navigable waters open for public use.

Forestier v. Johnson, 164 Cal. 24.

In this case it was held that the phrase "navigation" included hunting and fishing as incidental thereto.

Furthermore, this section of the present organic law deprives the legislature of the power to dispose of the tidelands fronting upon navigable waters so as to entitle the grantee to destroy or interfere with the public easement for navigation, and it to that extent repeals all laws which theretofore may have purported to authorize such alienation.

People v. California Fish Co., 166 Cal. 576, 587.

"The provisions of the constitution are mandatory and prohibitory. They are binding upon every department of the State government, legislative, executive, and judicial. (Art. I, Sec. 22.) All previous laws inconsistent therewith

ceased to be effective upon the adoption thereof. (Art. XXII, Sec. 1.) The effect of the section above quoted is that, no matter what effect a subsequent sale of tidelands may have to pass title to the soil of the tidal lands of a navigable bay such as that of San Pedro or Wilmington, it cannot be effective to give the patentee a right to destroy, obstruct, or injuriously affect the public right of navigation in the waters thereof. *Since the adoption of that constitution in 1879, if not before, grants of such lands by the State carry, at most, only the title to the soil subject to the public right of navigation.*"

The Code Section Dealing with Tidelands Appears to be a Mere Statement of the Common Law:

Civil Code, Section 670. Property of the State. The State is the owner of all land below tidewater, and below ordinary high-water mark, bordering upon tidewater within the State; of all land below the water of a navigable lake or stream; of all property lawfully appropriated by it to its own use; of all property dedicated to the State; and of all property of which there is no other owner.

III. Grants of Tidelands and of Lands Under Navigable Waters.

Any grants of such lands to private interests within two miles of an incorporated city or town, whether detrimental to the public easement or not, is prohibited where "fronting on the waters of any harbor, estuary, bay, or inlet used for the purposes of navigation."— *Constitution 1879, Art. XV, Sec. 3.*

However, the State, through its legislative authority may validly lease such lands with proper restrictions of time and proper regard to public use.

San Pedro R. R. Co. v. Hamilton, 161 Cal. 610.

Koyer v. Miner, 172 Cal. 448.

Furthermore, grants of such lands may be made to municipalities where such grant is for a purpose in harmony with the trusts upon which the State was invested with title to the same.

Cimpher v. City of Oakland, 162 Cal. 87.

City of Los Angeles v. Pacific Coast Steamship Co., 45 Cal. App. 15.

City of Long Beach v. Lisenly, 175 Cal. 575.

Also, such municipalities may in turn make valid leases of such lands for "all purposes which shall not interfere with navigation or commerce but for no purpose which would interfere with navigation or commerce."

Oakland v. Larue Wharf etc. Co., 179 Cal. 207.

Moreover, the Constitution of 1879, Art. XV, Sec. 2, provides that no rights shall be obtained by private interests which shall curtail the public easement of navigation or access to navigable waters, in and to tidelands on a harbor, bay, inlet, estuary or other navigable water in this State.

A. PURPOSES FOR WHICH GRANTS MAY BE MADE.
1. In Aid of Navigation.
Oakland v. Oakland Water Front Co., 118 Cal. 160, 183.

Here the power of the State to grant such lands in aid of navigation was thus stated:

"** * ** the State might alienate irrevocably parcels of its submerged lands of reasonable extent for the erection of docks, piers, and other aids to commerce. It was further conceded to be a proper exercise of the power of the State to establish harbor lines and to authorize the reclamation of mud flats and shoals where that could be done without detriment to the public rights. The filling up of such lands, it was said, was often an improvement of navigation and therefore lands susceptible of reclamation may be alienated irrevocably."

Koyer v. Miner, 172 Cal. 448.

Here the city of San Pedro made a lease of tidelands to defendant in consideration of his building a sea-wall in front of it which clearly was in aid of navigation. The court said:

"The State had the undoubted right to make the lease in question in order to procure the erection of a sea-wall with docks and slips and the improvements to be made to obtain public access to deep water, the better to fit the harbor for navigation."

See also, *People v. Kerber*, 152 Cal. 731.

2. Grants of Such Lands for Purposes Which Do Not Interfere With Navigation.
Eldridge v. Cowell, 4 Cal. 80.

In the plan and survey of the city of San Francisco lots and streets extended into tidelands so as to reach far enough into the water for the convenience of shipping. Defendant filled up this tideland to the line fixed by the city.

Held that defendant had a good title to such land by grant from the State. This may have been in aid of navigation but certainly did not interfere therewith.

Ward v. Mulford, 32 Cal. 365.

This decision upheld a grant of salt marsh land which was covered and uncovered by the ebb and flow of the tide and which was of no possible use for navigation, but could be made valuable for agriculture or other purposes if reclaimed.

Oakland v. Oakland Water Front Co., 118 Cal. 160, 185.

Here Beatty, C. J., after a careful review of the authorities thus stated the principal adopted by the Supreme Court:

"A grant by the State of California, therefore, of mud flats and shoals between high and low tide on the margin of the bay of San Francisco cannot be held to be in excess of the legislative power, in the absence of any proof that such grant has seriously impaired the power of succeeding legislatures to regulate, improve, or develop the public rights of navigation or fishery. * * * "

This statement appears to give the legislature too extensive powers in view of Constitution of 1879, Art. XV, Sec. 2, and to that extent is not correct. See *People v.*

California Fish Co., 166 Cal. 576, which holds that the legislature now does not possess the power to dispose of tidelands fronting upon navigable waters so as to entitle the grantee to destroy *or interfere with the public easement of navigation*.

3. Grants for Purposes Which May Interfere With Navigation.

Subsequent to 1879 when our present Constitution was adopted grants for such purposes would seem to be invalid. Art. XV., Secs. 1, 2 and 3.

However, prior to the adoption of this Constitutional provision such grants appear to have been valid, subject to revocation upon payment of the fair value of the improvements made. The rule is stated in *Oakland v. Oakland Water Front Co.*, 118 Cal. 160, 183.

"No grant of lands covered by navigable waters can be made *which will impair the power of a subsequent legislature to regulate the enjoyment of the public right.*"

The more sweeping statement in *Ward v. Mulford*, 32 Cal. 372, is couched in such language as to practically admit its inaccuracy.

"The right of the State is subservient to the public right of navigation and fishery, and *theoretically, at least*, the State can make no disposition of them prejudicial to the right of the public to use them for the purposes of navigation and fishery."

The unlimited power of the legislature to grant tidelands prior to the year 1879 when the present Constitution was adopted was rather clearly enunciated in the early case of *Eldridge v. Cowell*, 4 Cal. 80, where the court says:

"* * * there is nothing to prevent the exercise of her power, in certain cases, to destroy the easement, in order to preserve the general good, which, when done, subjects the land to private proprietorship."

IV. Agencies Through Which Such Lands Have Been Leased and Conveyed Into Private Hands.

In the first place all titles to such lands acquired under Mexican rule would be protected. Also where the United States has confirmed the title to land in this State acquired from Mexico, during Mexican rule, and which the State would otherwise have owned by virtue of its sovereignty, the State has no power to convey.

Ward v. Mulford, 32 Cal. 365.

The legislature by statute has conveyed to incorporated cities and towns the tidelands within its borders. Statutes, 1851, p. 309.

San Francisco v. Strant, 84 Cal. 124.

Statutes 1852, p. 181.

Cimpher v. Oakland, 162 Cal. 87.

Patton v. City of Los Angeles, 169 Cal. 521.

People v. Cal. Fish Co., 166 Cal. 576.

There are many other cases dealing with these legislative grants of tidelands to the different cities of the State. Also, there have been special commissions appointed to convey certain specified tracts of tidelands, as for instance, the commission appointed to examine and make sales of the interest of the State of property within the water-line of San Francisco.

Guy et al., v. Hermance, 5 Cal. 73.

The great bulk of the State grants, however, have been made by the State Board of Tideland Commissioners created by the Statutes and abolished by Amendments 1875-6, page 15, and after February 4, 1876, by the Surveyor-General who at present is the officer who makes such grants of tidelands. See Act. 8418, Gen. Laws 1923, Vol. 2, Stat. 1923, p. 677 as to swamp and tidelands. Chapter 303, Statutes 1921, approved January 25, 1921, deals with Oil and Gas Permits and Leases. See Amendment approved June 1, 1923.

Also, the different cities to which such lands have been granted may make valid leases of such lands.

San Pedro R. R. Co. v. Hamilton, 161 Cal. 610.

Koyer v. Miner, 172 Cal. 448.

Oakland v. Larue Wharf etc. Co., 179 Cal. 207.

Franchises for wharves, chutes and piers are granted by the boards of supervisors of the several counties, upon approval of the Railroad Commission.

Pol. Code, Chapter V, Sec. 2906, et. seq.

Within their corporate limits the municipal authorities of any incorporated city or town, except San Francisco, may grant authority to construct wharves, chutes and piers instead of the board of supervisors.

Pol. Code, Sec. 2920.

V. Title to Submerged and Tidelands Cannot be Perfected by Adverse Possession.

Parish v. Coon, 40 Cal. 33.

The location of such lands with school warrants held to not amount to such a color of title as would form the basis of a claim by adverse possession.

Land & Water Co. v. Richardson, 70 Cal. 206.

The plaintiff was in possession of a ranch lying immediately in front of the ocean, using the land as a "seaside resort." They had a hotel on the upland and on the beach a bath-house and benches for the patrons. They considered themselves in possession of all the beach and on several occasions had their employees order off "campers" and remove structures erected by other persons.

Held that it did not appear that plaintiff was in possession of the beach so that it could not maintain an action of forcible entry and detainer.

People v. Kerber, 152 Cal. 731.

This was an action under Pol. Code 2578 to recover possession of tidelands of the bay of San Diego. Defendant pleaded the ten years statute of limitation on the theory that it had obtained title by adverse possession. The tideland involved was back of the harbor line as fixed by the Harbor Commissioners, but the wall had never been built. The court reversed the judgment which had been for defendant on the ground that title

to such land could not be gained by adverse possession. The court through Shaw, J., said:

"Tidelands of this character vest in and belong to the State by virtue of its sovereignty * * * and when such tidelands are situated in a navigable bay and constitute a part of the water front thereof, as is the case here, they constitute property devoted to a public use, of which private persons cannot obtain title by prescription, founded upon adverse occupancy for the prescribed period. * * * This is the settled rule in this State with respect to all properties so devoted to public use, and tidelands, underlying waters forming part of the waters of a navigable bay used for navigation, are not, in this respect, to be distinguished from property used for other public purposes."

Cimpher v. City of Oakland, 162 Cal. 87.

To the same effect. This decision was more squarely based on Constitution 1879, Art. XV, Sec. 3.

Patton v. Los Angeles, 169 Cal. 521.

Held that no character or period of adverse possession can terminate or affect the public easement of navigation and fishery. Here by the construction of railroad embankments in front of plaintiff's land under license from the State, the land previously tideland was divested of that characteristic. The court refused to adopt the theory of plaintiff that by adverse possession plaintiff had procured the jus privatum of the State and when the easement for navigation was destroyed by the erection of the embankment plaintiff had the whole fee therein.

Also see:

People v. Banning, 169 Cal. 542.

VI. The Respective Rights of the State, and Incorporated Cities and Towns, Littoral or Riparian Owners and the Public.

1. The rights of the State in general are fully dealt with under main heading No. II.

(a) Title by adverse possession cannot be perfected against the State. See main heading No. V.

(b) As already indicated the title of the State to tidelands situated within the limits of incorporated cities and towns have been conveyed to such cities and towns.

2. The rights of littoral proprietors in and to tidelands.

(a) Enumeration of their rights.

(1) Such owners and possessors have a right of passage over such land which is a necessary incident to their right of access to navigable waters.

Eldridge v. Cowell, 4 Cal. 80.

San Francisco Sav. Union v. R.G.R. Petroleum Co., 144 Cal. 134.

Henry Dalton & Sons Co. v. Oakland, 168 Cal. 463.

Weber v. Harbor Commissioners, 18 Wall. 57.

(2) Littoral proprietors are entitled to the accretions added to their land.

Dana v. Jackson St. W. Co., 31 Cal. 118, 120.

Wright v. Seymour, 69 Cal. 122, 126, 10 Pac. 323.

Strand Improvement Co. v. Long Beach, 173 Cal. 765.

Here the court in construing Section 1014 of the Civil Code held that it did not abrogate the common law rule of accretion along the ocean shore. The court refused to follow the contrary decision of the United States Circuit Court of Appeals in *Western Pac. Ry. Co. v. So. Pac. Co.*, 151 Fed. 376, 397.

It should be remembered, however, that a riparian or littoral proprietor has no vested right in future accretions.

Cohen v. U. S., 162 Fed. 364, 370.

Similarly the title to future accretions may not be quieted.

Taylor v. Underhill, 40 Cal. 471.

The doctrine of accretion appears to be limited to gains made little by little, "by small and imperceptible degrees."

Dana v. Jackson Street Wharf Co., 31 Cal. 118.

The court indicated that additions due to driving piles in tidelands did not accrue to the littoral proprietor.

"This shows decisively that in cases of purpresture, the right of entry is not in the adjacent land-owner but in the crown."

In *Patton v. Los Angeles*, 169 Cal. 521, it was held that land located in the city of Los Angeles and bordering on the navigable bay could not benefit by an accretion to the mainland caused by the erection of an embankment leading from the upland by the Southern Pacific Railroad along the line of its road leading from the mainland across a part of the bay. The court said, in holding that the city still owned the reclaimed land,

"that it was once tideland and that this being so, it was reserved from sale, and was not alienable by any State officer under any law, during the time when the alleged accretions occurred, and, therefore, no artificial embankment, made by third persons, or made or suffered by State officers or agents, nor any accretion to the adjacent upland caused thereby, could operate to divest the State of its title to the tideland so reserved."

(3) It is possible that littoral proprietors have certain rights in the seashore of a purely aesthetic nature, although this is doubtful. However, the existence of such a right has been intimated in at least one Supreme Court decision.

S. F. Sav. Union v. R.G.R. Pet. Co., 144 Cal. 134.

This action was brought to obtain an injunction and to have abated as a nuisance a platform constructed by defendant in front of plaintiff's land on the seashore below the ordinary high tide. Plaintiff is the littoral proprietor. Defendant evidently was preparing to bore for oil.

The court quoted with approval the language of the judge below defining the rights of the littoral proprietor in tidelands and seashore.

"From time immemorial the sea has been treated as a vast waste not susceptible of occupation or private and individual ownership, except as herein indicated. Nations, governments and peoples have all been of one accord in treating it as exempt from appropriation by individuals. The occupation by defendants is in disregard of this universally conceded condition. Upon the strength of universal custom, conduct and tacit consent and understanding individuals and communities have acquired properties and rights, and have located lands, built homes and cities along the seashore, because not alone for its commercial advantages, but for the permanent and indestructible beauty of the environment. Unlike the location of the interior, where the incidents of private ownership may permit encroachments by way of unsightly and disagreeable structures, the prospect of ocean view is sacred from individual obstruction and contamination. So thoroughly has this been understood and acted upon by the whole world that no obstruction—not even wharves and docks—not built by the abutting owners have ever been attempted, except under license and control of the State. * * * This policy and mode of dealing had inured to the property-owner abutting thereon as an additional property right which though not involved in this case * * * I think is explanatory, if not the foundation of the principle enunciated by the courts that the abutting landowner has property in the sea by way of access thereto."

(b) Extent of the rights of littoral proprietors.

(1) Where an individual or a private corporation without any license or permit from the State or any of its agencies, interferes with the rights of littoral proprietors, such proprietors may have their rights as such proprietors protected by injunction.

S. F. Sav. Union v. R.G.R. Pet. Co., 144 Cal. 134.

(2) Where the State or an incorporated city or town in carrying out some project in aid of navigation interferes with such right such proprietor will not be granted relief by the courts.

People v. Cal. Fish Co., 166 Cal. 576.

Henry Dalton & Sons Co. v. Oakland, 168 Cal. 463.

Here plaintiff had for many years loaded small boats in front of his property. The city of Oakland now threatens to erect a sea-wall in front of plaintiff's land and thus cut off plaintiff's access to deep water. Plaintiff sought to enjoin the erection of the wall. The injunction was refused and the court distinguished *S. F. Sav. U. v. R.G.R. Pet. Co.*, 144 Cal. 137, on the ground that there the obstruction was erected by a private individual and not in aid of the public easement of navigation and fishery.

(3) Also, where private interests with permission of the State perform certain acts in aid of navigation, but which interfere with the rights of littoral proprietors, such proprietors have no legal or equitable remedy.

Koyer v. Miner, 172 Cal. 448.

Defendant was erecting a sea-wall in consideration

of receiving a 50 years lease to the land reclaimed under contract with the city.

(4) Our Supreme Court has not yet determined what are the rights of littoral proprietors to enjoin acts of individuals not in aid of navigation but with the express permission of the State upon tidelands. In *Dalton & Sons Co. v. Oakland*, 168 Cal. 463, 468, the court indicated, however, that before the littoral proprietor could be compelled to submit to an interference with his right of access to navigable water, this interference must be in aid of navigation. The court said:

"If such improvement have the effect of cutting off access over said tidelands from the upland lot of the plaintiff, it is no ground of complaint because, as pointed out, it had no right as an upland owner to the free and unobstructed access to navigable waters over said tidelands as against the right of the State to at any time devote them to the improvement of the harbor of Oakland *in aid of the public easement of navigation and commerce* * * * "

(5) Another undecided question is the right of the littoral proprietor to enjoin as a nuisance acts on the foreshore and tidelands by the State and individuals with the State's permission to remove oil or other minerals belonging to the State.*

Chapter 303, Statutes 1921.

See also, Amendment approved June 1, 1923.

Boone et al., v. Kingsbury, Surveyor-General, No. S. F. 12707, 12708, 12728, 12729, 12730 and 12743 now before the Supreme Court.*

3. The rights of the public in submerged and tidelands.

It is well settled that the public has large rights in submerged and tidelands. In fact it has been early recognized that title to such land was in the State for the express purpose of carrying out the public trust and protecting the rights of the public. The rule was thus well stated in one of the earliest California cases dealing with tidelands.

Eldridge v. Cowell, 4 Cal. 80.

" * * * her ownership is, by the law of nations, and the common and civil law, attributed to her for the purpose of preserving the public easement, or right of navigation * * *"

See also *Guy & Others v. Hermance*, 5 Cal. 79.

Moreover, this public right was recognized and secured by Article XV of the California Constitution of 1879. But prior to this constitutional protection the State through its legislature had the power to abandon and destroy the public trust. This is made apparent by the decision of *San Francisco v. Straut*, 84 Cal. 124, where the court held that the interest of the city and county of San Francisco in its beach and water-lot property is a legal estate for ninety-nine years under Statutes of 1851, p. 309, and the right of the city for that term is as absolute a title, and as free from public trust as if

*This question has since been determined: 77 Cal. Dec. 94.

held by a private proprietor, and may be extinguished by adverse possession, under the statute of limitation.

See to the same effect, *Holladay v. Frisbie*, 15 Cal. 631, holding that the interest of the city may be sold under execution. Field, C. J., speaking for the court said:

"In that property the interest of the city is absolute, qualified by no conditions and subject to no specific uses. It is therefore a leviable interest, subject to sale under execution * * * "

Knudson v. Kearney, 171 Cal. 250.

Ward v. Mulford, 32 Cal. 365.

Also, where the legislature by improving the water-front renders certain tideland inaccessible and useless for navigation, it may irrevocably and absolutely alienate such land free from any public trust, under the present Constitution.

People v. Cal. Fish Co., 166 Cal. 576.

Otherwise, it would seem that the legislature has no power to curtail or destroy the public easement or right of navigation.

People v. Cal. Fish Co., supra.

(a) The extent of this public right of navigation.

(1) This right or easement clearly includes what is commonly understood by the term navigation. This includes the right to build or authorize the building of wharves, chutes and piers. See Chapter V of Pol. Code. Also, of improving harbors, and expending public money therefor.

Henry Dalton & Sons Co. v. Oakland, 168 Cal. 463.

City of Long Beach v. Lisenly, 175 Cal. 575.

The city may issue its bonds for improving a harbor within its limits.

Weber v. Harbor Commissioners, 18 Wall. 57.

Held that a littoral proprietor could not enjoin the Harbor Commissioners from erecting a sea-wall in front of plaintiff's land, and a wharf he had erected out from his land.

Primarily, of course, the public has the right to propel ships over navigable waters, and tidelands may be used for that purpose. The court in *People v. Kerber*, 152 Cal. 731, said that

"for all practical purposes the bay is open to navigation to the actual shore line of high tide over the land in question * * * "

(2) It has been repeatedly stated that the public easement or right includes the right of fishing.

Forestier v. Johnson, 164 Cal. 24.

(3) The easement, also, has been held to include the hunting of wild game.

Forestier v. Johnson, 164 Cal. 24.

Here the plaintiff claims title from the State under a sale of the land as tideland, a patent being issued to him. Defendants claim that as citizens of the State they have the right to go upon the premises for the purpose of hunting, fishing and navigation. The land involved was known as Fly's Bay and was a side channel of Napa River. The court found that at mean tide the whole of the premises is used by vessels of small burden for the purpose of navigation and hunting. Held that the plaintiff could not exclude the public. The court said in regard to hunting that

"the authorities do not designate the hunting of wild game as an object for the protection and promotion of which the State holds title to and dominion over the tidelands and navigable waters. Nevertheless, it is a privilege which is incidental to the public right of navigation."

(4) The correct view would seem to be that this easement or right includes the public right to use the tidelands for the purpose of bathing. The courts, however, have not always been unanimous in declaring such a right. It has been indicated by the Supreme Court of California that even where tideland has been granted to a city for the purpose of public bathing that such public right is subject to the superior right of public navigation and fishery.

Santa Cruz v. So. Pac. R. R. Co., 163 Cal. 538.

Held that the Act of March 21, 1872, providing that

"all of the tidelands within the corporate limits of said town, between the line of high and low tide, are hereby dedicated as public grounds, and the title thereto is granted to the town of Santa Cruz in trust for the use of the public * * * but nothing herein contained shall in any manner be construed so as to prevent the construction * * * of wharves over, in and through said lands by authority of the laws of the State of California, or the free use thereof for fishing purposes"

was enacted in recognition of the fact that Santa Cruz has always been a summer resort, especially adapted to sea bathing and other sports and it was its purpose to dedicate the tidelands to such public uses, subject to the use for navigation and fishery. But the city's title is, therefore, subject to the paramount rights of navigation and fishery. An injunction was refused against the improvement of the wharf so as to interfere with the use of the beach for bathing and other like sports and uses.

"The principal thing complained of is the threatened act of the appellants in filling in the space under the wharf so as to prevent the use of that part of the beach for pleasure grounds. It may be conceded that if the appellants should place any obstruction upon the beach that was not appropriate for beach purposes and was not useful in aid of navigation, the city, having charge of the subordinate trust, relating to that land, would have the right to remove it or cause its removal, on the ground that it was an unnecessary purpresture upon that particular public use. This is the extent of the right and power of the city. It is not claimed or asserted that the filling in of this space is unnecessary to the use or preservation of the wharf, or that it obstructs or prevents the use of the beach for other purposes more than is necessary for the purposes of navigation.

It appears to be an appropriate method of strengthening the structure. Hence it follows that the city has shown no right to interfere with such improvement of the wharf."

The early cases which indicate that there is no public right of bathing in the ocean are really not in point as they go on another ground, namely, that of creating a nuisance in a public place.

Rex. v. Crunden, 2 Campbell's Reports 89 (1809).
Reg. v. Reed & Others, 12 Cox Cr. L. Cases 1.
Brinckman v. Matley (1904) L. R. 2 Ch. Div. 313.

In an early Pennsylvania case it was indicated that if such a right exists it is a qualified right. This case also, was complicated by problems of negligence.

Hunt v. Graham, 15 Pa. Superior Ct. 42.

"The right to bathe in a public stream is not an absolute right. It is qualified by fixed rules as those which determine the privilege. It is permitted only at certain places, and is of the same character as the right to use or take water from the stream."

In *Tiffany v. Town of Oyster Bay*, 182 N. Y. Supp. 738, plaintiff, a littoral proprietor filled in the foreshore in front of his property. The court in another action held that the title to the foreshore and this reclaimed land belonged to the town. Plaintiff then offered to remove the fill. The town contracted to have bath-houses erected on this filled in space and plaintiff sought an injunction on the theory that it injures his riparian right of access to navigable waters.

The injunction was granted on appeal to the Appellate Division. The court said:

"A public bath-house incidentally raises another question. The public has no right to pass over the foreshore in England to bathe in the sea. *Brinckman v. Matley* (1904) L. R. 2 Ch. 313. The public right to bathe, save at designated places, is doubtful in this country. *Hunt v. Graham*, 15 Pa. Super. Ct. 42."

The more modern decisions seem to indicate a trend toward recognizing such a right in the public. The Supreme Court of Florida in *Brickell v. Trammell*, 82 So. (Fla.) 221, says:

"The rights of the people of the States in the navigable waters and the lands thereunder, including the shore or space between high and low water mark, relate to navigation, commerce, fishing, bathing, and other easements allowed by law."

And in *Barnes v. Midland R. Terminal Co.*, 85 N. E. (N. Y.) 1093, there was a like holding. Here both plaintiff and defendant were littoral proprietors. Plaintiff alleged that defendant by the erection of certain piers and buildings extending out from his land obstructed the rights of the public in the foreshore. The injunction was granted on appeal. The court said:

"The same reasons which underlie the decision in the Brookhaven case as to the rights of littoral and riparian owners apply with even greater force to the rights of the public to use the foreshore upon the margin of our tidewaters for fishing, bathing, and boating, to all of which the right of passage may be said to be a necessary incident."

The injunction was modified in *Barnes v. Midland Railroad Terminal Co.*, 112 N. E. 926, but the rule as above stated was in no respect limited.

(b) However, there is no right in the public to cross private property to reach the ocean.

Bolso Land Co. v. Burdick, 151 Cal. 254.

In this case plaintiff sought an injunction to restrain defendants crossing its land to reach a navigable bay. The injunction was granted. The court here squarely held that the public has no right to invade and cross private land in order to reach navigable water.

F. A. Hihn Co. v. City of Santa Cruz, 170 Cal. 436.

Action by plaintiff to quiet title to beach between ordinary or mean high tide and extraordinary high-tide line. This was about 200 feet wide and covered with sand. Next to the tideland this was not built upon, but back of that the city had constructed a paved road and park. The city was held to have procured title to the latter part by adverse user, but not the sandy portion next to the ordinary high-tide line. Held that the State did not get title to this strip as tideland and so its grant to the city was invalid. Also, although the public had long used this strip in conjunction with the tideland beach below, it was held not to be dedicated to the public use, nor was title obtained by the city by means of adverse user. The court said:

"But where land is uninclosed and uncultivated, the fact that the public has been in the habit of going upon the land will ordinarily be attributed to a license on the part of the owner rather than to his intent to dedicate (13 Cyc. 484). This is more particularly true where the use by the public is not over a definite and specified line, but extends over the entire surface of the tract (13 Cyc. 484). It will not be presumed, from mere failure to object, that the owner of such land so used intends to create in the public a right which would practically destroy his own right to use any part of the property."

APPENDIX NO. VI

Extracts from a Report Made in 1924 by the Los Angeles Superintendent of Parks,
With Recommendations Similar to Those of This Report

DURING the period of nearly fifteen years in which I have been associated with the Los Angeles Park Department, I have from time to time given considerable thought and attention to the need of a comprehensive park system.

Fifteen years ago the city covered an area of 85 square miles, with a population of 300,000 and a park area of 4,000 acres, considerably over the accepted area of one acre to every 100 inhabitants. The system was only partially developed. The boundaries of the city had just embraced Griffith Park, which was so far from the center of population and without any means of transportation that no attempt had been made to develop it and very few people patronized it; but adequate provision in park area had been made at that time.

Today (1924) the city covers an area of 415 square miles, with a population of over 1,000,000, while the park area has increased less than 1,000 acres. It is true that the present park area of 5,000 acres is extensively developed and portions of it used to the point of abuse, but there are large areas of the city closely built up and thickly populated that have no provision for parks, and the present park area is less than one-half acre per 100 inhabitants, and poorly distributed.

The city ought to make provision for the future population by securing an additional 45,000 acres of land for park purposes before the price becomes excessive, and before other permanent improvements occupy the land. There is an immediate need of 5,000 acres additional park land to accommodate the present population.

In July, 1925, the method of providing money for park maintenance will be changed. Instead of indefinite amounts appropriated by the City Council, the new charter provides a direct levy of 7c per hundred dollars assessed valuation. Under this plan the Park Board can intelligently estimate and forecast expenditures, and they can outline a policy of park development years in advance. Under the 7c rate the Park Department will receive about $1,000,000 annually or nearly $1 per capita, almost 40

per cent more than the present allowance. The cost of providing all forms of park service for the past fiscal year was 57c per capita. On account of the increase in laborers' wages granted this year by the budget committee of the City Council, the per capita cost will be about 60c.

Several attempts have been made by former park boards to carry out a program of park expansion, notably the effort to acquire the Arroyo Seco and the Silver Lake Parkways, which was started in 1910. This was the first attempt in Los Angeles to create a parkway along a drainage channel from the mountains to the sea. Evidently the taxpayers within the assessment areas did not realize the necessity or advantage of acquiring this valuable addition to the parks, for both projects were protested out after several years spent in negotiations.

In 1914 a movement was started to establish a comprehensive system of parks and boulevards. This was intended to provide: mountain and beach reservations; parkways and special areas classed as rural or country parks; together with a system of neighborhood parks that would provide the same service in each radial mile, giving each four square miles a park; the system to be linked up by specially improved and traffic-regulated streets to form a boulevard chain around and through the city. Surveys were made, numerous maps were drawn, a comprehensive report was prepared, and steps were being taken to secure by legislation an adequate park law under which to function. And then America went to war, and for several years park projects were of minor consideration.

In 1920 the Los Angeles Planning Commission was created as an official advisory body, and, after a year's study and investigation of our civic problems, decided that in order to adequately meet the situation the political boundaries of Los Angeles would have to be ignored and co-operation brought about through the County government, with the result that Regional Planning Conference was called by the County Board of Supervisors in 1921. Committees of five were appointed to investigate and report on each physical civic problem, and were selected from the northeast, northwest, southeast, southwest, and central districts of the County, the central district representing the City of Los Angeles. I was accorded the very great courtesy of being selected to serve on the Parks and Boulevards Committee representing the Central District.

After eight months' field study and investigation, together with the preparation of a map, the Parks and Boulevards Committee submitted their recommendations in the form of a report so brief that I will repeat it:

Sec. 1. That all parkways and pleasure boulevards be established as separate features from traffic highways.

Sec. 2. That all parkways and pleasure boulevards when located along river channels, arroyos, canyons, and the sea coast be established so as to pass *under* all other lines of traffic, and when located on ridges and mountain crests that they be established so as to pass *over* all other lines of traffic by bridge or viaduct. Briefly, no grade crossings should be permitted to exist.

Sec. 3. That parkways and pleasure boulevards when established along channel enbankments can be beautified economically, artistically, and with great scenic effect at low cost; and as a utility they provide easy means of construction for trunk sewers and storm drains, and a rapid means of transportation in case of flood-control work.

Sec. 4. That parkways and pleasure boulevards when established along ridges and mountain crests should be located so as to reach the most advantageous viewpoints, and as a utility they will prove extremely valuable in providing rapid means of transportation in case of forest fires.

Sec. 5. That as a further consideration these parkways and pleasure boulevards serve to link up all beach reservations to be established, these reservations to be for the full use of the public and not controlled by private parties.

Sec. 6. We recommend that picnic parks and camps be established throughout the district.

Sec. 7. We recommend that all principal drainage channels be acquired and controlled by the community for the highest public use.

Sec. 8. That patents to land in the forest reservations be discouraged.

As a result of the conclusions and recommendations of the various committees of the Regional Planning Conference, the Board of Supervisors, in 1923, established as an advisory body the Los Angeles County Regional Planning Commission, who in their first report laid particular stress on the entirely inadequate provision for local parks supplying neighborhoods in the City of Los Angeles. . . .

During the past four years the City Planning Commission has been endeavoring to solve the problem, and has now reached the point where, assisted by the County Regional Planning Commission, the legal machinery is being built up to permit the establishment of a metropolitan park district. . . .

Under the jurisdiction of a metropolitan park commission, it will be possible to secure park territory lying outside the boundaries of municipalities within the metropolitan area, and the activities of the commission will be financed by a mill tax for acquisition and maintenance of such properties. The ultimate area of the park system will

be governed by the amount of money available for maintenance, the size of each park, and the relative service demanded by the locality, together with the type of improvement introduced.

Referring to the price of park land, it may be interesting to estimate what it will cost Los Angeles to acquire immediately the park land necessary to provide for a limited increase in population.

The 415 square mile area of the city contains 265,600 acres, which, subdivided into 5 lots per acre, will make 1,300,000 lots, exclusive of streets, the assessed valuation amounting to $1,368,000,000. The City Planning Commission, after an exhaustive study of the problem, estimates that a district bond issue amounting to about 2 per cent of the assessed valuation would be the proper ratio of expenditure for park purchase. The 2 per cent ratio would work out alike on high and low priced property, as the same pro rate area can be secured in each case. Two per cent of the assessed valuation amounts to $27,360,000. Assuming that recently subdivided property, selected where least desirable for residence purposes, can be secured for $1,000 per lot or $5,000 per acre, and outlying acreage in and around the drainage channels can be secured at $1,000 per acre, a fair average price would be $3,000 per acre, with variations in price according to location and surroundings. A 30-year district bond issue of $27,000,000 would secure approximately 9,000 acres of park land—the equivalent of 90 parks of 100 acres each, or 180 parks of 50 acres each, or any modification of that amount to suit the individual case. The 415 square mile area of the city, divided into sections of 4 square miles each, make 104 neighborhood park districts; and 9,000 acres provides the equivalent of 86.5 acres for each neighborhood park required, leaving the *special areas, parkways, and regional parks* to be acquired by the Metropolitan Park Commission. Adding 9,000 acres to the existing 5,000 will provide 14,000 acres of park land, or an allowance of park area considerably over one acre to every 100 inhabitants. To pay off the 2 per cent bond issue in 30 years would require an average tax annually of 12½c per $100 assessed valuation for sinking fund and interest at 6 per cent—very easy terms on which to acquire adequate space for neighborhood parks. There is no case on record where an expenditure for park purposes ever depreciated the value of the property assessed. If real estate subdividers keep on cutting up the acreage into lots without making adequate provision for parks, and the people who ultimately purchase and occupy the subdivisions persistently refuse to meet the cost of acquiring the necessary territory, then some drastic legislation will have to be enacted for the protection of the individual and to secure the welfare, health, and safety of the community.

Very respectfully,

FRANK SHEARER,

Superintendent of Parks.

INDEX

INDEX

THE POWER OF DICTION

An Interview with Laurie Olin
(Greg Hise and William Deverell)

Tell us about your training and the significance of the Olmsted firm for professional education in landscape architecture in North America.

I don't have the background and training that is typical for young people today in landscape architecture. I didn't set out to be a landscape architect, didn't go to school to study landscape architecture, and didn't go into the field for some time after leaving college. I began as a student of civil engineering at the University of Alaska, in Fairbanks, where I grew up, and I transferred into architecture at the University of Washington, where we got a heavy dose of Olmsted theory, planning, and history from Richard Haag who was a student of Stan White, E. B. White's brother. Haag trained at the University of Illinois which had some of the early ecologists in North America. White had worked in the Olmsted office before teaching at Illinois. So Rich made us read ecologists like Loren Eiseley, Paul Shepherd, as well as J. B. Jackson whom he knew. So we were absolutely pickled in vernacular American landscape, the traditions of Olmsted's planning and design, and Japanese art and architecture.

The period when I worked for Richard Haag, Fred Bassetti, Jack Morris and Ibsen Nelson—the best design firms in Seattle at that time—colleges and universities were in a huge building boom. There was a great deal of academic campus planning work. It was the luck of being born at the right time. If you come out of school in 1929, it is different than if you come out in 1946. Well, I came out of school in 1961, there was a huge building boom going on, a lot of academic institutional work, and people were beginning to talk about new towns. There was a lot going on. It was similar to my office now—almost irresponsible—with principals dumping work on talented young people, just loading them up and hardly able to supervise them adequately. For the people who have joined my office in the last year or so it is very much like it was when I was at Edward Barnes's office in 1964: "Here's a campus, kid. Do something and I'll see you in three days." When I went to Barnes's office we immediately won a competition, and I remember thinking "wow!" They had hired me for a couple of weeks' work and I stayed for three years. They put me on the State University at Potsdam, after that I went on to the Emma Willard School, after that there was a Christian theological seminary, some houses for the Rockefellers, housing in Puerto Rico and Chicago, Monterey Pacific College, and SUNY Purchase.

While I was living in New York, several people I had known in architecture school who had worked for Rich Haag also, who were talented and who also drew well, had decided to go to Harvard to get graduate degrees in landscape architecture. They would come down and stay with me and look at the city. Because they were interested in landscape architecture, I would give them walking tours of Central Park. We'd go in on 59th Street and Fifth Avenue, and we'd walk the whole length of the park. Or I'd take them up on the subway to 125th Street, and we'd enter the park from the north and walk down the whole length. Then we'd walk all the way down Manhattan to the Battery, take the Staten Island Ferry, come back and take the Lexington Avenue line to 53rd Street where I lived. So I had become interested in Central Park, and I had started to give tours to landscape architects of Central Park even though it wasn't my thing. But I had begun to come to the conclusion that it was really pretty damn good; it was an interesting and wonderful place, big and sprawling and full of ideas. Then I would go up and visit my friends at Harvard. They were studying under Hideo Sasaki, who was chairman at that time. Sasaki had just moved his office, Sasaki, Dawson, and DeMay, in Cambridge, into an old Masonic temple and my friends were working there, and they'd show me the work they were doing. There was a young guy named Pete Walker, who they'd sent out to open a West Coast branch which was called Sasaki Walker (later SWA). So I was around the edges of landscape design while I was working for Ed Barnes and all these young designers who were keeping tabs on each other's work.

By coincidence, Steven Currier, a wealthy man married to one of the Whitneys, and a man who liked his horses, offered to give the city of New York money to build a new police stable. The Polo Grounds in the Bronx had been torn down for a housing project, and the stables for rental horses on the West Side were starting to disappear under urban renewal. Currier offered to build horse facilities on the 86th street transverse of Central Park if he could give money to build a polo ring. This is at the north end of the Great Oval that's recently been restored, near the Metropolitan Museum of Art. There's a police pistol range there in a little Calvert Vaux building, as well as some police stables. Currier gave some money, and there was a limited competition. They invited Philip Johnson, Marcel Breuer, Ed Barnes, Davis Brody and Kevin Roche, the hot firms in New York at that moment. Because people rotated from one office to another we all knew what was going on in other firms; it was an interesting moment. Anyway, I was put on the competition team, along with a couple of other hotshot designers, and we had to do drawings—not only on the design for the polo ring, but also its context. I was elected to do all of Central Park, and I produced this long drawing, a beautiful ink rendering of every bridle trail, every path, every tree, every twig, every stone, every lake. It got me to study Central Park in a way I had not even known it walking around, taking my friends through it.

This was kind of an unusual exercise for a young architect. Among other things, I came to the conclusion that it was probably the single greatest work of art in America by an American artist, that it was *the* best. Maybe somebody else will do something better at some point, but I couldn't think of a single work of art in America that was more astonishing than that place. This idea never went away. So I have a strange education. I began working in and later teaching landscape architecture without ever studying it. But it turned out I had been studying it informally.

· · · · ·

The importance of the Olmsteds to the inception and nature of landscape education can hardly be overemphasized. Many of the first teachers came out of the Olmsted office. The curriculum of study in most landscape architecture programs today, which emphasizes a diversity of practical/technical methods and skills (grading, construction, road alignment, horticultural methods, drainage, and ecology), along with humanistic subjects such as history and studio art, the embrace of new technology, and social issues, is nearly a mirror of the ideas and practice of the Olmsted firm. If you look at the Olmsted firm, and the skills needed to work in their offices, how they approached projects, and how they broke them down and what their own interests were—they really formed the underlying basis of the curriculum in most landscape programs.

For several decades, graduates from the first schools, steeped in and influenced by the Olmsted example and body of work, fanned out across the country to practice and found other schools. Their office in Brookline really had a tremendous influence on all the schools. I would make the assertion that all successful and important landscape architects now practicing in the United States can trace his or her connection to the Brookline office in fewer than the six degrees of separation popularized by John Guare's recent play. In my own case it is three degrees. Rich Haag/Stan White/Brookline. Bang. Bang. Bang. For Pete Walker, it is Hideo Sasaki/Stan White/Brookline. For Lawrence Halprin, it was several faculty members at Harvard who had worked in the Olmsted firm. For Dan Kiley, it was Warren Manning, who worked for Olmsted. The lines are short for all the people over forty-five in our field and although it may be four degrees for today's students, still the connections, attitudes, methodologies, and values are more often than not direct descendants of the Olmsted office.

The agenda of the Olmsteds (Sr. and Jr.) of civilizing American cities, of suffusing urban design and planning with the benefits of healthy natural systems, of providing access to high quality open space for all citizens—young and old, commuter and resident—this idea of creating networks of parks, playgrounds, parkways, natural preserves, great civic spaces, and environmentally-sensitive suburban development has been largely taken up by the entire profession and forms the basis of much of our teaching curriculum and employment today.

It would be interesting to know who in the office was responsible for writing the 1930 report for Los Angeles County. The whole financial work, the tax work, is very smart. It is rather like a proposal we recently made to the University of California in Berkeley, where we said, "Yes, we can do a plan for Berkeley, but only if the University allows us to have direct access to the President and some of the Regents. We have to reorganize parts of how you manage capital projects; otherwise there's no point in it. We won't work for you unless you reorganize how the client deals with the real problems." We made

THE POWER OF DICTION

the presentation to middle management, to whom we were essentially saying we're going to go over you, around you, reorganize you. Needless to say, we didn't get the job. This is part of what happened with the Olmsted/Bartholomew plan for Los Angeles I suspect.

When you are asked to plan important things, you have to overreach. You just pitch your work as high as you can, because things are never better than at the beginning. You never achieve everything. So you want to aim high enough so that when you don't get everything, what you do get is worth the effort. Rarely does any whole scheme get built. Even Adolphe Alphand and Baron Haussmann didn't get it all done. The period that Alphand was working for Haussmann, who was Prefect of the Seine, was about fifteen years, and that was it. It was a very short period of time. There was a lot that did not happen, but a lot that did happen. Once their bureaucracies were established, they went on building even though leadership changed and people lost their vision or different tastes prevailed. It's the same with the Olmsted-Bartholomew plan; some of it got started, and then it developed a life of its own. Clearly, planning in Los Angeles County was very ad hoc and piecemeal beforehand.

If you look, you see an illustration in the report of proposed arterials and highway construction that some other group had proposed. They picked up on the whole concept of parkways and freeways and invented a broader system that really did develop a life of its own, even though it ended up nothing like what they intended. But then who knows what comes of most plans that any firm proposes? The Li Wu River Gorge study our office did, who knows about it? Only the Secretary of Interior and a bunch of bureaucrats in Taiwan and a couple of people who work in my office. Who knows about reports that Jones and Jones in Seattle has done or how about the Toronto waterfront study that McHarg's office did, who knows of these things? There is an enormous amount of excruciatingly considered professional work that is lost—although it's not really lost, it's just unknown.

Now that you have had a chance to review the Olmsted-Bartholomew report Parks, Playgrounds and Beaches, *we are interested in your thoughts about the plan, its objectives and intentions, the scale and scope and the feasibility of implementation. Do you have any thoughts about the value of this report for practitioners and students (planners, architects, landscape architects, policy-makers, urban historians)?*

My immediate response is to the ambition, the breadth, and the scope of the report. It is very impressive. It is rarely matched in the work of professionals I know today. I think it is a period piece, in its quality, its scope, its scale, and its ambition. One of the things I noted while reading is how well written it is, how literate it is, how numerate it is, the confident grasp of issues, whether they are social issues, fiscal issues, ecological, administerial, or judicial issues. The grasp of all that, and the confidence with which the report addresses them, certainly is unusual today.

It's not that the profession has dumbed down. It's just that these guys were unafraid of taking it all on. And they did, but with the clarity of mind and a diction that allowed them to address it so clearly. One of the things I noticed were the famous, wealthy, powerful public figures who formed the client committee and advisory group. These were real movers and shakers, some of whom were merely lending their name to support the effort, but clearly some of them were working for it. These are people from industry, from entertainment, Cecil DeMille, Mary Pickford, people like that. But there are numerous design professionals such as John Parkinson and Myron Hunt. Somehow this issue unified people from different backgrounds, all very powerful in their spheres of influence, who recognized this topic was important to society.

The report underscores several interesting and important facts of American urbanism and western expansion which should not pass unnoticed. One is that the western cities developed in a relatively short period of time, often in very dramatic and unique physiographic settings. Vancouver, Canada, San Francisco, or Seattle, all began as crass, bustling, business enterprises adjacent to landscapes that were almost universally deemed beautiful, healthful, and attractive—spectacular landscapes by almost any measure. As each of these cities grew, private enterprise was unable and unwilling to devote adequate land and financial resources to great public works and open space. There were several reasons. First, the land was deemed too valuable and people were too eager to maximize their opportunities to get rich quickly. Second, immediately adjacent to these crass commercial enterprises was a seemingly unlimited resource of beautiful wide open expanse— the beaches, the mountains, the agricultural valleys. People were in the habit of going outside the city for nature and recreation, which seemed near and in enormously great supply. This was a common factor in all these rapidly urbanizing centers in western America.

I think the Olmsted Brothers, coming from the East, were particularly sensitive to this phenomenon. They saw it very clearly, while people within the communities did not. It comes through as a subtext in this report. All of these cities—Los Angeles, San Diego, San Francisco, Seattle—now sprawl all over those once fabulously beautiful settings. Nature has been pushed to the horizon. Each city has serious traffic congestion, terrible air pollution, a great deficit of adequate parks and open space, and swollen populations. They're all deficient in profound ways, because they happened so fast. People thought, "Well, we'll do that next year." They never did. The Olmsted Brothers point that out. They say, "this is going to happen, and this is your moment to do something about it or you'll miss the chance." I think that's one of the most interesting things in this report. It's poignant actually.

The report spells out the probable outcome based on an already problematic situation in 1930. Interestingly enough, it is the first year of the Great Depression. Yet they propose a very ambitious plan at a time when the entire economic structure of America has collapsed. Talk about brave! And wildly optimistic. If you look at pages four and five, they offer economic rationalizations for the situation. One of the reasons they advanced to explain why park planning hasn't happened is that the financial capital is all tied up in the creation of basic economic and social infrastructure. There isn't any free capital, it's all invested in generating the city and the urban fabric. It's used up. All the bonding capacity is tied up, because of rapid expansion. Somebody working on the report understood the fundamental economic situation very profoundly. Yet ironically, if you think about this, the great park systems in the east and in Midwestern cities were all created at a time when their economies were expanding as rapidly as the economies expanded in western cities at the turn of the century. Just think about that. When were the great park systems built in Kansas City or Chicago or even New York? No one had platted it all out, they hadn't built out New York when Olmsted was thinking about expanding Central Park another ten blocks north. The earlier plans worked at a time when there was an increase in capital and there was considerable generation of wealth in those cities along with a series of financial panics, wars, and uncertainty. Yet there were people with social value who said, "We must do this," and a couple of people interceded effectively. But it didn't happen in Los Angeles. There were people who knew to do it; people on this committee knew to do it.

They understood they were in the same position as New York in 1885. "Oh God! We have to do this." So there is that sense of learning from history. Some of it happened, and some of it didn't quite make it. I find that interesting.

In the report there is an explicit discussion of what might constitute a park system. The authors distinguish between two kinds: local and regional facilities. They describe the representative characteristics and uses that would constitute such a system. That's great. They lay out what a park system is, and what are the parts you need. This is the stuff that operates at a micro scale, that is what operates at a macro scale, and these are the differences between them. They don't ask their clients to choose. They tell them to do all!

They go further and talk about larger physiographic and ecological possibilities. At page fifteen, there's a discussion of flood hazards and how to treat the corridors of floodways and floodplains, and how to incorporate them into a network. They suggest the cost to society if it doesn't do this, and what would happen in terms of dollars and public safety if they don't. The planners use a carrot and stick approach.

On page sixteen, the authors calculate it would take $40 million for park acquisition and local recreation improvements, plus the acquisition of virtually the entire Pacific shoreline for public use and access. Another $27 million is necessary for access facilities and improvements at the beaches. For the regional athletic facilities, they suggest $7 million. For natural and wildlife preserves, another $12 to $14 million for their acquisition and improvements. And for the pleasureway parks or parkways, another $100 million for the requisition of land and $45 million for improvements. They propose a project extending over forty or fifty years. The net result is they end up proposing $233 million in 1930 for acquisition and improvement and a build out period of forty to fifty years. Sounds like a lot. Sounds very ambitious. But of course if you turn around, and divide $233 million by forty years, that's only $6.8 million a year. Truly a modest sum. If you can figure out how to front end it and bond it, and do it in phases, paying it back over time, it's not such a bad, or unimaginable, deal.

When you look at their photos of Los Angeles in the 1930s, they are almost heartbreaking. You see this vast open space, with the strong presence of natural features so close to the city and all around. It's heartbreaking, also, when you consider the irony of how these planners had such a romantic vision of and love for the automobile that they coupled with a proposal for gracious scenic auto routes, a system of parkways that would bind the whole region together. Furthermore, they combine these with proposals to preserve floodways as a way to lower the social cost of flood damage to society. Put the two together and you get a dream of easy, leisurely movement through a spacious, generous realm of natural features. There is a vision of touring through a landscape paradise implied in this report that, of course, was a mirage that kept receding from us all as we tried to approach it.

Even so, their proposal is really a skillful and brilliant study, because they begin with an analysis of need, followed by a superb marshalling of statistics to their purpose. The executive summary is really terse and powerful. Then you go into the back-up report where they lay out their argument. The rhetoric is quite persuasive. There's a discussion of the rapid growth rate and the chaos of jurisdictions. They overwhelm you with the fact that the county is 1500 square miles, there are 40 municipal jurisdictions, there has been a twenty-fold growth in population in thirty years. They offered what proved to be remarkably accurate projections of growth over the next twenty years. In fact the population they predicted for 1950 was almost to the number. They absolutely saw it clear, and they were able to describe the situation and use statistics in a very careful way. It's not sloppy, and they don't fudge the figures. They are, in fact, quite cautious with them. They were extremely prescient, when they talk about the evil of the "friction of distance"—a wonderful phrase—and the problems of distribution even while they were absolutely enthralled with single family detached houses and auto travel. They foresee the problems of diffusion associated with low density development, remarking that such development is desirable "unless checked by traffic congestion and by the increasing length of travel through completely urbanized territory, etc." They imagine the likelihood of what everyone is going through in rush hour today on the 405, the 10, and the 101 freeways. What's out there now in Los Angeles County, they describe in their marvelous diction. They see it as one possible outcome, but then they as much as say "but you could design your way out of that." I find that really interesting. They are so smart, rather like the smart guys who brought us Vietnam. You can't design everything, you can't control everything, and they clearly lost control.

That sounds more snippy and vicious than I mean it, because I think the Olmsted office was fabulous. On page twenty-three and the following pages they discuss the loss of access to natural resources—especially the beaches, the canyons, and the hills. Clearly we still feel this loss and people continue to talk about it. They present a photograph of the San Fernando Valley that is nearly two-thirds groves in the image. It's quite beautiful. It's all citrus and irrigation with a few roads along the section lines. The loss of this agricultural land has something to do with why food has to travel so far and has become so expensive and so much less tasty. It has to be designed not to bruise in transit. The period of this report was a moment in American history when we had fresh food grown next to the people who actually consumed it. Well there's a lot of reading between the lines when you look at these pictures. There are all the other things you think of along with the things you are supposed to be thinking about.

There's another great observation on page twenty-four. They say, "the hills and sightly eminences in and around Los Angeles have never been properly worked into the expanding structure of the city." What a great phrase. Then the authors become very specific about Baldwin Hills, and they go on to identify places that should have skyline drives on them and so forth. They make a big plug at this point in the backup material for an arterial roadway network and scenic roads, insisting that these be free-flowing things. There's also a belief in the limited future growth and the utility for mass transit. They already see the future problems of mass transit in this region. We all know the story of the Red Line later—and of the role the American automobile industry played in the demise of Huntington's railroad, but the truth presented here is that even in the 1930s Olmsted and Bartholomew could see that there was a statistical problem. There was a physical, mathematical, statistical problem; if you spread people out in such broad areas, it will be very hard to come up with a transportation system that will serve them well. They understood that very clearly, and said it. They pointed out that the only way this kind of development pattern would make sense is to create a superior system of arterial roadways and a great local network of roads. But, they believed in mass transit, that it would be very efficient in delivering people to certain key destinations, like the beaches or major parks and downtown destinations. Therefore they proposed a both/and strategy, not an either/or.

There's a very interesting compilation of statistics about cities and their park acreage, and I think anyone reading this report then or now would be really interested in what the numbers were at that period (as best as anyone could tell). They note one exception to the rule in Los Angeles, the single, really well-planned place with a large amount of open space and access to natural features and amenities, Palos Verdes. This is interesting and self-serving because the Olmsted firm had helped to develop it, had a financial interest in it, and Frederick Law Olmsted Jr. had a house there.

Chapter three is devoted to administration and to legal and financial conditions. It is an extraordinarily interesting and powerful chapter. They propose a countywide park district funded by what I take to be something like a five mil property tax, with start-up money financed through bonds to be paid back over time. Essentially they determined that if you're going to do a system like this, you need some kind of tax increment financing. They begin laying out possible ways to do it. They point out that with tax increment financing, the rate would go down as the assessment goes up because additional development will be generating funds and the increase in property values means that your relative contribution would be going down. This is shrewd. These people are really bright. They were and still are light years ahead of most local politicians in their understanding of how public financing for parks might work. They tried to address the financing of infrastructure at the scale of the problem.

I do not know many landscape architects today, outside of academia, who could handle municipal finance and think at this level, to try to persuade a client to reorganize their government and their tax structure in order to produce a better environment. This is not the sort of thing taught, although it should be. You'd find it in the Wharton School of Business but you won't find in the design schools. You'd find municipal finance in the Stanford Business School, but not an interest in parks.

Given my experience at the Olin Partnership, I know that quite a few people and different hands go into getting large and important reports done. There are people who lead the team, but you delegate. Principals write some things and others write parts. As I read the Olmsted-Bartholomew report I kept wondering, "whose voice is this?" I'm not sure. I can't tell. I haven't read enough other work by them. But it would be very interesting to read additional reports and see if you could pick up phrases or if there's a turn of mind or certain strategies that repeat. I would be very interested to know who wrote the section on administration and finance because I think it is extraordinarily bold and extraordinarily intelligent. Clearly it was beyond the ken of the folks in Los Angeles. It left them in the dust, and they were either frightened or set about covering their ass, for they didn't get it.

Olmsted and Bartholomew clearly talked to important people in Los Angeles, but they were applying strategies they had learned elsewhere. They refer to Paris and New York, cities where civic leaders had done this sort of thing. I drew a diagram to figure out how they were proposing to do it. The text suggests there are these different curves. The first one is the cost of acquisition and infrastructure improvements, it starts slow, climbs very fast, peaks, and then begins to fall off. Meanwhile, maintenance and operating costs remain low for a time, but at a certain point these lines intersect and maintenance and operating costs continue to climb. As acquisition costs go to zero, the implementation costs begin to level off and eventually trickle down and stop. But clearly the authors and their clients were worried about cash flow. The whole discussion has to do with "well yeah, if it is 233 million over forty to fifty years, that's only 6–8 million a year," but they understand that in order to get it going they will need big chunks of capital up front. It's a cash flow problem, getting it up and running. Also, there is the haunting thought that "in the future, the operating costs are going to go on and escalate and continue." Even though they hadn't seen the kind of inflation that we've known since, you can tell they were thinking about it. Ironically this approach and the fiscal language which is so familiar to us today must have seemed like wishful thinking in the first years of the Great Depression. Their Keynesian discussion was rarefied, occurring among a group of worldly intellectuals at a time when everyone else in the country was running around saying "how am I going to feed my family? Twenty million? You must be out of your mind."

In essence, the authors challenge the city of Los Angeles to be as bold as Paris or as Westchester County, New York when these jurisdictions embarked upon the construction of parkways and parks. They assert that the parks in this plan will create value, they are not a money sink. If Los Angeles were to make this investment, it would be returned through increased property values. This is an argument we now know to be true in many cases but not always. The Urban Land

Institute (ULI) will tell you it's a mixed story. We have great examples like Bryant Park in New York and we have terrible examples. But Olmsted and Bartholomew were making the best case they could for why Angelenos should do it. They were trying every possible argument to get people to step up and dare to do it, to reshape their city and its relationship to the natural setting.

These consultants recognized that small, disorganized local agencies cannot do any of this. There was a need for a larger vision, the need for unity and for coordination and for broad sweeping powers, similar to a Panhellenic union. They flat out say it; they challenged the county to figure out how to deal with balkanized jurisdictions.

They were attempting to build upon the things they found. Many of the specific proposals predate their plan, which is kind of sad when you think about it. They were trying to say this is great, but let's keep going, let's do the next, bigger, more adventurous stuff.

They propose a series of playgrounds in a manner that we all recognize because several of the so-called New Urbanists have picked up some of these diagrams from the 1930s and before. One is the scheme for distribution according to a quarter-mile and half-mile radius, the distance a child can walk to school and local amenities. Andres Duany, Stefanos Polyzoides and others have been proposing this uniform distribution of small-scale spaces in the last few years. Here we have a perfect diagram of such a proposal. The authors also set standards for community centers based upon their understanding of the needs of children and the elderly. Once again, they harp upon finance; they keep hitting this topic hard, over and over again.

In chapter five, part two, they talk about public beaches, and it is interesting to see that statistically, Venice Beach had three-quarters of the total use of all beaches in the Los Angeles region. So you realize how these early imprints really do read through time. Despite the drilling for oil and the adjacent industry, despite everything that has happened to Venice, the fact is that people got there early and it stuck as a prime recreation area. Zuma Beach up toward Point Dume is great for surf and everything, but it never has had the quantum of use Venice Beach has had.

Public versus private, commercial use versus recreational use: the authors discuss the conflicts the beaches elicited. Should beaches be developed for urban uses? Who should have access? Only those who have money? They talk about this very intelligently. But they then make a proposal that in a way is wonderful and bold and brave and in another way it is really loopy. (Audacious would be too mild a term.) My notes on page sixty-six say "interesting and ambitious plan for oceanside park and harbor all the way from the Pacific Palisades to Marina del Rey."

What they propose is an offshore scenic drive. I put an exclamation point down in my notes when going through the report. If you look at their drawing there's this simple big arc—they make this great draftsman's gesture at one scale all the way across the bay—and then propose to fill along it creating a series of islands and breakwaters that produce a great inner lagoon for recreation, boating and swimming. Of course, if you think about power boats and the oil and everything—who would do that? What we see in plate 33 (p.66) is essentially the equivalent of Daniel Burnham's fabulous navy pier proposal in the Plan for Chicago, with a lagoon formed by a long jetty/breakwater with an inner harbor for pleasure craft. The darn thing must be fifteen miles long. And it appears one could drive along its length—there are places to stop. They even talk about the different kinds of places to park. It's an extraordinary proposal. In a way, it's truly American. The idea builds upon Venice, it builds upon Coney Island, it builds upon a lot of odd precedents that they pull together in order to make the scheme appear quite natural and very lofty. In fact, it's a very big deal! It's like building an Air Force base! It is amazing! It's like Kansai Airport in the ocean off Osaka. It would have been a truly remarkable piece of naval engineering, civil engineering, hydrology, oceanography. It is an amazing project they proposed.

I'm certain they really wanted to do it. I think they really wanted to try it somewhere. They'd built little fragments and pieces of it. They'd seen other people do bits. They'd seen jetties, they'd done this or that. People were building the highway to the Keys in Florida at that time. So the idea and precedent were in place for these ocean highways and they were kind of fun. We have to remember the romance of the private auto car at that moment, too. Here was an extraordinary vision! On the one hand, it is wacky and is truly an American fantasy. On the other hand, you could do it. It's simply civil engineering, right? We do this with harbors all the time. I have serious qualms, however, when I consider the environmental efficacy of a project like that, let alone the economy of means with which one hopes to achieve one's goals.

The authors also talk about large reservations in this section, and again, there are big sweeping visions and pronouncements especially having to do with the inland mountain areas, deserts, the Joshua trees. They talk about stream courses, the Channel Islands—they really did not make small plans! A lot of this has not been done. However, there are elements, bits and pieces of what they propose, that people did work on. Why? Because they were obvious things to do, people could agree with them. Somebody would get behind this or that section of their plan. So pieces of their plan went ahead and developed a life of their own. There are many parts of this section about regional athletic and regional recreation that were carried out piecemeal over the next thirty-five, forty, fifty years. Some of the things they proposed in the section about large reservations really don't happen until after World War II, but then they do happen. And they are still happening.

People are still doing things suggested in the Olmsted-Bartholomew report without even knowing it exists. I am convinced that most people don't know about this report, but I have the sneaking suspicion that it had a kind of half-life. There must have been many times between 1930 and the Korean War, say, when someone, some bureaucrat, said, "oh Antelope Valley, wasn't there a report?" And you can probably find a subsequent report that said "we should do this up there." Or Joshua Tree, "oh yes we should do this." So if we ask: "What is the effect of a report like this?" I have to answer, I don't think you can expect a report like this, a large-scale, comprehensive survey, to ever have an immediate impact, nor can you expect to have all of it get built. That almost never happens. You produce a report and years later people are pulling pieces out, they take on a discrete segment, or they say "Well, they said it would cost twenty million and now they tell me forty so we can't build out the entire plan but can do such and such." This is inevitable. People pick off the parts that they want to work on or that meet their agenda. About two-thirds of the way through the report, after reading about the big regional stuff and realizing that some of it actually had happened, I concluded that such efforts are never foolish. We must attempt proposals of this scale and character and quality.

Chapter eight talks about the need for parkways and large preserves. There's a fold-out diagram that superimposes the Boston parkway system with all of its properties over Los Angeles County.

Wow! That should be a great diagram to impress local citizens. Plate 48 (following p.98) shows a series of alternative parkway sections intended for different situations. It shows that there are many ways to create a high-quality roadway system. In particular, they show that at night, it's dangerous and difficult on some of these mountain roads because headlights from opposing cars shine in your eyes. What can one do? Separate the cartways, or make them different. In effect they proposed more sophisticated highway standards than what we have on our interstates today. One of the roadways has a 225-foot right-of-way, an extraordinarily gracious road, very beautiful and in the best tradition of the greatest highways ever designed.

They also proposed developing a wildlife refuge and wetland at the mouth of Ballona Creek, a project I can happily say I helped advance. It took a long time—fifty years—but we got it done. So here's to them. Olmsted and Bartholomew talk about a Baldwin Hills parkway—it is really too bad that never happened. As it is, there is a nasty road through the oil fields and some sad public planting beside it. They made some proposals that were really smart and wonderful. Many of these referenced the topography of the region. They worked with the shape of the land and the roadways were designed to explicate its form so that people would have more sense of orientation, so they would be able to find their way around better. We would all be able to read the landscape better following some of the road systems they proposed. It would have been quite special had they been built.

I think landscape architects always take the long view. We have a sense of time that is different from many of our contemporaries. We know the trees won't look as we planned for awhile—we are different that way. We also have a sense that there are certain natural things that have meaning, that you have to advocate for. Whether I am the advocate or not, somebody in the profession will be. Whether they know about a scheme I did or not, another person is going to have a similar thought. You just hammer away at it. Estuaries count. Wetlands really matter. The people who finally build Bolsa Chica may not have known this report, but this report had an echo in the next report, and in the next report. Somebody knew there was a report, and since no one had acted upon it, they beat the county commissioners over the head. Some of the big regional environmental ideas Olmsted and Bartholomew proposed are now pretty much in place.

Because those were the regional environmental things that had to be done, that mattered. We didn't get them all, but they were the important ones. They put their sticker on the important ones. They did their homework, they spent time going around looking: "wow, look at this river—what do you call this river?" I go to a place and say "show me the place," and look around and ask, "what it this?" Somebody tells me this is an important old place. And I say, "well I thought so, it feels good." So too, I suspect, Olmsted and Bartholomew had local people help them and they obviously loved to get in their cars and drive about. You can hear that they liked to drive around Los Angeles as it was then. The authors of this report knew what they were writing about.

It's uncanny that they propose a 225-foot parkway from Los Angeles to Palos Verdes. In 1985, I proposed a 200-foot parkway from Los Angeles International Airport (LAX) into the city. This is the scale of street that would form a grand entry to connect the coast to downtown. The one I proposed isn't getting built either. But the point is that landscape architects think like that. Olmsted and Bartholomew saw this place and said "wouldn't it be great to have a fabulous street that led you along with trees this far apart and cartways like this." I made a drawing almost exactly like this one (see above). The point is, I knew what this drawing of theirs would be like without ever seeing it. It is part of the DNA of landscape architects. Olmsted and Bartholomew called for the Los Angeles River to be developed with an embankment and a parkway, a grand proposal that is still talked about and is still not realized. And they talk especially about the upper reaches of the river alongside Griffith Park. They hammer away at how to use the lower stretches, the middle stretches, and the upper stretches of the Los Angeles River. Today many people are working on similar schemes.

What I find humbling is the range and the sweep across the region, their sense of the different towns and municipalities and the character of them. I really find this a humbling report. It is so correct in its ambition and in its vision about what a great society might aspire to and how it relates to its land and to its socialization in that land—it is a fabulous report. It shows what brilliant people in our profession can achieve when they are fully focused and are working at the top of their form. They master all this detail, but they don't lose track of the big picture. Other people should be amazed by this report. Contemporary practitioners will be struck by its extraordinary sweep, by the authors' grasp and their approach to broad social and environmental problems. It is also a model of expository writing and organization. In the end, I'm impressed and pleased by their insistence on big regional plans.

Today we would expect more graphic material in a report like this. Their audience must have found this sort of discourse accessible, adequate, and exemplary. They didn't feel the need for more graphics. Any city, agency, or client I have would want me to be quicker to the point. They'd want less text and more visuals: "show me more pictures, what's it look like?" The style of presentation we see in the Olmsted-Bartholomew report would be unacceptable to most of my clients today.

I think the report underscores the lack of physical environmental planning taking place today. It makes you realize how dumbed down and inconsequential a lot of the work that passes for planning in our regions and our cities really is. I think it is a damning critique of the lack of accomplishment in Los Angeles County. This report shows a combination of analysis, of vision, of financial savvy, and implementation strategies that is truly masterful. It is like a lost civilization.

Are there particular facets of the plan that you find especially inspired? Alternatively, are there aspects that are pedestrian or formulaic?

Inspired? Yes.

Setting goals so high, aiming for genuine excellence: that is inspirational. I think their notion of a vast network of linear parkways would have been breathtaking (as opposed to the freeways of today). I think it is sad, and it is complicated, because they proposed something that, had it been done, I don't know what the hell we'd think of it, but it would have been marvelous and unique and the world would have never seen anything like it.

That said, there are aspects of the plan that are pedestrian. They barely develop what recreation is. You can read the whole report and they don't really tell you what they mean when they say recreation. I think it's because they share a normative idea of recreation that was common then. Nor do they talk about what activities might occur in these athletic fields and parks that they are proposing. They are really kind of quiet and simple about that. They don't say much about what the inner-city playgrounds should be, what they might contain, how they might help people. Because of this lack of definition, the recreation facilities they propose seem dull, repetitive, ill-defined, and undeveloped. But that may be because everybody—client and professional—were so much of a social class and of a shared set of values that they didn't have to specify it. So possibly it's our lack of sympathy that we read the report and find it missing or lacking in this area. I don't want to privilege my own perspective and not be sympathetic to all the known, understood, shared intelligent things of another group. It would be wrong to abuse them by using the standard of another period. So there's an intellectual problem here, what is the unsaid of any period of history—the problem for historians.

Although it does not fall into the pedestrian category, I was a bit shocked by their unquestioning embrace of single-family housing and their enthusiastic embrace of the private motor car. They acknowledge the shortcomings of diffusion in the report but don't seem to understand how inevitable and serious these problems would become. I think this is worth pointing out. Even the most thoughtful, environmentally conscious, prescient people in America had no idea of the transformative nature of the automobile. On a similar note, I was surprised by their absolute hostility to compact urban centers and to congregate living, especially in the form of apartments, which would provide a critical mass and make public services such as neighborhood parks and civic spaces work better without the need for autos or so much travel. If you think about what they are proposing in terms of walking to neighborhood centers and if you think of the notion they have of regional and local facilities, the two-tiered system, density offers certain advantages, but in their own plans they encourage low density. Like all mere mortals, they carry contradictions forward with them. Finally, their proposal for the ocean-going parkway on the breakwater of islands across the entire Santa Monica Bay, while appealing to me in some ways in terms of its boldness and freedom and imagination, nonetheless would be strange and might wreck the entire Bay and the beach. It was a beautiful and naïve notion; wrongheaded—but that's ok, it didn't happen.

Given your understanding of development in Southern California, how do you view the Olmsted-Bartholomew proposal? More specifically, how do you read the plan in light of current projects in the region (for example, the Getty Center, Figueroa Corridor, Union Station, greening of the Los Angeles River)?

Some of us never work at more than one scale or certainly not at multiple scales at one time. Here, however, we see the Olmsted office comfortably working at several scales—juggling planning, design, management, and finance simultaneously. Today landscape work in Los Angeles, whether it's that of my firm or others, is far more opportunistic, and far more piecemeal. Unlike Olmsted and Bartholomew, a lot of our work doesn't really push for change at the same scale, certainly not change in terms of institutional structures. In fact, all the work in the region barely links up. It doesn't speak to the deep needs of vast portions of the region. The Olin Partnership does really wonderful projects, and a few people come and get it. Maybe hundreds of thousands of people come and get it, but not tens of millions. In a way, Playa Vista (in southwest Los Angeles between Venice and Westchester near the Los Angeles International Airport) was almost a scale model in 2000 acres of what Olmsted-Bartholomew were talking about over 1500 square miles! That's a great difference. Ironically, at Playa Vista the designers and developer did attempt nearly every one of their strategies. We talked about dispersed small neighborhood parks, we talked about taking advantage of the hydrologic cycle, we talked about wildlife and landscape restoration. We talked about scenic drives, we talked about preservation of steep land that would be held in public domain and not developed. We included just about everything that is in the Olmsted-Bartholomew report in the Playa Vista report, but it was 2000 acres instead of 1500 square miles. So the strategies in the 1930 report are what my colleagues and I still try to bring to citizens in a dense urban community and in a landscape like this.

Ironically, I am no longer working on Playa Vista but from what I know of the first phase of buildings and the inadequate budgets for the parks, they may well ruin it despite thirteen years of my efforts on the project. So I find that disappointing, as I'm sure the Olmsteds found their project disappointing. Many of us have wrecked our ship on Los Angeles. My admiration and my hopes really go out to the stalwart folks who are working on the greening of the Los Angeles River, the people who are tirelessly trying to get trails to connect things together. I can't feel more positively toward them. Only local residents can harangue their government and force them to do these things. I might be able to accomplish that in Philadelphia but I can't accomplish it in Los Angeles, because I'm not here all day everyday. I can't call the commissioner, I can't bug him, and I can't turn up after dinner at community meetings. I can't make these guys do it. So the people who are here, who are advocates, are absolutely on the side of the angels, so to speak. If you don't live here full time, you can't force things into being. You can only work on the pieces you are allowed to work on. We did a plan for the La Placita, and for decking the freeway to connect the Plaza site with Union Station and the Civic Center. We did studies of the Civic Center. I've done plans for Chavez Ravine and how to connect it to Chinatown. We've done a series of studies of great, green boulevards throughout the region for the MTA's trolley buses, a scheme that would have encouraged complementary development along transit corridors. I've done a study to remake Veterans Parkway and a plan for the Figueroa Corridor. We also did a scheme for greening Ballona Creek and enhancing its watershed. But none of this has happened, and yet I keep trying. We are currently working on plans to rebuild Grand Avenue as a fabulous *ramblas* connecting the new cathedral and the Music Center and the civic center with Disney Hall and the Coburn School for Performing Arts with MOCA and the urban office areas. However, there are few firms that could match the resource planning and the regional planning that we see in the Olmsted-Bartholomew report and combine that with the excellence they demonstrated in terms of the design of specific parks, squares, and other urban amenities.

In many ways, the national reach of your own practice is similar to that of the Olmsted firm and the Bartholomew office in the first half of the twentieth century. What is the nature of the similarity? The differences?

It is hubris and unseemly to compare oneself and one's firm to these offices. They were pioneers. They were operating in somewhat uncharted territory, whereas our horizons are a bit more constrained.

The Olmsted office in particular had an affinity for what I would say is an American landscape type—the campus or the university plan. It is interesting to note that following the Korean War, American colleges embarked on an explosive period of construction, one that nearly wrecked so many campuses, when buildings of incredible insensitivity were dropped all over them as though from airplanes. This moment coincided with the final closing of the Olmsted office in Brookline, the firm which for nearly seventy years had so much to do with the careful planning and development and husbandry of all these campuses. Now the Olin Partnership is being asked to come to campus after campus and try to pull them back together and rescue them, to fix them and undo things and put them back together. And in many cases, extend and complete the work of earlier planners—the Olmsted office included—that hadn't been brought to full form and to now provide coherent form and a kind of grace to another generation of construction.

Like the Olmsted office we have had the extremely good fortune to have a series of important urban design projects come our way, projects where we really thought we could help the public realm. In terms of streets and squares and parks we've been blessed with opportunities including Battery Park City (New York), Playa Vista (Los Angeles), and Mission Bay (San Francisco). Really good urban development projects. These have been laboratories for testing which principles of the Olmsted legacy still have currency and value and which are now empty or passe or have lost their energy. You're not going to be surprised to hear that I have found that a great number of the principles that I draw from their work—not necessarily the architectural expression, but the principles behind them—are still vital and really useful. These were real urbanists. These people were clearly devoted to community and society, and so are we.

Many places would be totally uninhabitable today without their work, without their generous parks and site plans. Think of Manhattan without Central Park. Cities bonded themselves heavily to under-

THE POWER OF DICTION

take these projects, projects they considered important public deeds or public works. But now cities aren't doing that. Cities today aren't putting themselves in hock to build public parks the way they did when the Olmsted office was active. Private developers cannot build a great city by themselves. At least not as projects are currently financed they can't. I'm not sure that they ever could. The public really must contribute if we desire an adequate public realm. It is like any other service—whether it's transportation, or airports, or harbors, or whatever. If the public wants this public good, the public has to get involved. One of the things about the Olmsteds is that they were masters of logistics and management. We may think of them as designers, but they were also good businessmen and financiers, and adept manipulators of electoral politics.

However, our office is like the Olmsted office in one way: we are a great teaching office. We are engaged in the future of the profession and in trying to help people become good practitioners and to understand the values I have been talking about. Great offices are always a clearinghouse for talent.

It is an enormous burden to get out from under the weight of the great people in your field. And yet the obligation is that you must. The obligation is that you must feel as strongly about the value of the field and your work as they did, you must find your own way, and you must do it without denying the value of their work. There are times when it is important not to be inventive or not to change things but keep something going that has value or merit that is unfinished or is worth doing. The French geographer Augustin Berque described our field as "the art of milieu." It is about all of the things that comprise our culture. Nobody can control all of that. It is an uncontrollable thing that you set out to do. It is a paradox.

One of the principal motives for going into landscape architecture is a value placed upon the rich environment of the natural world, some feeling for nature, some appreciation of the forces and the energy and the richness of it. But often landscape architects are asked to change things and they're taking down parts of what exists to substitute something that is speculative. Probably two-thirds of the landscape architects in North America are engaged in new development which often consists of bulldozing farms or woodlots or nature to build urban settings of mediocre or questionable value. So there's an enormous melancholia that hangs over my field and my profession, a sense that "I came into this field for one set of values and what am I doing for a living?" That affects this field, and it's not talked about openly, but it is there. So when one encounters a report produced by professionals in top-notch firms that is saying, "these are the things that matter; this is how you build a great city in a natural setting that takes advantage of the setting and doesn't ruin it and brings it to the fore, that puts you more in contact with the forces of nature while being in a grand urban place," your response has to be "That's what I am supposed to be doing!" I can't imagine another landscape architect of any seriousness not having a similar response. As you read it, you ask, "am I doing as well with my life as these guys did with theirs?"

J. B. Jackson said that every American is entitled to a landscape that is biologically sound, socially just, and spiritually rewarding. Holy smokes! What an agenda! That's the agenda of the Olmsted-Bartholomew report! And it is as old as Vitruvius. These are the values that we hold self-evident. We will produce a place that is well-built, that makes sense ecologically, that is biologically and structurally sound. Then there's the socially just; everybody has equal access to the important amenities of the region, regardless of their age, ability, wealth or whatever. And then there are the things that lift the spirit in ways that put us in touch with the universe. You know, those are pretty deep things. And they're in the report. They don't say it that way but those are the values that underlie every decision in it. They're trying to make an argument to persuade the audience they thought they were dealing with; they know that if they stood up there and said you have to do this because it is going to be so pretty and your kids will love you for it that it wouldn't work.

Something to keep in mind is that there are the spoken and unspoken things in our profession. If you're a designer you're supposed to understand these things. You don't have to spell out spiritual things to people who are your social class and your peers, right? They should understand. You don't put that on a questionnaire. And so one of the problems of a report like this is reading what's between the lines. I don't think that because they don't say it you should assume that it isn't there. You have to be very careful about that. Because good professionals always know what's not said. Whether they act on it appropriately or come through, that's another story.

I think that in this case there was a disconnect between the consultants and the client. The client was not able to rise to the important measure they were getting. Great clients rise to the occasion. Clients also set the scale of intervention. Although I have colleagues who are working in cities in Asia that are expanding rapidly, who are inventing the equivalent of Central Park rather than restoring it, very few of my own projects are of the type that initiate the form of the city or the park system that might come. We are often working in highly developed urban areas. So it is a different type of insight and knowledge and skill that we bring to bear on our projects.

There are other things that define practice today. Frederick Law Olmsted Sr., when he was working on the Stanford campus plan, would ride west on the train. He'd get on the train in Boston and he'd slowly wind his way to California, and as he was going west, he'd work and he'd write letters and he'd do stuff and at every station he'd send letters east to the office saying "do this" and "I've thought about such and such and here's my letter to Senator so and so." He'd keep sending stuff east as he went west, and then he'd get to Stanford and he'd get off the train and go down to Palo Alto. He'd be there a week or two working day and night, away from his wife and his office and his family so he'd work late, write letters, take notes and work hard. Then on the trip back east he'd write job reports, he'd write the minutes, he'd make sketches and notes, and he'd keep sending them back to Stanford. So that by the time he got back to Brookline, he had gotten Stanford and its concerns under control. There was a balance to it all. Compare this with practice today. I composed my thoughts about the Olmsted-Bartholomew report during the five-hour plane flight out. I had just enough time on the plane. But that's it. That's the biggest chunk of time I can usually get to think about anything. I don't get two days. I don't get a train ride across the country. Five and a half hours, six or seven to London, maybe. That's the longest time a professional gets these days to think without being interrupted.

Clearly from my remarks, there's nobody I admire more. Everybody has to have heroes.

INDEX

Design and Composition:	Star Type, Berkeley
Text:	10.5 / 13 Janson Text
Display:	Janson Text
Printer and Binder:	Edwards Brothers, Inc.